COMMUNITY AND ALIENATION

COMMUNITY AND ALIENATION

ESSAYS ON PROCESS THOUGHT AND PUBLIC LIFE

DOUGLAS STURM

University of Notre Dame Press
Notre Dame, Indiana

Library of Congress Cataloging-in-Publication Data

Sturm, Douglas.
    Community and alienation.

    Includes index.
    1. Public interest.   2. Common good.   3. Justice.
4. Individualism.   5. Process philosophy   I. Title.
JC330.15.S78   1988   320'.01'1   87-40614
ISBN 0-268-00768-3

CONTENTS

ACKNOWLEDGMENTS

I WISH TO EXPRESS appreciation to the many persons who assisted in the preparation and revision of these essays. My secretary, Linda Bresenhan, has been diligent and patient in the typing and retyping of these pieces as they underwent several transmutations. My companion and home-mate, Margie Jean Anderson Sturm, has exactly the right balance of concern and distance appropriate to such projects. My mentors, James Luther Adams and Bernard Eugene Meland, have been supportive without remaining uncritical of my extensions of their insights and teachings. My colleagues and friends at Bucknell were generous in their reactions to my proposals and ideas. The Scholarly Development Committee at Bucknell was gracious in providing financial support for the revision of the essays and their collection into book form.

Most of these essays were originally presented in various academic institutions or at professional society meetings. The first essay was among the inaugural lectures of a three-year project at the University of Chicago Divinity School. The second essay was delivered at a meeting of the American Academy of Religion. The third was given in a lecture series at Southern Methodist University. The fourth essay was a public lecture presented at the University of Chicago. The fifth was initially a Presidential Address at the Society of Christian Ethics and delivered in revised form at St. John's College in Santa Fe. The sixth was delivered at an International Congress of Learned Societies in the Study of Religion in Los Angeles. The seventh was presented at a seminar at the University of Southern California under the auspices of the Visiting Firestone Professorship. The eighth essay was among lectures on economics and ethics given at a University of Chicago Divinity School Association conference. It was also delivered as the opening plenary of the annual meeting of the College Theology Society. The ninth was presented as part of the Cordell Hull Speakers Forum at Cumberland School of Law.

All of the essays have been revised since their original presentation as lectures or publication as essays. I respectfully and gratefully acknowledge the permission granted by the following to include in this collection materials published in their publications:

"Religious Sensibility and the Reconstruction of Public Life: Prospectus for a New America," *Religion and American Public Life*, ed. Robin W. Lovin, pp. 53–87. Published by the Paulist Press. Copyright 1986 by Dr. Robin W. Lovin. Used by permission of Paulist Press.

"Process Thought and Political Theory: Implications of a Principle of Internal Relations," *The Review of Politics* 41, no. 3 (July 1979): 375–401. Copyright 1979 by the University of Notre Dame. Permission to republish granted.

Subsequent republication, slightly revised, in *Process Philosophy and Social Thought*, ed. John B. Cobb, Jr. and W. Widick Schroeder, pp. 81-102. Copyright 1981 by the Center for the Scientific Study of Religion, Chicago. Permission to republish granted.

"So What's the Problem: Three Ways of Talking Politics," previously unpublished.

"On Meanings of Public Good: An Exploration," *Journal of Religion* 58, no. 1 (January 1978): 13–29. Copyright by the *Journal of Religion* 1978. Permission to republish granted.

"The Prism of Justice: E. Pluribus Unum?" *The Annual of the Society of Christian Ethics 1981*, ed. Thomas W. Ogletree, pp. 1-28. Copyright 1981 by the Society for Christian Ethics. Permission to republish granted.

"Corporations, Constitutions, and Covenants: On Forms of Human Relation and the Problem of Legitimacy," *Journal of the American Academy of Religion* 61, no. 3 (September 1973): 331-354. Copyright 1973 by the American Academy of Religion. Permission to republish granted.

"Corporate Culture and the Common Good: The Need for Thick Description and Critical Interpretation," *Thought* 60, no. 237 (June 1985): 141-160. Copyright by Fordham University Press 1985. Permission to republish granted.

"Toward a New Social Covenant: From Commodity to Commonwealth," *Christianity and Capitalism: Perspectives on Religion, Liberalism and the Economy*, ed. Bruce Grelle and David A. Kreuger, pp. 91-108. Copyright 1986 by the Center for the Scientific Study of Religion, Chicago. Permission to republish granted.

"American Legal Realism and the Covenantal Myth: World Views in the Practice of Law," *Mercer Law Review* 31, no. 2 (Winter 1981): 487–508. Copyright 1980 by the Walter F. George School of Law. Permission to republish granted.

"Contextuality and Covenant: The Pertinence of Social Theory and Theology to Bioethics," *Theology and Bioethics*, ed. E. E. Shelp, pp. 135-161. Copyright 1985 by D. Reidel Publishing Company 1985. Permission to republish granted.

INTRODUCTION:

PUBLIC LIFE AND INTERNAL RELATIONS

WE LIVE, ALAS, at a time and in a place when public life, while increasingly important in determining our fate, is not highly valued. The corporate world and the professional guild are more respected than the town meeting or the congressional caucus. Production of goods and services is more treasured than the deliberation of political policies and the struggle for social reform. There is a strong tendency to think of public life as a tiresome necessity to be tolerated only so long as it conduces to a more secure private life. John Locke is often cited as a proponent of this judgment, although what Locke himself intended is currently under debate. Nonetheless, many passages from his famous treatise on civil government might be and have been used to support this understanding of public life as of but instrumental worth. Take as a paramount example Locke's thesis on the purpose of civil society: "The great and *chief end* therefore, of Mens uniting into Commonwealths, and putting themselves under Government, *is the Preservation of their Property*."[1] Government's purpose is to secure the individual's property; public life is for the sake of private life; civil society is subordinate to the happiness of the individual.

Since the seventeenth century, these sentiments have been widely held in the Western world, especially in the Anglo-American community. While they give expression to an idea of eminent importance—namely, it is the individual who lives, suffers, grieves, and dies—they belie the actual condition of our life and constitute a threat to a fuller happiness that, in principle at least, is possible for us. That is the negative thesis underlying the essays collected in this book. Individualism, including its curious transmutations into the forms of corporativism, racism, and nationalism, is a constraint, depriving us of a deeper, more complex understanding of ourselves and a richer, more thickly textured sense of the goodness of our lives.

1

The alternative to individualism promoted throughout these essays derives from the tradition of process thought, in particular its principle of internal relations. Process thought has had an appreciable effect in philosophy of science and in theology. In philosophy of science, for instance, Alfred North Whitehead promoted a shift from scientific materialism with its principle of simple location to an organic cosmology with its sense of the relatedness of all life. In theology, Bernard E. Meland is among those introducing a change in imagery from God as the Wholly Other to God as the Ultimate Efficacy in the creative passage of events. But the full implications of process thought as it bears on the interpretation and evaluation of social and political life have yet to be developed. These essays are intended as a contribution toward that end.

Meland's theological reflections have had a deep and lasting influence on my mind. At the heart of his reflections is the idea that we are participants in a creative passage whose communal character is the ground of our existence. In that sense "community is a constituent of the individual."[2] Yet, Meland warns, this does not mean that the community absorbs and dissolves our individuality. Rather we as individuals must claim the community as integral to ourselves, necessary for ourselves. Our lives as individuals are fulfilled within concrete existence through our relations with others, including God, whose creative intent bears its impress on each event. Everyone, Meland reminds us, encounters a tension among three simultaneous demands upon one's being: "the creative intent of God, the impulse toward solidarity, and the demands on the subjective experience."[3] Our relatedness, we must note, extends to all aspects of reality. To paraphrase Meland, we are microcosmic as surely as we are individualistic: the sea water flows through our veins; the very minerals and chemicals embedded in the earth give form to our bodily structure; in each moment, we are at once individual persons, national citizens, denizens of humankind, and creatures of the creative passage that fashions the whole of existence.[4] Our lives manifest a polarity between individuation and participation. That, in brief, is the meaning of the principle of internal relations that informs my effort to reconsider the meaning and place of public life in our existence.

I do not intend to identify, in any simple way, the ordinary forms and institutions of public life with the communal ground of our existence. Quite the contrary. These forms and institutions touch our lives in various, sometimes countervailing, ways. They may be supportive and enriching in their influence. Take, for example, the institution of public education when it works as it should. But the forms of public life may also be, indeed have often been, crushing in their impact upon us; they have been destructive of our humanity; they have run contrary to the legitimate expectations of those to whom, presumably, they are responsible. Yet the principle of internal relations, as I intend it, bears on the construction of the meaning and place of public life in our existence in two related ways. It is a basis for understanding what public life is and what it ought to be.

First, it declares that public life is an inescapable dimension of our lives. We are, in a profound sense, solitary creatures. The joys and sorrows, the anxieties and expectations of our inner selves are ours alone. The lonesome valley is one side of the pathway of our lives. Yet, even in our solitariness, our lives are publicly significant in a twofold way. First, our individuality is an emergence, a coming together in creative synthesis of a vast universe of things and people. The food we ingest, the words we speak, the images we contemplate, the steps we take could not be were it not for a heritage bequeathed to us. That heritage may be more or less enabling, but without it, we could not be at all. Second, what we do in our individuality adds to the common store. The acts we perform and the symbolic meanings we embody are a giving, however much they enrich or impoverish others, to future generations. In this twofold way, public life is a natural part of our existence, not an artificial Leviathan created to remedy some inconvenience. At least in this sense, Aristotle's dictum that we are by nature political animals is more apt than Hobbes's social contract theory. To denigrate public life is to deny an essential aspect of our being.

But there seems to be good reason to denigrate public life. The historical evidence is all too clear that the forms of our public life, despite patriotic pretenses to the contrary, are rife with corruption if not downright evil. Richard Rubenstein, for instance, has declared that ours is an "age of triage."[5] For centuries, our officials have disposed of unwanted peoples through various forms of genocide, direct and indirect. The crematoria of the Nazi

concentration camps were a blatant and crass instance of the policy; but long-term structural unemployment in industrial societies
has much the same effect. Again, the Marxian tradition has argued, justifiably, that the apparatus of the state operates as an
agent of the powerful to subdue and to exploit the powerless.
Moreover, the ordinary citizen is wont to conclude without undue
cynicism that politicians are more likely to be driven to act in their
own self-interest than for the common good of the people they are
meant to serve. Thus public life may be an essential aspect of our
existence, but it seems deplorable as it is played out in our
day-to-day experience. The anarchists who would have us do
away with all things political have a persuasive point.

On the other hand, I would contend that the corruption and
evil that pervade the traditional forms of our public life can be
discerned as such only by contrast with the deeper meaning of our
lives. That is, corruption and evil are identifiable as such because
they contradict the normative bearing of the principle of internal
relations. This is the second way in which the principle of internal
relations stands related to the meaning of public life in our existence. By virtue of what we are, given the principle of internal
relations, there are more and less appropriate ways in which to
conduct our selves both as individuals and in the forms of our
common life. Within the tradition of process thought, there are
various formulations of the more appropriate ways. Henry Nelson
Wieman uses the language of "creative interchange."[6] Daniel Day
Williams writes of "community"—"the order in which the members of a society are so related that the freedom, uniqueness, and
power of each serves the freedom, uniqueness, and growth of all
the other members."[7] Community to Williams is an implicate of
the law of love. Alfred North Whitehead promotes the ideal of
"civilization" with its qualities of truth, beauty, art, adventure,
and peace.[8] Meland suggests the ideas of open awareness ("recep-
tiveness to the full datum of experience"), appreciative awareness
("readiness to establish an interchange of meaning that may well
require a reorientation of [one's] own outlook or situation"), and
creative awareness ("a transformative power of social magni-
tude").[9]

Thus the principle of internal relations is simultaneously
metaphysical and moral. It tells us both who we are and what we
ought to be. It informs us that public life, understood broadly, is

an inescapable dimension of our existence. And it instructs us about the character and form that public life should, most appropriately, assume. It provides a grounding for a political ethic. In these essays, I have called that political ethic "communitarian." Moreover, I have associated that political ethic with an ancient covenantal tradition out of the conviction that at least some aspects of that tradition might be illuminated by and, in turn, find a forceful re-presentation in the more recent tradition of process thought. This association is reinforced by Meland's thesis that covenant is a root-metaphor of the Judaic and Christian communities and is, as such, a central component of the mythos of Western history.[10]

Process thought, although sometimes criticized as overly optimistic about the course of human possibility, shows keen awareness of the depth and diversity of evil—from inertial tendencies and protective hierarchies to the intentional subjugation or utter destruction of creative forms of life.[11] "Human evil," Meland writes, "is the dissolute and destructive turn of events which arises from human nature itself and from the accumulative results of human behavior."[12] In these essays, I have appropriated the term "alienation" to designate the central evils of our public life. Alienation, in my usage, is a negative form of belonging. Alienation is manifest in the immediacy of personal relations and in the complicated structures of institutions. Child abuse within the family is a stark case of alienation in the family. Parent and child belong to each other; abuse is the reversal of that sense of their connection. Both parent and child are deprived in the act of abuse. Slavery is a classic case of alienation in the economic and political sector. The slave is clearly degraded in the relationship. But so also is the master. Any institutional form in which and through which persons are entrapped—even if by their own acquiescence or volition—in a process that runs contrary to the mandate of community is an instance of alienation. Thus alienation, as a negative form of belonging, is the reverse side of community; it constitutes a distortion or degradation of the normative dimension of the principle of internal relations. As a result of alienation, whatever its precise forms, the whole world suffers.

Unfortunately, at the present moment in our history, virtually every sphere of relationship between self and world is seriously scarred with the marks of alienation. Roberto Mangabeira

Unger, in his masterful critique of classical liberalism, distinguishes three such spheres: the individual's relationship to nature, to other individuals, and to the individual's own work.[13] In the first sphere, we confront massive and systemic problems of environmental pollution and decay. The question of the disposal of nuclear wastes compounds the problem in untold ways. In the second sphere, we have yet to deal in any adequate manner with the severe consequences of racism, sexism, and ethnocentrism. And the nation-state system has far outgrown whatever positive functions it may have fulfilled in times past. In the third sphere, work has become sheer employment, and employment is itself in short supply in many industrialized societies. In brief, we are entrapped in the support and reenforcement of organized systems of interaction that, despite their promise and benefits to some, run contrary to the possibility of the communitarian vision.

In Unger's prognosis, however, the next stage of our common life is open. We confront alternative futures. Among them, given the pressures and trends of the present moment, is a highly regimented society captured in the idea of "conservative corporativism," a tightly organized, hierarchical system of social control. But among them is also the prospect of an "egalitarian or open community."[14] I share Unger's yearning for the latter possibility. But the yearning is not, at least by intention, sheer fantasy. It is grounded, by claim, in the metaphysics of internal relations. That, I would suggest, is the realism of a communitarian political theory. Realism has, for too long a time, borne the connotation of cynicism or, more modestly, pessimism. But a deeper realism contains within its purview the grounds for that persistent hopefulness that sustains the human spirit and is supportive of movements for social and political transformation. In that sense, I would claim that the essays in this book constitute a new kind of realism, a realism that rejects despair even in the face of the darkest realities of human history which the twentieth century has experienced in manifold abundance.

While the essays brought together in this book were originally prepared for different occasions, they cohere as efforts toward the construction of a communitarian political theory. The opening essay sets out an agenda for inquiry into the future of public life in America. Throughout the essay, I contrast two perspectives on public life, individualist and communitarian. Its central thesis is that the principle of individualism, as incorporated in the culture and forms of American society, is unable to support the kind of public life needed for our immediate and long-range future. The particular themes outlined on the agenda, each discussed briefly in this essay, are unfolded at greater length in later essays.

The second essay, for instance, attends to the grounds and meaning of public life. In this essay, I suggest that process thought, with its organic cosmology, is a basis for thinking of the public realm that is closer to Aristotle than to Hobbes. Politics is more a matter of sustaining a community as a whole than a struggle for power. Moreover, I propose that the political orientation of process thought is not classical liberalism, but a kind of communitarianism in which human rights are encased in a doctrine of responsibility.

The third essay is given to the issue of how to identify problems of public order. What constitutes a problem and how a problem is delineated are matters of theoretical determination. Isolating three alternative theoretical perspectives—rights theory, interest theory, relational theory—I show how they deal with several current questions of public order—the quality of the environment, the equality of women, and the impact of plant closings.

The fourth and fifth essays are devoted to principles of public life. The fourth essay discusses meanings of public good which I have deemed "the first virtue of social institutions." Contrasting a relational view of public good with a range of other alternatives, from analytic perspectives to traditional understandings, I use several Supreme Court cases to illustrate the angle a principle of internal relations takes on problems of property rights and civil liberties. The fifth essay, appropriating the metaphor of a moral prism from Dorothy Emmet, distinguishes four facets of the meaning of justice—liberty, equality, community, wisdom. Holding these facets together, I suggest they are attributes both of civility (as a matter of personal character) and of civilization (as a social ideal).

The sixth and seventh essays deal with the dominant institution in modern American society: the large business corporation. The central question of the sixth essay is the legitimation of the corporation. Three forms of legitimation are distinguished: legal, consensual, and ontological. I argue that the full legitimation of

the business corporation would require its transformation. It
should be reconstructed to conform to principles of constitutionalism and to represent the qualities of covenantal community.

The seventh essay is a critique of prevailing studies of corporate culture as superficial if not devious. To comprehend fully the
culture of corporate life, a range of dimensions must be discrimi-
nated and each examined closely. The corporation does not stand
alone; it is an agent within a complex global set of agents, all of
which are undergoing gradual, but significant historical change.
Ultimately, corporate culture must be measured by its compatibil-
ity with the common good.

In the eighth essay, the idea of democratic capitalism is examined and found wanting. Here, again, I argue that public good
or common good is the supreme virtue of social practice. Sec-
ondly, I advance the thesis that capitalism and democracy, despite
their historical association, are in principle in tension with each
other. And, finally, I argue that social democracy is a form of
public life closer in character to the common good than democratic
capitalism.

The ninth essay draws together areas of discourse often held
apart: jurisprudence and religious inquiry. Acknowledging the
judgment that legal realism is the everyday jurisprudence of the
practising lawyer, I use Karl Llewellyn's thought to set out its
characteristics and to reveal its limitations. I then use Meland's
doctrine of the "new realism in religious inquiry" to suggest a
deeper, more critical ground from which to view the meaning of
legal practice.

The final essay poses three methodological questions of the
discipline of bioethics: questions of scope, focus, and grounding.
In scope, I propose the need for a contextual bioethics; in focus, I
concentrate on the social and historical aspects of professional
practice; in grounding, I explore the meaning and implications of
Whitehead's reformed subjectivist principle. What applies to the
discipline of bioethics may apply as well, *mutatis mutandis*, to other
disciplines pertinent to public life.

Throughout all the essays, I have retained the original language of quotations from others' books and essays, including the
language we might now view, with good reason, as "sexist." The
principles of a communitarian political theory require, among
many other things, the responsible use of language. Yet, in the

interests of sustaining the historical record as written, I deemed it best not to alter the original texts, however offensive they might seem at the present time.

The first essay was initially delivered as a lecture during the inaugural conference at the University of Chicago Divinity School of a three-year study of religion and public life in America under the direction of Robin Lovin. Subsequently, I spent a year at the Institute for the Advanced Study of Religion under the auspices of that project. Work on several of these essays was accomplished in that setting. The inspiration of those with whom I associated during that time is incalculable and has proven to be invaluable. This collection may properly be conceived as among the products of that project.

1. ON THE RECONSTRUCTION OF PUBLIC LIFE IN AMERICA: *AN AGENDA*

WE ARE CONFRONTED with a question of far-reaching theoretical and practical import. What is the future of public life in America? What will it be? What can it be? What should it be? The question pertains to our destiny. But our destiny is not a matter of fate. It is not predetermined, a script set down before we were born. Our destiny is, in no small part, a possibility to be shaped by our imagination and our action. Our destiny, at least in the historical realm, rests on the character of our religious insight and political action. This is the importance of theology and political theory and of their connections with each other.

To those sophisticated in current trends in theology and political theory, we need not bother with an apology about connections between them. We can accept as a working premise Alexis de Tocqueville's assertion that

> Every Religion has some political opinion linked to it by affinity. The spirit of man, left to follow its bent, will regulate political society and the City of God in uniform fashion; it will, if I dare put it so, seek to harmonize earth with heaven.[1]

There is an interplay between social order and social consciousness, and religious sensibility is the deepest dimension of social consciousness.

> The religious conception of reality is the basic level of social consciousness in several senses. Religion represents the most general expression of the beliefs that nourish and unify the several branches of a type of social consciousness. It exhibits the characteristics of social consciousness in their purest and most complete form. And it is always involved, more or less directly, in every change of social ideals and beliefs. Thus, the religious consciousness deals with the whole of experience.[2]

To pose the issue of the future of public life in America assumes two things. First, it assumes that public life is not a given. However indomitable its current structures appear, it is a construction. It is a work never fully accomplished. It is an enactment. By what we are, do, and say, we are engaged in a process of its formation or reformation. Only thus can we speak meaningfully of a future.

Second, it assumes the current conditions of public life are unsatisfactory. As Vincent Harding has observed,

> I see all of America as a kind of contested territory. The old definitions and the old visions of what America is and ought to be are passing away. They have, in many cases, been crashed aside by the events especially of the past 25 to 30 years. At this moment new definitions, new visions, new understandings are in the throes of construction and creation. . . . We must try to create and project a courageous vision of what ought to be, of what *must* be, not only for the humanizing of America, but also for the safety of the world.[3]

Many declare we are in a state of crisis, whether it be a "legitimation crisis" (Habermas), the "decline of business civilization" (Heilbroner), a movement "beyond liberalism" (Kariel), the "twilight of authority" (Nisbet), or the "twilight of capitalism" (Harrington).[4]

The assumption of crisis is as much a question as it is an assumption. There *is* a sense of malaise, serious malaise, that pervades many segments of American society. But what are the roots of that malaise? How are we to name the crisis? Naming the crisis is a preliminary, yet paramount question for our inquiry.

The naming of a crisis is ultimately an expression of religious sensibility. In medicine, a crisis is a turning point, a moment of life or death. In drama, a crisis is a decisive event in the development of the protagonist's story, an event determinative of the protagonist's future. In public life, a crisis is a time of potentially radical social change. It portends some transformation of the human condition. It marks a transition in historical epochs. It signifies the beginnings of new religious insight.

Alfred North Whitehead avers that "the topic of religion is individuality in community."[5] One way to construe historical epochs is the manner in which "individuality in community" is embodied in social order and social consciousness. In simplified form, the transition from the medieval to the modern world is the shift from a principle of organic hierarchy to a principle of individualism.

American society has been organized, according to recurrently stated intentions, to honor the principle of individualism. The liberty of the individual has been the "prospective image" of the New World.[6] That principle constitutes the heart of American liberalism. But American liberalism has soured. In part it has soured because of its exclusiveness. Significant populations within the American community have yet, despite two hundred years of the democratic experiment, to experience the benefits of its promise. Furthermore it has soured because of its perverse use to justify concentrations of wealth and power that redound not to the freedom of the human spirit, but to the perpetuation of control, witting or unwitting, by an elite.[7]

The crisis which gives rise to concern for the future of American public life is centered in the inability of the principle of individualism as it has been embodied in the institutions and consciousness of American society to ground and to support a genuinely public life as needed at this point of history.

An alternative that is not without roots in the American experience is a principle of internal relations. Here I appeal to the tradition of process thought in its philosophical and theological expressions. According to the principle of internal relations, everything in the universe is conjoined with everything else in a continuous process of becoming. Each entity has its own integrity, yet stands in dynamic relationship with all other entities. The universe is self-transcending. It is always to some degree and in some sense a moving beyond.[8] In Whitehead's formulation,

> The actual world, the world of experiencing, and of thinking, and of physical activity, is a community of many diverse entities; and these entities contribute to, or derogate from, the common value of the total community. At the same time, these actual entities are, for themselves, their own value, individual and separable. They add to the common stock and yet they suffer alone. The world is a scene of solitariness in community.[9]

Within this metaphysic, religious sensibility is responsiveness to the full context of one's existence, to its limitations and its possibilities, and to the burden of responsibility one bears for its enrichment or degradation. God is "that sensitive nature within the full context of nature, winning the creative passage for qualitative attainment."[10] The principle of internal relations can be understood as a conceptual rendition of the covenantal tradition, a not insignificant strain in American history, religious and political.

In political thought, this principle of internal relations is communitarian. As such it provides a ground for preserving what is of value in the liberal tradition, but casts it within a new framework which, I would contend, is more adequate to the needs of our time.

From this perspective, I offer six topics for inquiry into the future of public life in America, some topics of which will be discussed more extensively in subsequent chapters: (1) the absence, (2) the ground, (3) the meaning, (4) the problem, (5) the principles, and (6) the study of public life.

1. THE ABSENCE OF PUBLIC LIFE: ISOLATION VERSUS PARTICIPATION

Concern has long been expressed over the extent and depth of political alienation in American society, measured at times by low voter turnout. But, more importantly, serious doubt has been voiced for several decades about whether a genuinely public life is at all possible in modern times. There are features central to the character of modern culture militating against the formation and maintenance of an effective polis.

Sixty years ago, for instance, John Dewey argued there has been an "eclipse of the public."[11] To Dewey, a public is a group of persons mobilized for action because it suffers from the indirect consequences of a transaction effected by other parties. In the early years of the American republic, the mobilization of such groups was an easy matter because the society was organized around small local centers. But social conditions are totally transformed by the growth of modern commerce and technology. The town meeting is virtually a thing of the past. "The machine age has so enormously expanded, multipled, intensified and complicated the scope of the indirect consequences, [has] formed such immense and consolidated unions in action, on an impersonal rather than a community basis, that the resultant public cannot identify and distinguish itself."[12] Dewey cites the First World War as a case of the enormity of the problem. What might he say today? He also notes the contortions by which the principle of individualism has become a justification for its very antithesis.

> At the outset, it was held by "progressives," by those who were protesting against the inherited regime of rules of law and administration. Vested interests, on the contrary, were mainly in favor of the old status. Today the industry-property regime being established, the doctrine is the intellectual bulwark of the standpatter and reactionary. He it is that wants to be left alone, and who utters the war-cry of liberty for private industry, thrift, contract and their pecuniary fruit.[13]

In a vivid interpretation of our political condition shortly following World War II, Hannah Arendt insists that an enduring public realm is possible only where grounded in an authoritative tradition which provides the social expectations and social space in which and through which a people might act in concert. But critique of traditionality and loss of authority are central features of the modern mind before which all inheritances are susceptible to skepticism. The ultimate break with tradition in the realm of the practical was effected by totalitarian movements which hold nothing sacred. Given the full iconoclastic force of modernity, each individual remains in isolation, vulnerable to the sufferings of meaninglessness. Save for rare moments—moments of revolution or resistance when persons may be thrust temporarily into common action—the public realm, the realm of practical freedom, is a mirage.[14]

Even during the 1960s, a decade of significant political action and political resistance, the absence of an authentic public realm is recorded. Robert J. Pranger, writing at the time, argues that a citizen's primary task is to participate in the doing of public business, but in the modern Western world, a politics of participation has given way to a politics of power. Not participation but domination characterizes the American political scene. The bureaucratization of organizational life has sharply delimited areas of citizen engagement. Resistance movements are efforts merely to counter power with power. The reduction of the public realm to a point of insignificance has resulted in the "eclipse of citizenship."[15]

More recently, Richard Sennett announced the "fall of public man." According to Sennett, the dislocations of life produced by capitalism have given rise to an ideology of intimacy.[16] The kind of social distance and psychological courage needed for public action are identified with the impersonality and dehumanizing effects of capitalist structure and are resisted for the warmth of immediate relations. Even within the political realm, matters of personality predominate over issues of policy. Civility—the attitude which enables transactions to proceed without close acquaintanceship—is shunted aside for kinship and chumminess, resulting in a trend toward a tyranny of localism and tribal identity. The exaltation of personal warmth as a reaction against the dissociative tendencies of industrial capitalism signals the end of public culture.

As Thomas Luckmann so ingeniously argues, a similar phenomenon has occurred in the religious realm.[17] In previous periods of history, religion provided a sacred cosmos diffused throughout and legitimating all aspects of the social world. However, a radical transformation has occurred in the age of industrialization. Institutions are now legitimated not by an encompassing religious myth, but by norms of functional rationality. Specialized areas of life are separated from each other, each with its own function to fulfill. Individuals may still seek out a sacred cosmos, but no single, overarching official model is available. Religious faith has become privatized, individualized, in effect, "invisible." That is the new form of religion in modern times. A radical bifurcation has been created between the inner religious world and the world of social interaction.

Thus even as the public sphere has become eclipsed given features of modern life—the force of modern technology, the loss of traditionality, the politics of power and domination, the escape to intimacy—so religion (with significant exceptions which Luckmann ignores) seems to have lost its public significance.

But has it? The complaint of political theology is that it has not. Religion, especially popular religion, has taken a subjective turn. Existentialist theology, concerned with the dehumanizing structures of modern industrial society, points to the intensely personal divine-human encounter as the source of meaning and fulfillment. The I-Thou relation between God and the individual transcends, it is claimed, the processes and patterns of historical life. But, political theologians shrewdly charge, the privatization of the religious encounter reflects and reinforces the individualism of bourgeois ideology. Indirectly, it supports the inhumane effects of bourgeois institutions by failing to challenge them for what they are. The argument of political theology is that the intended privatization of religion is a deception because of the solidary character of reality. Personalized religion is necessarily of public significance, but in a negative if not ultimately perverse way.[18]

2. THE GROUND OF PUBLIC LIFE: ATOMISM VERSUS CONTEXTUALISM

Questions of the ground and the meaning of public life are intertwined and finally inseparable. But for the moment I shall separate them. The question of ground asks about roots or origins. At its most basic level it is a question of cosmology. Its concern is the setting of public life. The question of meaning, on the other hand, asks about the structure of public life as such. Its concern is with the "orienting concept"[19] or categorial definition of politics.

Classical political theory, as, for instance, in Aristotle and Thomas Aquinas, reflects a fundamental understanding of the character of the world. The Aristotelian and Thomistic approaches to political life are comprehensible only within the framework of a teleological view of nature. Public life is intrinsic to the development and maturation of the human species.

The emergence of the modern world, however, is marked with a radically different vision of the world and of the beginnings of public life. Therein lies the genius of Thomas Hobbes. His "politics of motion"[20] gave voice to the new vision in a clear and direct manner. But the new vision has become more than a theory debated by philosophers. It has come, declares Roberto Unger, to "occupy a central place in our everyday thinking as well as in the specialized branches of social study."[21] It is the "unreflective view of society" generally presupposed and acted upon throughout liberal culture. Furthermore, Frank M. Coleman argues "that American constitutional tradition is the product of a revolutionary movement in political thought whose directions and nature are embodied in Hobbes's major works and that Hobbes, not Locke, is the parent source of American constitutional philosophy."[22]

In C. B. Macpherson's telling phrase, the central assumption of the new vision is "possessive individualism."[23] Given that assumption, public life is not of primary significance in human existence. It is not essential to the development of the human species.

It is an artifice. It has a remedial function to perform. Behind public life stands the "state of nature." "The State of Nature," declared Coleman, "is the literary vehicle employed by Hobbes to advance the claims of modern egoism."[24] As such, it betrays what humans are conceived to be in their most pristine condition. They are individuals in action—atoms in motion—reaching out to grasp whatever is pleasing to them. They are propelled by self-interest. The image is that of market society.

Given a relative scarcity of resources, persons are seized in a competitive struggle which, in its extremity, becomes a war of all against all. Without the construction of some principle of order, without, that is, the restraints of public life, existence would be "solitary, poor, nasty, brutish, and short."[25]

Public life is thus grounded in the limitations and frustrations of the state of nature. The social contract through which persons consent to be governed is a compact of convenience. It may be functionally necessary, but it is an intrusion into the primary activity of life. Political order is secondary to economic pursuit. Politics is alien to one's most fundamental inclinations. It goes against the grain of personal desire.

But times change. Shifting historical conditions provoke new imageries of thought and action. In William Ernest Hocking's phrase, we are now, on the far side of the twentieth century, at a point of "passing beyond modernity,"[26] of moving toward a principle of intersubjectivity. That sense underlies John MacMurray's thesis "that the self is constituted by its relation to the Other; that it has its being in its relationships; and that this relationship is necessarily personal."[27] With the shift from an atomistic to a contextualist cosmology, the setting of public life is altered. The self is not a subjective or isolated ego, but a person in relation. Bernard Meland has pointed to developments in the natural and social sciences tending toward a contextualist view of reality in general and a holistic understanding of humanity in particular. Within this understanding, both individuation and relatedness are essential features of existence.

> The integrity and authenticity of the person present one aspect; the claims of our communal ground present another. These are not antithetical aspects merely, for their occurrence simultaneously in any society and their interaction upon one another assures a depth

of freedom and solidarity which is spiritually greater in sensitivity and creative power than either individualism or communalism taken singly.[28]

In John MacMurray's rendition, this understanding of human existence lies at the heart of religious sensibilities, for the function of religion is "to create, maintain, and deepen the community of persons and to extend it without limit, by the transformation of negative motives and by eliminating the dominance of fear in human relations."[29] Religion, in its purest and truest form, is the celebration of communion through worship of the One in relation to Whom all entities are cherished.

The cosmology of contextualism provides a new setting for reflection about and the practice of public life. From this perspective, the initiating impulse of public life is not primarily to construct conditions for the maturation of a prescribed and pre-given set of potentialities. Nor is it to construct defenses to delimit the war of all against all. It is instead to give deliberative expression to the interactive processes that constitute the stuff of life in such a way to enhance the experience of each one. To be sure, regardless of the originating vision of public life, perversion is possible. But without an originating vision, perversion is unrecognizable. The ground of public life is the foundation for constructing the meaning of public life.

3. THE MEANING OF PUBLIC LIFE: PRIVATE INTEREST VERSUS
SUSTAINING COMMUNITY

If our concern is the future of public life in America, we must have some sense of what it means to speak about "public life." We must specify, albeit generally, what typifies the public, as distinguished from the private, side of our existence. Definitions of this kind are elusive, but indispensable and revealing. Their indispensability was addressed some time ago by David Easton in his inquiry into the state of political science: without an "orienting concept," he averred, any inquiry remains diffuse and unfocused. But definitions are also revealing. They disclose a way of thinking and acting. They bear the risk of ideological bias.

"Each generation," Easton asserts, "redefines its own image

of political science, with greater insight, one might hope, as our understanding of political life increases."[30] Maybe, however, understandings of public life are not cumulative. Whatever the reasons for paradigm shifts in history, they seem not to be merely the functions of increased knowledge. Insight and viewpoint are bonded in complex ways, but, of the two, insight occupies the place of priority. Whether the insight of any one generation is greater than another depends on how responsive it is to the needs of the time.

Harold Lasswell's presentation of politics as "who gets what, when, how" was a stroke of insight.[31] With Lasswell, public life is discerned as transactions of influence and power. Institutional form, however designed in constitutional documents, may or may not represent actual happenings. But public life is a matter of actual happenings. On that level, individuals and groups jockey for advantage. Such movements are characteristic of both domestic and international politics. There are winners and losers; yet the process is perpetual and the sides change. Governments are dominant places of exchange. Their form, procedures, and results betray the transactional processes in which the whole society is engaged. The lesson to any group feeling deprived is to organize. Underlying this construction of public life is the "Myth of the Liberal Enlightenment":

> The myth to which the Americans keep returning as they sense themselves to be under pressure can be seen in its most explicit form in the writing of its originators—that is, in the political theory of eighteenth-century English liberalism. Determined to defend a new regime in opposition to repressive feudal institutions, Thomas Hobbes, John Locke, Adam Smith, and James Madison were *compelled* to elucidate, and they did so unashamedly. They frankly proclaimed that a society was wanted in which everybody would be committed to the rational pursuit of self interest. They elaborately announced their faith in salvation through private endeavor.[32]

Under the spell of this myth, government is conceived to have two purposes: to protect private interest and to defend society as a whole from external and subversive threats. Questions about the overall quality of the common life, the goals of human existence, the justifiability of prevailing organizational patterns are bracketed as improper subjects for public debate and determination. They are matters reserved for individuals to decide in the privacy of their homes, religious communities, and local associations.

The paradoxical twist is that, over the course of time, "private interests" have come to mean the interests not of individuals and local groups but of corporate enterprise. "Under the aegis of the Myth of Liberalism, corporate business has emerged as virtually sovereign in America. Elite-governed industrial and financial giants have become the effective integrators of conflicting interests; they have emerged as the all-absorbing determinants of opportunities for generating options for the whole of society."[33]

Within the context of corporate America, political processes are still conceived as consisting in transactional relations, with government assigned the role of conflict-management. Ultimately, however, such an understanding of the meaning of public fails: "If public order is presented with some new and severe trial, requiring a more creative use of public authority, the sovereign will be incapable of action."[34] Frank Coleman names four such trials currently confronting American public life: structural unemployment, pollution and energy use, urban decay, criminal recidivism.[35] Others are not hard to imagine. Transactional politics cannot deal adequately with pervasive problems of public life.

An alternative understanding of the function of political processes is stated by A. D. Lindsay: "to serve the community, to remove the disharmonies which threaten its common life and to make it more a community."[36] To Lindsay, the political ideal is a form of democracy in which principles of equality and liberty are infused and informed by the religious sensibility of love. Sebastian de Grazia similarly discerns the conformity of the political and religious impulse:

> Those responsible for knowledge of the connectedness of things within the community and the order of them toward the highest good are the statesman and the theologian. . . . The communities they represent, the political and the religious communities or the great community, take in all of man's life. Theirs is the task of raising and holding before men's eyes the vision of the ideal community.[37]

Politics so construed is not simply "who gets what, when, how." More basically, it is an explicit manifestation of the quality of our living together. The purpose of public life is to pursue ways and means of improving that quality. It is to create and to sustain those relationships in which the actions of each enhance the life of all. On these grounds, de Grazia is critical of the competitive principle of the business ideology.[38] He insists that economic activity be made subservient to political and religious considerations.

While public life cannot and should not ignore issues of private interest, its more critical function at this point in history is with issues of "belonging," for, in Philip Hefner's judgment:

> Today we have a renewed sense of (1) our belonging to our fellow human beings, across all barriers—racial, sexual, economic, geographical, national, and age; (2) our belonging to the ecosystem of which we are a part, the natural environment which is the womb of our emergence and the support system for everything human; and (3) our belonging to the matrix of evolutionary development out of which our total ecosystem has unfolded.[39]

However few are actually vested with this sense of belonging, Hefner's judgment is an insight into what is needed in our times.

4. The Problem of Public Life: Allocation versus Alienation

Religious movements and political processes have in common a sense of something wrong with the world. This sense is particularly keen in the religious sphere. The realism of religion is found in what John Smith calls its "dark side."[40] Religions are imbued with a clear perception of the pervasiveness and depth of evil in existence. The political realm, however, is not without its own moments of darkness which provoke exceptional response. Hannah Arendt, in a striking parallel, associates specifically public action with religious miracle. Significant acts of public initiative like the miracles reported in the Gospels are responses to instances of dire need. As such, they are "interruptions of some natural series of events, of some automatic process, in whose context they constitute the wholly unexpected." Indeed, "the more heavily the scales are weighted in favor of disaster, the more miraculous will the deed done in freedom appear; for it is disaster, not salvation, which always happens automatically and therefore must appear to be irresistible."[41]

Even in the more ordinary run of events, however, political processes are motivated by some feeling of need. Recall John Dewey's interpretation of a public as a group called into being when it suffers the consequences of actions its members have not themselves directly initiated. A public is a reactive group seeking to gain control over the quality of its life. There is no public life without provocation. But what counts as a provocation varies according to perspective on the meaning of public life. (In chapter 3, I shall explore this idea more extensively.)

The liberal tradition, for instance, although devoid of a tragic sense of life, has two alternative means of ascertaining when something has gone awry and why corrective action is needed. In its utilitarian form, its measure is the greatest happiness principle. Given that measure, its concern is with the felt pleasures and pains of life as these are registered in the political process by groups mobilized to press their interests. Intensity of protest backed with organized power is the mark of a political problem. That is what signals the need for readjustment in the distribution of social and economic benefits.

In its human rights form, the liberal tradition possesses a more durable and fixed standard of need. At least in principle, any violation of human rights should provoke corrective public action even in the absence of organized protest. Thus the judicial process is presumed available to protect the rights of each and every citizen however lowly in social status and however lacking in political power. The Bill of Rights is a promise of benefits that belong to everyone, irrespective of utilitarian calculus. As such it is a gauge of public wrongs, a means of ascertaining when something has gone wrong and demands public response.

While the utility principle and the human rights principle are somewhat different versions of the problem of public life, in a sense they are the same. From both perspectives, the problem is one of allocating benefits to individuals and groups. Both tend to treat the wrongs of public life in piecemeal fashion. Both are blind to the more deep-seated and systemic distortions that permeate modern life. Neither perspective is searching enough to penetrate to the central problem of our time, the problem of structural alienation.

By alienation I mean a negative form of belonging. Sometimes, alienation means psychological and social distancing, a separation of person from person. But here I take alienation to mean a special kind of relationship, a relationship that is inherently contradictory. It is a relationship in which people are caught in a pattern of activity contrary to their own good. It is an institutional pattern in which a people suffers from the pernicious consequences of its own life-activity. It is a social form of Frankenstein's monster, a creation that turns back upon and against its creator.

Each self exists in a web of relationships—to nature, to others, to work. The good for the self depends on the quality of these relationships. When they are mutually enhancing, the good for the self is realized. The problem of public life in our times is that these relationships are mutually destructive. Thus we confront an ecological crisis, a social crisis, and an economic crisis, which, in their conjunction, constitute a dire threat to human life. Some argue that these crises, serious though they be, are overshadowed by the "exterminism" of the nuclear weapons crisis.[42] The curiosity is that all these crises are of human making. And they persist and intensify because of institutional forms and policies we continue to support and to reinforce. Neither the utilitarian calculus nor the resolution of conflicts over rights—at least as these procedures have been carried out heretofore—will do to confront the current problem of public life.

Nothing less than a radical transformation of our common life will blunt the self-destructive drive of current policies and practices in the ecological sphere. John Cobb calls for an "ecological asceticism" that would affect forms of transportation, residential patterns, industrial strategies, military technology, land use, energy usage, waste disposal, and population control.[43] But, he argues, such a change in style of life rests on the emergence of new forms of philosophical understanding and religious commitment, for without an altered state of mind, the urgency of institutional revision cannot even be discerned.

The same argument applies to the social crisis. The persistence and virulency of racism and sexism throughout American history are evidence of the thesis. Despite valiant efforts over decades to overcome these self-induced diseases of the human spirit through traditional forms of political pressure and judicial process, the results have been peripheral. The cultural and institutional hegemony of the white male is a seemingly ineluctable datum of American society and constitutes a central feature of the problem of public life from which, though they know it not, even white males suffer.[44] Only through an understanding that each of us belongs essentially to the other can the problem adequately be perceived.

In Michael Harrington's interpretation, the economic crisis is similarly of a structural character. Unemployment, inflation, and poverty derive from the nation's pattern of investment, which is governed by the priorities of the corporate world. "There is no doubt," he writes, "that the corporate domination of the economy and the attendant ideological assumption that private control of investment yields a maximum public happiness are basic causes of the current crisis." The key to the solution is "the democratization of the investment function."[45] Unless the community can gain control over the productive process to direct its energies toward the enhancement of the community and of the ecosphere, we will simply continue to participate in and contribute to a system that contradicts our own best interests. The issue is how to subordinate the economy to public control.

5. The Principles of Public Life: Compromise versus Justice and Common Good

There is merit to the slogan that politics is the art of compromise. Where society is conceived as an arena in which individuals engage in a process of give-and-take, where the supply of things to be given-and-taken is limited, and where stability of relations is favored, compromise is an honored form of interaction. In the lexicon of American politics, compromise is a positively charged word: "Essentially, for us, compromise means that politically interested groups or parties have contended, seriously but not fatally, in a relatively free market with their various strengths of argument and social power in order to reach a transient settlement that is, for a time, acceptable to most, though maximally pleasing to none." As such, compromise is central to the ethics of American public life.

> "Compromise" is at least on the edge of being a virtue in Anglo-Saxon discourse. It does not solve the world's problems once and for all, but it at least provides for the world's ongoingness. It per-

mits us to rise in the morning after knowing that certain of our complaints have been met, that the garbage will be taken, that the police will not strike, that a minority group will not reach a boiling point. Politics, is, after all, the art of the possible; compromise might seem to be its code of manners. Compromise avoids disgrace, and it may reconcile.[46]

We should distinguish, however, between conflicting *interests* and conflicting *principles*.[47] Where there are conflicting interests and all pertinent parties share a concern for the duration of the process of social interchange, compromise is an acceptable norm. Compromise is more difficult and less acceptable where principles are at stake. Firmly held political ideologies and deeply felt religious beliefs are not easily qualified when threatened by countervailing claims.

The force of American liberalism, however, has been to soften the edges of ideologies and creeds. The principle of individualism subjectivizes beliefs. Principles become interests and compromise becomes possible, if not mandatory, between political parties and religious groups. That is the force of Robert Paul Wolff's dictum: "The genius of American politics is its ability to treat even matters of principle as though they are conflicts of interest."[48] The liberal form of religious tolerance is a supreme instance of that trend. The "balancing test" in judicial decisions is another case of the same tendency. The sanction for the rule of compromise is the suspicion that, in its absence, everyone loses. The more sophisticated form of the rule is the utilitarian calculus.

But, as noted, the utilitarian calculus as applied in America has not served us well. Procedures for striking a compromise have not been so benign as pretended. They have taken the form of what Martin P. Golding calls "offensive bargaining": "In offensive bargaining the positions of the parties are almost asymmetrical as can be. One side is powerful, the other weak; one side has a large threat potential, the other's is small."[49] What Golding calls "offensive bargaining" might more appropriately be labeled exploitation or oppression. In the vocabulary of ethics, it is injustice or dehumanization. Its forms in American public life are legion, as those who are black, female, Native American, unemployed, or of Hispanic or Oriental origin can testify.

When the powerless are brought to the bargaining table, they may have more to gain than to lose, but the odds are they will not gain what is needful for full participation in the public life of the nation. That is the point of those who rightly claim that compromise should give way to justice as the paramount principle of politics.[50] The centrality of the principle of justice has long been recognized in the Western religious tradition from the ancient utterances of the Hebrew prophets to the modern reconstructions of neo-Thomism[51] and political theology.[52]

Precise meanings of justice vary.[53] But whether justice is understood as liberty, equality, mutuality, or wisdom, it signifies respect for the intrinsic dignity of human existence, perhaps, indeed, for the entire world of being. It is a judgment against offensive bargaining. It is a declaration that some forms of compromise are intolerable. It is a directive that every person should be granted those rights and resources needed for effective participation in public life. Justice, in the context of modern industrial society, mandates a form of "affirmative constitutionalism" for all large organizational structures, political and economic.[54] As Carl J. Friedrich argues, the roots of Western constitutionalism have their beginnings and find their sustenance in the Hebraic-Christian idea of transcendent justice.[55]

Justice, when construed as a distributive principle, is, however, only one side of the coin of political ethics. The other side—at this juncture of history the more prominent side—is an aggregative or holistic principle, the common good.[56] Robert Bellah distinguishes three forms of political pluralism, one of which demonstrates the character of this principle (which will be more fully depicted in chapter 4). Liberal pluralism is atomistic; it dissolves all non-contractual solidarities. Romantic pluralism is tribalistic; it reinforces a love of one's own. But there is also a "pluralism open to transcendence":

> It will be a pluralism that (1) is in search of universality while recognizing that every universal is apprehended only in particularity and concreteness; (2) can assert the validity of one's own and the right not to have that trampled on by anyone else; and (3) is developed in the context of the assertion of the good of the whole, not just the good of the national whole, but the good of the global whole.[57]

The common good is the good of the whole, which is "derivative from the interrelations of its component individuals, and also necessary for the existence of each of these individuals."[58] On the level of small groups, the common good is the goodness of friendship. On a political level, it is the goodness of there being a public at all. On still a third level, it is the goodness of the entire "biotic pyramid."[59] In an image drawn by Scott Buchanan:

> The purpose of the city in the valley would be the enhancement of nature including human nature in the valley. Human beings would no longer be exploiting nature or themselves. They would be free citizens in a constitutional kingdom of nature.[60]

The common good does not always rest easily with the demands of justice. There are moments when, for the sake of the community, the sacrificial commitment of the individual or of a group is demanded. Personal goals and communal needs may exist in a perpetual tension. Yet it must be insisted that justice and common good are not contradictory principles of public life. Neither is possible without the other. Both are expressive of religious sensibility as framed by Alfred North Whitehead:

> The moment of religious consciousness starts from self-valuation, but it broadens into the concept of the world as a realm of adjusted values, mutually intensifying or mutually destructive. . . . Religion is world-loyalty.[61]

6. The Study of Public Life: Empirical Analysis versus Dialogical Holism

Modern political analysis was launched as a distinct discipline in America near the end of the nineteenth century.[62] Behavioralism is its culmination. The analytic principle, a particular form of individualism, is its guiding spirit.[63] Analysis means the separation of things into parts. Analysis divides, distinguishes, brackets, sorts out in order to understand. It supposes that separation results in clarification. It favors the qualities of specialty, objectivity, neutrality, predictability. As Heinz Eulau casts it:

> A science of politics which deserves its name must build from the bottom up by asking simple questions that can, in principle, be answered; it cannot be built from the top down by asking questions that, one has reason to suspect, cannot be answered at all, at least

by the methods of science. An empirical discipline is built by the slow, modest, and piecemeal cumulation of relative theories and data. The great issues of politics, such as the conditions and consequences of freedom, justice, or authority, are admittedly significant topics, but they are topics compounded with a strong dose of metaphysical discourse. I don't think they are beyond the reach of behavioral investigation, but before they can be tackled, the groundwork must be laid.[64]

Specialization is the institutional form of the analytic principle, a form whose power is manifest in the growth of the knowledge industry: the consulting firm, the public opinion center, the think-tank, the technical expert.

The technical expert is, presumably, objective and neutral. Both these qualities require a bracketing. Objectivity requires bracketing personal judgments and hunches in order to represent the world for what it is; it assumes the world is external to oneself. Neutrality requires bracketing evaluation and assessment in order to let the bare facts be what they are; it assumes that values are not grounded in factuality but are imposed on the world as a matter of personal orientation. Thus the analytic principle effects a radical dualism between objectivity and subjectivity and between factuality and evaluation.

In addition, the analytic principle presses toward the formulation of judgments enabling one to predict the course of events at least within the limits of probability and, paradoxically, gives rise to the hope that one may, to some degree, gain increased control over events.

Despite Eulau's description, however, modern political analysis may not be as free from metaphysical discourse as it pretends or desires. Metaphysics and epistemology may not be siblings, but they are akin. The analytic principle makes sense only against the backdrop of the cosmology of scientific materialism with its notion of simple location.

There are good reasons, theoretical and practical, to hold the notion of simple location in doubt. On the theoretical level, Whitehead charges the notion of simple location with the "Fallacy of Misplaced Concreteness."[65] The alternative is a cosmology according to which "actuality is through and through togetherness."[66] In Bernard Meland's interpretation, this outlook assumes:

(1) that things exist in relations; (2) that relations are dynamic; (3) that the synthesis of meanings gives rise to a qualitative significance that is not apprehended among isolated events; and (4) that the accumulative effect of attending to such significance is the creation of a qualitative meaning that is over and above pure functional interests. This is the level of meaning that elicits our profounder emotions, such as appreciation and gratitude, and, under other circumstances, awakens concern and responsible action.[67]

From this perspective, while the analytic process has its contribution to make in the economy of understanding, it is secondary to the act of appreciative consciousness which attends to the communal context and the creative, as well as destructive, potentialities of events.

Moreover, from this perspective, the act of understanding is itself a mode of practical action. Mind and world are not wholly discrete entities. Human interests infuse all efforts at knowing, whether those interests are directed toward technical control, cultural understanding, or the emancipation of human action from structures of domination.[68] The study of public life is always an act of public significance.

Jürgen Habermas would carry the argument a step further: namely, that all efforts at knowing presuppose in principle, even as they may in their actual forms contradict, the paramountcy of interest in full-fledged communicative competence and therefore the overcoming of all forms of alienation.[69] There is, in short, a link, often neglected, between the search for knowledge and the good life.

Out of another, but sympathetic, tradition of thought, John MacMurray suggests that that link entails a religious dimension:

> The function of religion is the representation of the community of agents, and of the ultimate conditions of action, both in respect of its means and its ends. Religion, we may say, is the knowledge of the Other as community, and is the full form of reflective rationality. It is the knowledge which must inform all action for the achievement of community, and therefore the ground of all really efficient and really satisfactory action whatever.[70]

With a strong note of practical urgency, George Cabot Lodge presses toward the same conclusion:

Humanity is discovering that, like other species, it is bound by the S-curve that governs growth in any environment. It is clear that the ideology which was effective in governing man's conduct during the first part of the curve, when survival depended upon individual initiative and competition, tooth and claw, must be different from the ideology that will govern the second part of the curve, when survival requires cooperation. . . . The need for social, political, and above all, religious systems by which to recognize and allow for the interrelation of all things—to recognize and give consent to the laws of the whole, whatever we may discover them to be—is the inescapable conclusion of countless modern scientific studies.[71]

Thus Lodge calls for a new structure in the organization of knowledge, a structure in which holism replaces specialization. Holism "is the recognition that everything must be considered in relation to everything else; that mankind is one; that it lives on a spaceship, earth; that the resources available to it are limited; that to survive, men must become harmonious with each other and with all the rest of nature."[72]

From this perspective, there is need for both a critical theory of religion and a critical theory of public life, each of which requires the other for its completion. The ultimate interest of both would be to identify and to overcome structures of alienation wherever they may be found, even in the academy. The ultimate aim of both would be to effect that kind of emancipation that is directed toward a community of belonging. Perhaps, however, the most that can, at the moment, be expected, is the initiation of an elementary community of discourse, a dialogic process cutting across customary disciplinary lines and focused on the meaning and the problem of being a responsible citizen within the contemporary world. That in itself, however modest, might epitomize the possibility of reconstructing public life in America. It might recapture a dream that seems almost forgotten.

2. PROCESS THOUGHT AND POLITICAL THEORY:

A COMMUNITARIAN PERSPECTIVE

A FUNDAMENTAL AIM OF political theory is to disclose the grounds and meaning of political activity. But that is no simple matter. As Alfred North Whitehead remarks, "theories are built upon facts; and conversely the reports upon facts are shot through and through with theoretical interpretation." Facts are not a given; they constitute an issue. What counts as factual depends in no small measure on theoretical vision. The notion of "history devoid of any reliance on metaphysical principles and cosmological generalizations, is a figment of the imagination."[1] The task of political theory cannot be undertaken apart from considerations of cosmology. At this point, process thought is relevant to political theory.

I shall here present four proposals, expanding on ideas sketched more briefly in the first chapter. The proposals deal, respectively, with methodological perspective, categorial definition, historical problematic, and constructive orientation in the study of politics. In each instance, the grounds for the proposal will be a principle of internal relations.

According to this principle, relations are constitutive of the individual, although the individual synthesizes these relations in a selective and unique fashion. To understand an event (or an agent), one must attend not only to its unique character, that which sets it apart from other events, but to its communal ground without which it could not be and to its impress on the future which is its legacy to the ongoing world. The context and consequences of an event are dimensions of its meaning. An event is, indeed, laden with a depth of continuities and contradictions that elude clear analysis, but are part and parcel of its existence. The principle of internal relations, understood as signifying these dimensions and depths of reality, is a basis for interpretation and evaluation. On the human level, it means we are members of one another and depend on one another for the quality of our lives. To comprehend the identities and responsibilities of peoples, individually and institutionally, we must take account of their embrace of and influence on the world.

Throughout the discussion of these proposals, various doctrines of Alfred North Whitehead will be invoked. It is not presumed that the proposals have been derived directly from Whitehead's philosophy. It is only claimed that process thought is the angle from which these themes have been approached.

In summary, the first proposal is that among the dominant contending schools of thought in contemporary American political science, process thought is more akin to post-behavioralism than to either behavioralism or traditionalism. Process thought should thus be counted among the philosophical movements pressing toward the reconstruction of social and political thought in the West. The second proposal is that process thought provides a basis for thinking of the public realm in a way closer to Aristotle than to Hobbes. That is, politics is more a matter of polity than a struggle for power. It is concerned more with the formation of creative community than the systemic containment of interest groups. The third proposal is that the Marxist concept of alienation as a statement of the central problem of the modern epoch can be construed as an expression of a principle of internal relations and therefore as compatible with process thought. The final proposal is that the constructive political orientation of process thought is not liberalism, at least in its classical individualistic sense. It is rather a form of communitarianism in which the doctrine of human rights must be modified by a doctrine of responsibility.

1. Methodological Perspective: Post-Behavioralism

In *Science and the Modern World*, Whitehead contrasts two types of cosmology: scientific materialism and the philosophy of organism. Scientific materialism is the dominant view of modern science. It emerged in the seventeenth century and persists into the twentieth. "Every university in the world," he writes, "organizes itself in accordance with it."[2] He summarizes the view in this compact statement:

There persists . . . throughout the whole period the fixed cosmology which presupposed the ultimate fact of an irreducible brute matter, or material, spread throughout space in a flux of configurations. In itself such a material is senseless, valueless, purposeless. It just does what it does do, following a fixed routine imposed by external relations which do not spring from the nature of its being. It is this assumption that I call 'scientific materialism'.[3]

Central to scientific materialism is the principle of simple location according to which entities are taken to exist in definite regions and for definite durations. Their essential meaning requires no reference to other regions or to other durations. Save as they suffer from interference from other entities external to themselves, they exist in blissful isolation. Newton's first law of motion, the law of inertia, is a succinct statement of the principle. Conjoined with the theory of simple location is a doctrine of substance and quality. Of any particular entity, one may distinguish primary and secondary qualities. Primary qualities, quantitatively specifiable, are essential characteristics of the entity. They are its real substance. Secondary qualities are projects of the mind. They reside in the eye or ear of the observer. In itself, the world of natural entities is without them: "Nature is a dull affair, soundless, scentless, colourless; merely the hurrying of material, endlessly, meaninglessly."[4] The distinction between primary and secondary qualities is a translation of the distinction between matter and mind. Where the balance between them is not resolved monistically into either term—as in Thomas Hobbes or Bishop Berkeley—it is the basis for the dualisms, so characteristic of modern thought, between observed and observer, fact and value, reality and imagination, nature and history.

The principle of simple location provides a way of viewing the world of nature, but a way that is contrived and abstract. The error of the "century of genius" (the seventeenth century) was not in using the principle of simple location for scientific analysis. The error was in the failure to acknowledge the principle as an abstraction from experience. Modern science, in short, is guilty of the "Fallacy of Misplaced Concreteness."[5] The irony is that, in its reaction against the "unguarded rationalism of the Middle Ages,"[6] the intention of scientific materialism was to *attain* concreteness. In place of a search for inner essences, modern science sought out material facts. Instead of explaining events according to ultimate purposes, the concern of modern science was to measure distance from antecedent conditions. In contrast to the scholastic procedure of rational deduction, the method of modern science was observational and inductive.

We cannot but admire the creative outburst of scientific research and insight that accompanied the emergence of the new scientific philosophy. The mechanistic theory of nature was vindicated by its pragmatic results. Yet its inadequacies, critiqued over the years in various movements of thought in philosophy, literature, biology, and physics, provoke, as an alternative, an organic theory of nature. The organic theory

> involves the entire abandonment of the notion of simple location as the primary way in which things are involved in space-time. In a certain sense, everything is everywhere at all times, for every location involves an aspect of itself in every other location. Thus every spatio-temporal standpoint mirrors the world. . . . There are no single occasions, in the sense of isolated occasions. Actuality is through and through togetherness—togetherness of otherwise isolated eternal objects, and togetherness of all actual occasions.[7]

The primary unit of reality is not a substantial essence; nor is it a bit of matter; it is the event, the actual occasion, a concrescence of prehensions. An event is a process of becoming which issues from other events but forms and presents its own originality for all other events. An event is what it is because of the character of its relationships to its past and to its anticipated future. Where the principle of external relations is central to scientific materialism, the principle of internal relations is at the heart of the philosophy of organism. Negatively, the principle of internal relations means that apart from its relationships, an entity cannot be what it is. Positively, it means that an entity is what it is through its creative synthesis of the multiplicity of relata into a unique character. What an entity can be depends in part upon antecedent conditions; possibilities are not unlimited. But what an entity becomes depends as well on its own prehensive character which is shot through with valuational orientation. Value inheres in each entity as its mode of receiving, selecting, and integrating those prior occasions relevant to its final satisfaction. Upon attaining its final satisfaction, an entity becomes a condition, a datum for all future occasions.

What pertains to the general run of entities pertains as well to conscious entities. Knowing is but a special case of prehending. Knowledge is thus limited by conditions, is perspectival, is value-laden, and bears a responsibility for its adequacy to the past and its implications for the future. The dualities that seem so clear in scientific materialism between mind and matter, value and fact, theory and practice are blurred in the philosophy of organism. In substitution for the doctrines of the objectivity of the observer, the neutrality of observation, and the simple location of the observed, the organic theory of nature and of knowledge presents the concepts of perspective, valuation, and internal relations.

Whitehead's primary concern in *Science and the Modern World* is with the cosmology of modern physical science. Given that concern, he does not observe explicitly that the "century of genius" was a turning point not only in the history of science, but also in the history of political thought, though the cosmology of scientific materialism has its counterpart in the individualistic tendencies of Hobbes's political philosophy. In his conclusions, however, Whitehead does describe the general cultural influence of scientific materialism—the privatization of morality, the deadening of nature, the instrumentalization of the environment, the narrowing of the professions, and the glorification of competitive struggle. The cosmology of scientific materialism was not without practical import. The mentality of a people asserts itself in the manner of its living. Institutional formation is the ultimate triumph of the idea.

Scientific materialism was influential in the emergence of the psychological and social sciences in the nineteenth century. The legacy of Newton is evident in psychological and political behavioralism.[8] More generally, the dynamics Whitehead discerned among the physical sciences have their counterpart among the social sciences. It is instructive to parallel three currently dominant schools of thought in American political science with scientific materialism, the scholastic rationalism against which it reacted, and the organic theory of nature Whitehead outlines as an emerging alternative. The three dominant schools of American political science in contention with each other are behavioralism, traditionalism, and post-behavioralism. Behavioralism is, in principle, empirical and analytic; traditionalism is philosophical and ethical; post-behavioralism is dialectical and practical.[9]

Political behavioralism dispenses with traditional philosophies about politics in order to get at the real world, to observe facts in their stubborn facticity, to uncover the forces that determine the behavior of individuals and the actions of states.[10] In that sense, political behavioralism is empirical. Its interest is to formulate regularities of interaction among clearly distinguishable variables. Where possible, variables are quantifiably identified to avoid subjectivity of judgment and to secure precision in result. Verifiable mathematical formulae are the stuff of knowledge. Empirical theories, susceptible to scientific inquiry, are distinguished from prescriptive theories, which are of extra-scientific concern. In Thomas Spragens's summary, the most significant features of political behavioralism are: "nominalism, the myth of the total detachment of the knowing subject, the notion of the absolute heterogeneity of facts and values, a belief in the fundamental homogeneity of knowledge and of the world, and an essentially static cosmology."[11] Political behavioralism, the dominating methodology in American political science, shares with scientific materialism its principles of simple location and its distinction between primary and secondary qualities. Whether political behavioralism gets at the real world it intends depends on the character of the reality that is sought.

The question of the reality that is sought provokes the traditionalist critique of political behaviorism.[12] Traditionalism claims that the most basic philosophical problem—the nature of reality—is unavoidable in any serious political inquiry. Traditionalists find in Plato and Aristotle a more persuasive view of reality than in Newton and Descartes. Political communities are forms of life directed toward some view of good. No political community can be understood apart from its view of good and its claim—implicit or explicit—that its view of good is valid and superior to alternative views. The central task of political science is the philosophical critique of such claims. It is to disclose, as far as possible, the essential order of reality against which existing political communities are to be judged. Thus political knowledge cannot be "value-free." The knower cannot be "detached" from the object of knowledge. And the known is the meaning of human excellence.

Post-behavioralism, which emerged in the 1960s, is more diffuse than either behavioralism or traditionalism. Its critique of behavioralism tends to center on the status of political knowledge.

In one summary,

> A knowing act . . . is a dialectic between a personal agent and an
> external reality upon which the person is contingent. Each pole of
> the dialectic is equally essential, so while the transcendent reality is
> conceived of as existing beyond the knower, it is not seen as exist-
> ing wholly apart from him. The condition of knowing something is
> not a simple correspondence between subjective impressions and a
> wholly impersonal and objective reality but rather a felicitous in-
> dwelling of the knower in the world.[13]

Bluntly, political knowledge cannot be divorced from political action. Political scientists bear responsibility for the practical import
of their thought. On this point, post-behavioralists stand close to
traditionalism. But they stand apart in basic cosmology. The contrast is between a philosophy of becoming and a philosophy of
being. To the post-behavioralist, the aim of politics is not conformation to a transcendent structure of reality so much as participation in the shifting historic struggles in which the values of a
humane existence are constantly threatened. Political science is
part of the dialectic between reflection and action that constitutes
human experience; its methods should manifest that interactive
process.

In brief, behavioralism's methodological perspective is akin
to scientific materialism with its principle of simple location; traditionalism reiterates the classical doctrine that "the final real things
are permanent, eternal, and change and process are simply an
apparent unfolding of them in time"[14]; and post-behavioralism is
closest to the philosophy of organism with its principle of internal
relations. Process thought should be counted among those movements of doctrine—linguistic philosophy, phenomenology, and
critical theory—that Richard Bernstein notes are pressing toward a
fundamental restructuring of social and political theory.[15]

2. CATEGORIAL DEFINITION: THE POLITY

Whitehead's *Adventures of Ideas* opens with a discourse on the
dawning of the idea of the human soul; it closes with a discourse
on the meaning of civilization. Thus as psyche and polis are conjoined in the philosophies of Plato and Aristotle, they are similarly

conjoined in Whitehead's vision of history. But the conjunction raises a question: What is the meaning of the political in human experience? In what sense is the psyche political? What is the location of politics in human life?

The specification of the political is of more than scholarly interest. Orienting concepts do delimit fields of study; but they also, in a sense, constitute reality. That is, they elevate some dimensions of experience, subordinate others, and may distort some forces that nonetheless are vital in the field of action.[16] As such, orienting concepts make a difference in the way institutions are formed and lives are lived. Definitions of law, for instance, are not without significance in shaping the professional life of the lawyer. Just so, specifications of the political instruct citizen and official on how to approach political life.

Leo Strauss argues that "the founder of modern political philosophy is Machiavelli."[17] Machiavelli himself claims to have articulated a new way of thinking about politics. It is a way of thinking about politics without eternal reference. The world of human action is a world of becoming, a history without end. The key to his political thought is in his term "virtue." Where virtue to the scholastics signified moral perfection, to Machiavelli it means virtuosity. Politics is not a means to direct people to a just life and civic friendship. It is a shaping of the stuff of history by whatever means are necessary and available to win greatness and glory. In politics, prudence and power are paramount considerations in a never-ending struggle with fortune. Machiavelli's break with the cosmology and politics of the scholastics was dramatic and was perceived as such. In that sense, Machiavelli is a harbinger of modernity in political theory.

Yet, in a more critical sense, it is Hobbes whose political thought is characteristically modern. Hobbes was attracted to the newly emerging form of scientific thought. Contacts with Descartes, Harvey, and Galileo stimulated the formulation of a "politics of motion."[18] Reality is matter in motion. In Hobbes's words,

> The world . . . is corporeal—that is to say, body—and has the dimensions of magnitude, namely length, breadth, and depth; also every part of body is likewise body and has the like dimensions; and consequently every part of the universe is body, and that which is not body is no part of the universe.[19]

"Life," Hobbes writes, "is but a motion of limbs."[20] While Hobbes thus joins Machiavelli in repudiating the cosmology of the scholastics, Hobbes's uniqueness is his appropriation of the cosmology of the "century of genius," the cosmology of scientific materialism. Without pretending to resolve the controversy over how Hobbes's doctrine of nature and theory of politics are related,[21] I would claim the latter cannot be understood apart from the former. While Leviathan, civic society, is an artificial being, it is brought into existence precisely because of the conditions of the natural world. The structure, meaning, and justification of political formation make sense only within the framework of the materialist cosmology.

From Hobbes's perspective, the analytic method which requires the dissection of objects into their simplest components, is central to understanding. In politics, the simplest component is the individual acting in accordance with the passions, all of which are reducible to two kinds, aversion and adversion. In contemporary terms, the simplest component of political behavior is interest. Good and evil are nothing but functions of interest. The attainment of interest depends on available power, so Hobbes proposes as "a general inclination of all mankind a perpetual and restless desire of power after power that ceases only in death."[22] Interest and power are the central stuff of politics; yet they do not by themselves constitute the political realm for, by themselves, they are simply those conditions which, without containment, make human life a struggle, if not a war, of all against all.

Passions thus present us with a predicament. To suppress them causes unhappiness; but to pursue them invites destruction. The resolution of the predicament lies in the deepest passions, namely, fear of death and desire for self-preservation. The pursuit of all other interests rest on the avoidance of death. Survival is, in this sense, a *raison d'Etat*, for out of the passion to survive emerges the inclination to peace and the artificial creation of political sovereignty. The political sovereign thereby established becomes the source of all law and justice, peace and order, adjudication and security. Politics is therefore the institutionalized means of containing the war of all against all so as to optimize the possibility for individuals to pursue their own interests in their own way within the limits imposed by sovereign authority.

This understanding of the political is not without continuing valence. The argument that a Hobbesian orientation underlies dominant strains in the practice and the study of American politics and law is more than slightly plausible. It has been asserted that it is more Hobbes than Locke whose spirit stands behind American constitutionalism, American liberalism, and American pluralism.[23]

The contrast between Hobbes's and Aristotle's understanding of politics is stark. The difference is rooted in their respective concepts of nature and principles of motion. To Hobbes, motion is change of place. To Aristotle, motion is fulfillment of potentiality. To Hobbes, human motivation consists in passion and interest. To Aristotle, human motivation is a matter of need and self-realization. To Hobbes, there are no final causes and no ultimate destiny that guide human conduct. But, to Aristotle, human conduct must be interpreted, judged, and instructed by the inborn yearning of the person for fulfillment. To Hobbes, the laws that restrain behavior are externally imposed and are acceptable only out of fear for the consequences. To Aristotle, the most fundamental principles of behavior derive from the natural conditions and causes of human life. To Hobbes, laws are needed and political communities are formed because of the inconveniences of the state of nature, for nature is by itself dissociative. Its members are at odds with each other. Their relations are external and inherently threatening. To Aristotle, on the other hand, political association is itself part and parcel of the nature of human life even though there is human creativity in its constructions and its manifest forms may be perverse. In their grounding, associations are formed out of the natural belongings of persons with each other. Nature, in itself, is harmonious and coherent.

On a cosmological level, process thought stands in opposition to both Hobbes and Aristotle, for the doctrine of internal relations is incompatible with both the principle of simple location and the category of primary substance. Yet, on the question of specifying the political, process thought is closer to Aristotle than to Hobbes. Aristotle's *Politics* opens with the proclamation that the polis is a species of community (*koinonia*). The polis is distinguished from other communities by its inclusiveness. Each type of community—familial, educational, economic, municipal—has its specific purpose, each pertaining to human need. The political community is the inclusive association because it incorporates all the associations and activities, resources and responsibilities desirable for the development of a human life. In that sense, a political community is self-sufficient. It needs nothing beyond itself; it is the community of communities; it is that set of relationships which enables people to become what they are meant to become. To Jacques Maritain, incidentally, under the conditions of the modern age, the nation-state system is a poor excuse for political community. Given current economic, cultural, ecological, and military circumstances, a genuine polis cannot be attained on anything less than a global scale. Within the Aristotelian tradition, the political is specified as the kind of inclusive human community providing all the conditions needed for human fulfillment. It is this specification that is more akin to Whitehead's philosophy of organism than is Hobbes's doctrine of Leviathan.

To Whitehead, of course, the human self is profoundly social. It is, in itself, a dynamic interconnection of nexus ruled over at any one moment by a presiding occasion whose character endures through time. But the self is social in a more extensive sense. The irreducible individuality that characterizes each self is not an isolated or merely private individuality; it is public in its dependency and in its implication. The possibilities of the self are heavily dependent on its forms of social inheritance and the determinations of the self constitute a legacy to a social future. The self's identity cannot be comprehended apart from its past or its future, its given environment or its creative formation.

In short, there is a dialectical relationship between self and society, between psyche and polis. In this connection, I would compare Aristotle's thesis that the faculty of language makes political association possible with Whitehead's doctrine of the uses of symbolism. "Language," Whitehead writes, "binds a nation together by the common emotions which it elicits, and is yet the instrument whereby freedom of thought and of individual criticism finds its expression."[24] Thus he judges Edmund Burke correct in pointing to the importance of precedent, of the inherited symbolism of language and act as a political force holding together a throng of persons in organized society. But Burke was wrong in negating the desirability of progressive change and political transformation. In contrast, Whitehead writes:

> The art of free society consists first in the maintenance of the symbolic code; and secondly in fearlessness of revision, to secure that

the code serves those purposes which satisfy an enlightened reason. Those societies which cannot combine reverence to their symbols with freedom or revision, must ultimately decay either from
anarchy, or from the slow atrophy of a life stifled by useless shad-
ows.[25]

The counterpart to Aristotle's concept of polis in Whitehead
is, in brief, the idea of civilization in its institutional form. That is,
polity is the inclusive form of coordinated activity among persons
and groups that incorporates more or less adequately the conditions and qualities of civilization: truth, beauty, art, adventure,
peace. In the total absence of the conditions and qualities of civilization, human life would be impossible. Yet civilization in its full-
ness remains an elusive ideal, a distant telos calling for constant
transformation of given political forms. Psyche and polis depend
upon each other for the fulfillment of their respective aims. Both
are part and parcel of the meaning of human life. The beginning
and the end of *Adventures of Ideas* are related dialectically. Taken
together, they constitute a treatise on politics as polity.

3. HISTORICAL PROBLEMATIC: ALIENATION

Political consciousness is stirred by a sense of something
wrong, of crisis, disorder, injustice, victimization. One of the initial questions to ask of any political theory is: What is the problem
provoking its articulation?[26] The first major portion of Whitehead's *Adventures of Ideas* focuses on the issue of slavery as an
ancient mode of social coordination and contrasts the system of
slavery with modern declarations of freedom and human rights.
Against that background, Whitehead formulates a test of political
order: "In any human society, one fundamental idea tingeing
every detail of activity is the general conception of the status of the
individual members of that group, considered apart from any special preeminence."[27] The superiority of modern political thought
is its acknowledgment of the freedom and rights of the individual.
Despite repeated declarations of human rights, however, there
has been a curious twist of fortune in modern times, such that, in
nineteenth-century capitalist society, the "doctrines of freedom,
individualism, and competition, had produced a resurgence of
something very like industrial slavery at the base of society."[28]

Developments in corporate forms and in the law of corporations in advanced capitalism have but compounded the problem. Doctrines of contract and private property, once symbols of liberal society, have become largely fictions without correspondence to actual social conditions.[29] There is a discrepancy between the rhetoric of freedom and the reality of corporativism.

Slavery in its contemporary form is called alienation by the young Marx. There is controversy over whether the more mature Marx repudiates the concept, yet, in Morton Kaplan's judgment, "Much of the moral power behind the idea of socialism lies in the concept of alienation."[30] Alienation means contradiction, paradox, strains of experience radically out of kilter with each other. Understood this way, the concept of alienation rests on a principle of internal relations.[31]

To locate the concept of alienation in Whitehead's philosophy of organism, I suggest it means a certain lack of conformation between appearance and reality. In its political expression, that lack of conformation is found in any institutional form that, however grand in technical proficiency and organizational elegance, is sadly deficient in moral truth and thus in the qualities of civilization.

More technically, according to Whitehead, actual entities are prehensive in character. They are events of becoming constituted by a creative grasping of prior events throughout the world. Each entity is thus a concrescence, a merging of many things into a new unity in accordance with its subjective aim or "final cause." It is teleologically structured, although its aim is not predetermined in the order of things. Upon attaining satisfaction, it becomes a datum for all future entities; it takes on the role of objective immortality; it continues to be efficacious for good or for ill. The doctrines of prehension and objective immortality are explications of Whitehead's principle of internal relations.

Relations among entities, however, are never that of simple identity. There is always some selectivity, some show of difference, however trivial, in the flow of events. The range of novel possibility open to various entities varies considerably such that a difference of degree becomes a difference in kind. Crystals, flowers, humans are not the same, although metaphysically all are composed of actual entities.

Selectivity in the composition of an actual entity occurs at

various phases of its development. This is especially true of entities with a high degree of mentality. Whitehead's notions of negative prehension, perspective, transmutation, consciousness, symbolic reference indicate various processes of selectivity. Yet, it
must be noted, that which is inhibited or suppressed through
selectivity retains an effect. Even through negative prehension,
the elimination of data initially given from incorporation in an
emerging entity, something is contributed to that entity, for

> A feeling bears on itself the scars of its birth; it recollects as subjec-
> tive emotion its struggle for existence; it retains the impress of what
> might have been, but is not. It is for this reason that what an actual
> entity has avoided as a datum for feeling may yet be an important
> part of its equipment.[32]

On the level of human experience, this same dynamic is even
more importantly present in processes of transmutation and symbolic reference.

Transmutation is the lifting up of a common characteristic
out of a number of otherwise discrete data. Transmutation is a
generalization, classification, a fusion of many into one. It sub-
dues the unique for the sake of the orderly. Without transmutation, life would be unimaginably chaotic. Yet with transmutation
there is a risk appearance will dominate reality.

Symbolic reference is a translation between phases of experience: "The human mind is functioning symbolically when some
components of its experience elicit consciousness, beliefs, emotions, and usages, respecting other components of experience.
The former set of components are the 'symbols' and the latter set
constitute the 'meaning' of the symbols."[33] In more technical
terms, symbolic reference is interchange between perception in
the mode of causal efficacy and perception in the mode of presen-
tational immediacy. It is at the point of translation and interchange that error—"the mark of the higher organisms" and "the
schoolmaster by whose agency there is upward evolution"—is
possible.[34] So declares Whitehead. I would insist, however, that
some schoolmasters are incompetent or worse. Their classifica-
tions are distortions, their simplications are perversions, their
generalizations suppress the truth even when they aim at a certain
kind of beauty. Error, at times creative, does not always have a
happy conclusion. On the level of praxis, the failure of appearance

to conform to reality is near to the heart of injustice, especially when such failure assumes systemic and institutional form.

To illustrate this point, consider John T. Noonan's study of the "masks of law."[35] In the laws enforcing American slavery, processes of simplification and symbolization concealed the reality of persons enslaved. Through those laws, appearance became reality, but not without contradiction. Paradoxically, the slave was both slave and non-slave, person and non-person, and was understood and treated as such. The contradiction resided uneasily in the structure of experience itself. A similar dynamic is discernible in Martin Buber's interpretation of the generation of a lie,[36] Don Browning's notion of the distortions of symbolization in the psychotherapeutic relation and the theological situation,[37] Walter Lippmann's concept of the stereotype,[38] Albert Camus' study of the rebel,[39] and Jürgen Habermas's theory of systemically distorted communication.[40] In each case, fictionalization results in distortion and contradiction. Appearance does not mesh with reality, even though it takes on the force of reality. There is a denial of truth. Relations that ought to prevail for civilized society are corroded.

In Marx's understanding, alienation is the kind of contradiction between appearance and reality particularly characteristic of relations in the capitalist epoch. As Bertell Ollman summarizes the meaning of alienation, it is a dissimulation of those relations that constitute the species-being of humanity.

> Man is spoken of as being separated from his work (he also plays no part in deciding what to do or how to do it)—a break between the individual and his life activity. Man is said to be separated from his own products (he has no control over what he makes or what becomes of it afterward)—a break between the individual and the material world. He is also said to be separated from his fellow men (competition and class hostility has [sic] rendered most forms of cooperation impossible)—a break between man and man. In each instance, a relation that distinguishes the human species has disappeared and its constituent elements have been reorganized to appear as something else.[41]

In capitalism, creative abilities become marketable skills. The worth of products is calculated by exchange value. Value may assume various guises—land, interest, organization, physical facilities—but in all guises it is, most succinctly, capital. Everything and everybody has its price. The character of the cash nexus permeates class relations, political activities, cultural institutions, as well as economic forms.[42] The commodity is the reality of capitalism. But the commodity glosses over a deeper reality that is distorted, though not destroyed, by capitalism. That deeper reality is the species-being of humanity whose central features include creative freedom, productive activity, social cooperation. Alienation is the tension between the reality of capitalism and the deeper reality of humanity. As such, from a Marxian perspective, alienation is the central problematic of our historical epoch. Alienation is not, as some would have it, that distancing of self from others needed to attain autonomy.[43] It is rather a paradox in historical experience, a dialectical tension running throughout modern life. It is institutionalized in structures of oppression and exploitation that have had a deleterious effect on peoples and environments the world over.

I do not mean to identify the Marxian concept of alienation with process thought in any simple way. But there are suggestive parallels between these two modes of thought bearing on political theory.[44] Whitehead and Marx are both critical of scientific materialism. Whitehead's doctrine of internal relations is a counterpart of Marx's principle of dialectic.[45] Whitehead's understanding of high-grade organisms, especially those with consciousness, is analogous to Marx's doctrine of species-being. Whitehead's construction of the problem of appearance and reality is a way of casting the inner dynamics of Marx's notion of alienation. A comparison of Whitehead's doctrine of the qualities of civilization with conditions of life under advanced capitalism would likely be supportive of a Marxian interpretation of human existence in capitalist society.[46] Finally, to both Whitehead and Marx, "nature does . . . contain within itself a tendency to be in tune, an Eros urging toward perfection," "a general drive toward the conformation of Appearance and Reality."[47] The presence of this drive in each actual entity constitutes the anguish of experience. Without that presence, the sense of something gone awry and the impetus for transformation would be ungrounded.

4. CONSTRUCTIVE ORIENTATION: COMMUNITARIANISM

The adequacy of a cosmology lies in its bearing on all phases of experience. Several efforts have been made to demonstrate the bearing of Whitehead's cosmology on social, political, and cultural experience. It has been appropriated as a basis for an "organic political philosophy,"[48] a "politics of civilized humanism,"[49] a "civilization of experience,"[50] a "city of reason,"[51] and a "process social paradigm."[52] Samuel Beer's "philosophy of liberalism" grounded on Whitehead's cosmology is among the more extensive of these efforts. But Beer's formulation is seriously flawed by its neglect of the dialectical relation between psyche and polis.

Beer concentrates on three aspects of Whitehead's thought— his theory of actual entities, his theory of soul, and his theory of God. In each case, he stresses the two-fold character of things: inheritance and creativity.

On the one hand, at the heart of the theory of actual entities is the "notion of mutual immanence": "an actual entity is a compounding of other actual entities. An actual entity is primarily composed of its past."[53] On the other hand, an actual entity is a unity, a concrescence, a unique drawing together of its past into a new creation. The human soul, because of its organized memory and its consciousness, is a special variation on this theme. The richness of its past and the range of its creative possibilities far surpass those of lower grade entities. God, as well, is inheritor and creator, for God receives and cherishes whatever the world has to offer, but God also projects on the world a supreme aim—to attain as keen a degree of balanced intensity as is seasonably possible.

At this point, however, Beer interprets Whitehead as radically distinguishing between the responsibilities of the divine and of humanity. God's concern is the problem of togetherness. It is in God that a final unity is located. God is the solution to the issue of continuity and completeness. God's responsibility is preservation—the harmony of harmonies. But the responsibility of the human soul is creativity. It is to engage in a personal adventure of self-realization. Individuality of thought and action is of the essence of humanity.

This distinction of responsibilities leads Beer to assert:

There is a perfect community of real togetherness in which we are all members one of another. But that society cannot be on earth; it is in heaven . . . Only to this final community and to the Purpose which is making it from the materials we help to provide do we owe unconditional loyalty [sic], not to any earthly community now or later.[54]

Beer thus presses to his conclusion, that Whitehead's thought leads to a politics of liberalism. To Beer, "the metaphysics of this philosophy is collectivist, but its ethics and politics are strenuously individualist."[55] He argues that the individualism of process thought is closer to the natural rights tradition than to utilitarianism because the obligation of self-realization entails a right grounded in the nature of the soul. Even so, process thought, in its political implication, is thoroughly individualistic. In Beer's interpretation, the principle of peace prevails only in the kingdom of heaven; in the kingdom of earth, the law of liberty is supreme.

The ethics of politics is essentially liberal. Its central value is the creativity of the individual soul. It directs our attention to that moment when novelty ingresses into the process of human experience. But that moment is a moment of solitude for the individual. . . . It exhibits the inner liberty of man.[56]

The political task is to protect that liberty and to provide the external conditions and means requisite to its enhancement.

At first glance, Whitehead's social theory in *Adventures of Ideas* seems to lend credence to Beer's interpretation. The social theory is constructed on the analogue of the actual entity. As the actual entity consists of two poles, inheritance and creativity, so social history is composed of two aspects: senseless agencies and formulated aspirations; instinct and wisdom; steam and democracy. In the transition from age to age, both factors are at work. At times, blind forces of necessity are dominant; at other times, ideas and beliefs are in control. The interplay between these poles, however, seems to be transformed by Whitehead into a doctrine of social progress. Higher grade societies are those in which factors of wisdom, consciousness, liberty, the humanitarian ideal triumph. Of force and persuasion as two forms of relations, the latter is the mark of humane society:

Civilization is the maintenance of social order, by its own inherent persuasiveness as embodying the nobler alternative. The recourse to force, however unavoidable, is a disclosure of the failure of civilization, either in the general society or in a remnant of individuals.[57]

But the identification of political liberalism in its classical sense with this doctrine is too simple. Whitehead explicitly calls liberalism to task for both its practical consequences and its theoretical deficiencies. In practical life, its effects contradict its own vision of the free society. In theory, it denies the dialectic between inheritance and creativity that pertains to all forms of life. A key passage directly critical of Sir Henry Maine's famed liberal dictum about the progress of civilization (from custom to contract) and generally critical of liberal doctrine as a whole is as follows:

> The whole concept of absolute individuals with absolute rights, and with a contractual power of forming fully defined external relations, has broken down. The human being is inseparable from its environment in each occasion of its existence. The environment which the occasion inherits is immanent in it, and conversely it is immanent in the environment which it helps to transmit. The favorite doctrine of the shift from a customary basis for society to a contractual basis, is founded on shallow sociology. There is no escape from customary status. This status is merely another name for the inheritance immanent in each occasion. Inevitably customary status is there, an inescapable condition. On the other hand, the inherited status is never a full determination. There is always freedom for the determination of individual emphasis.[58]

This doctrine, through which Whitehead joins Burke's conservatism with Mill's liberalism, is a reminder that each actual entity is essentially social. It is a gathering of the world unto itself. Its character is shaped by data that "constitute the display of the universe which is inherent in the entity."[59] The social and cultural process is an intrinsic part of the stuff of the individual. There is a depth of meaning and a complexity of relations to personal existence that tend to be glossed over in classical liberal theory. Political life is not merely a means to self-realization. Rather polis is integral to psyche even as it is psyche that creatively enacts and reenacts polis. It is this dialectical relationship between polis and psyche that Beer neglects.

Historical progress, when it occurs, is not from tribe to individual, but from one mode of coordinated activity to another, from primary dependence on instinct and compulsion to increasing reliance on power of persuasion, respect for reasoned judgment, toleration of discord.[60] It is in this context that the principle of human rights is allied with social advance, but context conditions meaning. Thus, first, Whitehead notes that the principle of human rights pertains not only to expressive and literary activity; it is, more importantly, a mandate that pertains to social and economic activity for "the essence of freedom is the practicability of purpose" and the practicability of purpose is contingent on the economic facts of life.[61] Prometheus procured for humankind not freedom of the press but fire, not an idea but a technology.

Second, the principle of human rights is subsumed under the notion of moral responsibility. Each entity is subject and superject. Responsibility accompanies both these features. Each entity is responsible, first, for being what it is, for making something of its world, for the creative composition of its own self, for the embodiment of its version of the natural and political world. How and what an actual entity comes to be, given the parameters of its environment, is the initial phase of moral responsibility.[62] This marks the relevance of Beer's doctrine of self-realization. But each entity is also superject. It enters into the composition of other entities. It gives of itself for the formation of future worlds and is responsible for what it delivers.[63] This marks the limits of the doctrine of self-realization.

Without intending to overstate the case, I would suggest that the principle of rights in process thought is closer to an organic political theory than Beer admits. The individual's political duty is not merely to respect the rights of other individuals. It is to contribute to the common good, the good of the polity. Rights are not ends in themselves. They are requisites to creative symbiosis. As requisites, they are abused when suppressed, for their suppression is a denial of human agency. But they are also abused if not employed for the common good.

The common good, in a broad sense, is the realization in social life of the qualities of civilization. In a more pointed sense, the common good is the particular quality of peace in its historical modality. Peace, in human life, signifies a deepening and broadening of experience. It is a reaching beyond prescribed boundaries. It subverts the egotism of self and society. It is an acceptance of the world for what it is, even with its tragedies, but also for what it might be and should become. In relation to peace, human rights—personal and civil, economic and cultural—are enabling. They remove barriers and provide conditions for its realization.

Peace is both a religious and a political concept.[64] As a political concept it is more than the absence of war. It is a certain manner in which people live in, through, and for one another. It bears on the problem of appearance and reality, for "The attainment of Truth (i.e., the conformation of Appearance and Reality) belongs to the essence of Peace."[65] There is

> a factor in each occasion persuading an aim at such a truth as is proper to the special appearance in question. This concept of truth . . . would mean that the appearance has not built itself up by the inclusion of elements that are foreign to the reality from which it springs.[66]

Peace is a quality in experience running counter to those contradictions between appearance and reality that constitute alienation. Alienation in its attitudinal and institutional forms is a violation of peace and thus destructive of civilization. It is degenerative of the common good which is the purpose and meaning of political life.

The primary thesis I am promoting is that the constructive political orientation of process thought with its principle of internal relations is not individualistic liberalism; it is a form of communitarianism.[67] The central value of its political ethic is not the creative act of the individual taken by itself, but how fully that creative act is responsive to the communal ground of its being and how richly it contributes to the communal future. The aim of communitarian politics is not simply the fulfillment of the individual, but the conjunctive participation of each person in a unity of adventure.[68]

3. IDENTIFYING PROBLEMS OF PUBLIC ORDER:

A RELATIONAL APPROACH

SIR THOMAS MORE, THE "man for all seasons," once sketched the outlines of life on an island of Utopia where men and women live and work in communal bliss with each other without greed, without envy, in absolute equanimity. In many respects the vision is attractive. Yet it gains in power when viewed less as an ideal than as a reaction to the dark realities of his times.

Utopianism has a positive function to play in our experience; it is intended to inspire, to spur us to positive action. But it may also blind us to the contradictions and confusions of our actual existence. At such moments, realism is the ready antidote, for realism would turn our attention to the pressing problems of our common life; it would force us to stare directly at the underside of our personal and institutional relations. All is not right with the world. We must learn to confess the distortions of our psychic and social life for what they are.

As John Smith, exploring the experiential basis for knowledge of God, notes, an apprehension of the reality of evil resides at the heart of religious experience: "All religions of scope and depth are filled with a clear sense of the negative judgment on existence. . . . Far from being the complacent celebration of a transcendent goodness existing above and beyond historical life, the religious perspective forces us to acknowledge the reality of evil."[1] Similarly, Thomas Spragens asserts that serious political reflection originates in an unshakeable discernment of something having gone wrong.

> Political theories are like pearls; they are not produced without an irritant. Most political theories . . . are written as attempts to deal with some very real and urgent problems. The problems *demand* the attention of the theorist; they don't merely invite inquiry. The theorist writes out of compelling practical necessity—the need to under-

stand a political situation that is causing real trouble and real pain
to those caught within it.[2]

Spragens's thesis, however, provokes a series of questions.
How do we know when we in fact confront "some very real and
urgent problems"? What constitutes an issue in the public realm?
What are the marks of something having gone wrong? Is it not
possible that some perceived problems, if we thought about them
deeply enough, are but pseudo-problems, not really problems at
all? Moreover, even if we agree on a troublespot, mightn't we
disagree on the sense in which it is troubling? If we do so differ,
what is the basis of the difference?

Sometimes differences are matters of superficial opinion, offered without much forethought. At other times, however, they
are matters of considered opinion. They arise out of a larger vision
or theory about the meaning of public life or, more generally, the
meaning of human existence. Political theories, produced out of
discernment of "some very real and urgent problems," are, at the
same time, the bases for the diagnoses of those problems. They
are ways of talking politics. They underlie considered efforts to
determine problems of the public realm, to define what is going
wrong. But political theories stand in tension with each other and
may have a seasonal quality about them. The political theory that
was prominent at one time and place may be viewed as irrelevant
if not suspect at some other time and place.

With that background, I shall explore the following thesis.
During the seventeenth and eighteenth centuries, two political
theories emerged in strength tending to set the terms for defining
the problems of the public realm in the West well into the twentieth century. While they do not set well with each other, both are
expressions of modern individualistic liberalism. The two positions are rights theory and interest theory. But these two theories,
visions of public life, while not without merit, are inadequate at
the present time. They should be replaced by, or incorporated
within, relational theory. I shall, first, characterize each of these
ways of talking politics and then relate them to three current questions of public order—the quality of the environment, the equality
of women, and the character of plant closings and plant
relocations.

1. Rights Theory

Rights theory and interest theory, as means of determining when something has gone awry in society, are pervasively characteristic of the modern Western world. I am taking John Locke as representative of rights theory and Jeremy Bentham of interest theory. Granting that each may be read in different ways—Locke, for instance, as a constitutionalist protector of civil liberty[3] or as a bourgeois protector of property[4] or as a Calvinist preoccupied with eternal happiness[5]—I am more concerned to appropriate their political visions as they have been played out in the everyday arenas of political discourse and debate.

The seventeenth century was a watershed in social and political thought. John Locke was among those whose reflections mark a radical turn in the manner in which Anglo-American peoples looked at and engaged in public life. The shift, in brief, was from a concern for ultimate human fulfillment to an obsession with human liberty; from the imposition of social duties to a clamor for individual rights; from the educative use of law to inculcate a virtuous disposition to the coercive use of legal means to safeguard external goods.

To John Locke, civil society is established only because there is a problem to be solved. In the absence of the problem, people would have no reason to create or to sustain institutions of law-making and law-enforcement. The public realm is not an intrinsic good; it was formed as a remedy for a preexisting issue. To understand the character of that issue, one must imagine what life might have been or might be like without a political order. This imaginary moment is what John Locke meant by his construct of the state of nature.

Under such conditions, people would live in "a state of perfect freedom to order their actions, and dispose of their possessions, and persons as they see fit, within the bounds of nature, without asking leave, or depending on the will of any other man." Moreover, a state of nature is "a state . . . of equality, wherein all the power and jurisdiction is reciprocal, no one having more than another."[6] Yet, though free and equal, all are under the burden of the law of nature: "no one ought to harm another in his life, health, liberty, or possessions."[7] But if anyone violates the law of nature, then everyone "hath a right to punish the offender."[8]

We have no reason here to untangle all the intricacies of Locke's doctrine of property. We must, however, understand the following. In Locke's own language:

> Every man has a property in his own person. This no body has any right to but himself. The labour of his body and the work of his hands, we may say, are properly his. Whatsoever then he removes out of the state that nature hath provided, and left it in, he hath mixed his labour with, and joined to it something that is his own, and thereby makes it his property.[9]

Thus, prior to the formation of civil society, everyone possesses a set of three rights, innate and God-given—a right to life, to liberty, and to property, which Locke at times aggregates under a single rubric, a right to property. These rights everyone possesses in the imagined state of nature. While they may be, under specific circumstances, waived or qualified, they are in principle inalienable. Moreover, in this imagined state of nature, the force of human interest gives rise to a work of human ingenuity—money—a convention through which the quantity of one's property might be extended indefinitely, for money does not spoil as other goods do.

But if life with its rights and with the prospect of an indefinite expansion of property is available in the state of nature, what is the problem provoking the formation of a public order which seems to constrain us so with its laws and regulations? Locke poses and answers the question in these words:

> If man in the state of nature be so free, as has been said; if he be absolute lord of his own person and possessions, equal to the greatest, and subject to no body, why will he part with his freedom? Why will he give up this empire, and subject himself to the dominion and control of any other power? To which 'tis obvious to answer, that though in the state of nature he hath such a right, yet the enjoyment of it is very uncertain, and constantly exposed to the invasion of others. For all being kings as much as he, every man his equal, and the greater part no strict observers of equity and justice, the enjoyment of the property he has in this state is very unsafe, very insecure. This makes him willing to quit a condition, which however free, is full of fears and continual dangers: and 'tis not without reason, that he seeks out, and is willing to join in society with others who are already united, or have a mind to unite for the

mutual preservation of their lives, liberties, and estates, which I call by the general name, property.[10]

In sum, the chief purpose of people placing themselves into commonwealths and under governments is the preservation of their property. Without organized society, one's existence, liberty, goods are always in jeopardy. That is the moral apology for political organization which, supported by the people's consent—tacit or express—promises security through three things: an established law which declares publicly what one's rights are; an independent judiciary which resolves conflicts over rights when they arise; and a power of enforcement which executes the laws and implements judicial decision.

Locke himself, it has been argued, was concerned with preserving only the rights of the bourgeoisie, more particularly, the Anglo-Saxon, male, Protestant bourgeoisie. Nonetheless, in subsequent centuries, rights theory has been widely invoked to define what is amiss in human relations and to rectify those wrongs. It has been called upon to explain the fundamental need for law, to justify revolutionary change in government, and to place pressure on public assemblies and courts in their day-to-day workings. Rights theory was the ostensible drive behind the American and French Revolutions in the eighteenth century; it inspired the abolitionist cause and fired the women's suffrage movement in the nineteenth century; it was a vision sparked anew by the atrocities of the Nazi holocaust and given dramatic form in the United Nations Declaration of Human Rights in the twentieth century.

2. INTEREST THEORY

The language of rights may be limited, as with Locke, to life, liberty, property. Or it may be expanded to embrace almost anything one wants, as with a recent book on rights for "people under age," declaring: a "right to sunshine," a "right of fathers to be present in the delivery room," and a "right to a sex-break."[11] But to declare a right is serious business; it is to call on all forces of government to protect one's claim and to rectify any alleged wrong. It is to lay out non-negotiable demands against the world. Under some conditions, rights may be defeasible, but otherwise one's rights set strict constraints on all other agents regardless of consequences. Thus the legal dictum: Let justice be done, though the heavens may fall.

That is the reason Jeremy Bentham was riled up with the French Assembly's Declaration of the Rights of Man and Citizen and with rights theory generally. The idea of innate rights is silly, if not mischievous:

> Natural rights is simple nonsense: natural and imprescriptable rights, rhetorical nonsense, nonsense upon stilts. But this rhetorical nonsense ends in the old strain of mischievous nonsense; for immediately a loss of those pretended natural rights is given, and those are so expressed as to present to view legal rights. And of these rights, whatever they are, there is not, it seems, any one of which any government can . . . upon any occasion whatever, abrogate the smallest particle.[12]

Rights theory, to Bentham, is, in its effects, a stumbling block to the political process. It stands in the way of government doing its proper job. It is an illicit way of perceiving what is wrong in the body politic and what should be done to remedy that wrong. It is, basically, a fiction: "Rights are fictitious entities—*the people* real ones. Realities on this occasion, as on all others, realities I prefer to fictions."[13] But how should we understand "the people"? Understanding them aright provides an alternative to rights theory in the perception of public problems and in the design of appropriate solutions.

The alternative is interest theory, stated summarily in the opening paragraph of Bentham's *Introduction to the Principles of Morals and Legislation*:

> Nature has placed mankind under the governance of two sovereign masters, *pain* and *pleasure*. It is for them alone to point out what we ought to be, as well as to determine what we shall do. On the one hand the standard of right and wrong, on the other the chain of causes and effects, are fastened to their thrones. They govern us in all we do, in all we say, in all we think: every effort we can make to throw off our subjection, will serve but to demonstrate and confirm it. In words a man may pretend to abjure their empire: but in reality he will remain subject to it all the while. The *principle of utility* recognises this subjection, and assumes it for the foundation of that

system, the object of which is to rear the fabric of felicity by the
hands of reason and law. Systems which attempt to question it,
deal in sounds instead of sense, in caprice instead of reason, in
darkness instead of light.[14]

Some years following initial publication of this statement, Bentham added a note announcing that the principle of utility might better be rendered the greatest happiness principle. But they amount to the same thing for each "approves or disapproves of every action whatsoever, according to the tendency which it appears to have to augment or diminish the happiness of the party whose interest is in question. . . . I say of every action whatsoever; and therefore not only of every action of a private individual, but of every measure of government."[15]

Given conflicts of interest, the responsibility of government is to seek the most expeditious means toward the most beneficient end, the optimization of pleasure of all citizens and subjects concerned. That is the felicific calculus, a calculus still very much in fashion. As one commentator notes: "Much of the argument for such welfare measures as Medicare, rent subsidies, and so forth is couched in latter-day utilitarian terminology."[16]

What kinds of interest count in the felicific calculus? To Bentham, any interest whatsoever: "Quantity of pleasure being equal, pushpin is as good as poetry."[17] On this point, John Stuart Mill demurred: "It is better," he wrote, "to be a human being dissatisfied than a pig satisfied; better to be a Socrates dissatisfied than a fool satisfied. And if the fool, or the pig, are of a different opinion, it is because they only know their own sides of the question. The other party to the comparison knows both sides."[18] However, Mill provides no criterion to distinguish higher from lower interests, and interest theory in general has heeded Bentham over Mill.

Where, then, are there social ills in need of diagnosis and remedy? Wherever individuals, severally or collectively, suffer pain or dream of pleasure; wherever interests clash and require adjudication; wherever the yearnings of people might be met and happiness increased; wherever by redistributing wealth or rearranging relations the agonies of a people might be alleviated. How might problems so described be resolved? In interest theory, there are two ways, not always consistent with each other: a free market and a democratic polity.[19]

Regarding the former, Bentham's appreciation for the ideas of his contemporary, Adam Smith, is notable. The marketplace is, by design, an apt means to respond to the stated needs and interests of a population, assuming they have the wherewithal to make their demands effective. The felicific calculus, translated into the curves of supply and demand and the equations of cost/benefit analysis, is at the heart of classical economics. It is no accident that James Mill and David Ricardo were among Bentham's staunchest disciples.

But interest theory gives warrant to the interventionist actions of a democratic polity as well. A government, directed by the principle of utility as its raison d'etre, will guide, manipulate, even coerce the forces of the public order deliberately and unashamedly to maximize pleasure and minimize pain.

Thus utilitarian theory may be appropriated as an apology for both laissez faire economics and the welfare state. Yet, despite their differences about the role of government, these two fundamental public policies are conjoined in their avowed objective: to serve the interests of as wide a range of individuals as possible. In both cases, it is the expression of self-interest that registers a problem in need of attention; the more intense its articulation, the more likely its satisfaction. These institutions are designed not to honor innate rights, but to respond to stated interests. To the market, everything has its price; to the welfare state, nothing is beyond its calculus.

3. Relational Theory

Rights theory and interest theory are not identical. In the former case, a political ill is announced when one declares, "I have been wronged," and seeks a remedy through the courts or through a revolution. In the latter case, a political problem is declared when one cries, "I am in pain," and searches for relief through marketplace or parliament. Yet, despite their differences, they have been synthesized in various permutations. Understandably so, for in deepest origin they are akin. As I have represented them, using John Locke and Jeremy Bentham as proponents, they betray all the marks of the modern liberal, bourgeois world. Both rights theory and interest theory are expressive of the "Myth of

the Liberal Enlightenment." Those who adopted this myth
"frankly proclaimed that a society was wanted in which everyone
would be committed to the rational pursuit of self interest. . . .
None feared that selfish pursuits would destroy the public interest, the general welfare, the common good."[20] As Henry Kariel
unfolds the myth, it discloses three assumptions, all questionable.

The first assumption is of the benevolent potentiality and
segmental character of natural resources. Nature—non-human reality—is nothing but a set of resources to be appropriated and
used as one has a mind to. One cannot strictly "harm" nature, for
nature has no rights or interests of its own. And whatever unfor-
tunate effects one has on natural resources are limited and local.

The second assumption is of the essential innocence of private power. Individuals, alone or in association, are thought to be
basically reasonable and to act, by and large, responsibly, if not
out of pure intentions, then out of enlightened self-interest. Whatever one's motives, honesty is understood to be the best policy
and prudence is considered a sufficient protector of the general
interest.

The third assumption is of the necessity but inherent treach-
erousness of public power. Government is best kept limited and
bound by internal checks and balances. Apart from national defense, the proper function of public power is to secure private
rights and to promote private interests, resolving conflicts where
need be, but never, save in the direst of emergencies, to assume a
directive role for the society as a whole, if, in fact, it makes sense
to speak of society as a whole.

These assumptions are no longer viable. We now confront a
kind and range of public problems which require an alternative
theory, a different vision of the meaning of our common life.
Consider such issues as the disposal of toxic and nuclear wastes,
famine and poverty across the mid-belt of the entire globe, conur-
bation and the savaging of urban life, institutionalized racism and
sexism, the irony of a nation-state system bent, for purposes of
national survival, on exterminist policies. Such issues are of a
structural character. Rights and interests are tangled up in them.
But if traced out in their causes and consequences, they are complicated and intricate; they engage our lives in multiple ways,
directly and indirectly. Taken altogether as pieces of the mosaic of
modern living, they are indicative of a principle of understanding

neglected in rights theory and interest theory: a principle of connectedness.

Given this principle, our lives, individual and associational, are caught up with each other. They cannot be lived in splendid isolation, each pursuing an independent pathway, regardless of all others. That may have been true in other times and places, but it is no longer true today. While in some significant sense we are solitary beings, we nonetheless bear the burden of the world in every breath, in every bite, in every thought, in every act.

If that be the case, we must alter our assumptions. First, nature is not a warehouse of supplies from which we may take at will without concern over consequences. We should speak instead of a biosphere in which the line between the natural and the human is not so hard and fast as we once thought. Second, private power, concentrated nowadays in large corporate organizations, is no more innocent than public power. Both are treacherous. Both may be beneficial. Neither is justified in its doings by good will alone. The retriculations and repercussions of their policies must be carefully monitored and assessed. Third, there is need for a public space and a directive agency through which the peoples of the land—the whole land—may debate over the meaning of the common good and may plan for the future. In sum, rights theory and interest theory must be subsumed under relational theory.

Relational theory introduces a new way of understanding the self. As a self, I am an agent, one who acts. But action is always interaction. While there is an irreducibly solitary dimension to my being, I am not simply an isolated individual possessing innate rights or driven by personal desires, pursuing my own private pilgrimage through the world in my own self-determined way. My life has both a private and a public side. What I can be and do is contingent on a host of relationships of which I am an inheritor. With that inheritance, the possibilities for my life are enhanced, or, as is often the case with whole classes of persons, oppressively crimped. However, in turn, what I am and do sets the context and fixes the conditions for other agents and beings.

There are three theaters of interaction within which my life is lived.[21] Each theater is characterized by the two dimensions of relationality: separateness and connectedness, individuation and participation, solitariness and togetherness. The three theaters are the self's relationship to nature, to other selves, to one's own work and station. Taken together, they constitute the self's relationship with the world. Pervading all theaters, there is an ideal form of relationship, specified, respectively, as natural harmony, sympathy, and concrete universality.[22] In the absence of harmony, sympathy, concrete universality, both self and world are deprived.

Thus, in relational theory, a political problem is delineated not so much as a violation of rights or a delimitation of interests as a perversion of relations. Its traditional name is alienation. Alienation is a distortion or twisting of connections; it is a negative form of belonging. Under conditions of alienation, one is ensnared in webs of interaction that run contrary to one's own good. One is led to the reproducing of institutional structures which result in one's anguish.

The classical instance of alienation is slavery. In a master-slave relationship, the slave is, on the one hand, a tool of the master, an instrument to be employed as the master dictates, to be disposed of as the master alone wills. But the slave, on the other hand, is a person, possessed of the dignity of humanity, a free spirit, a reflective and responsible being. The system requires the slave repeatedly to enact and to reenact a structure of interaction that goes contrary to the very capacity that enables the slave to act at all in a responsible manner.

Consider other cases, closer to our own time: women in male-dominated institutions; Hispanics in an Anglo society; a consumer culture producing a constant flow of lethal wastes; the lot of the nations driven to militaristic frenzy out of fear for their survival. In each case, one may speak of the violation of rights and conflicts of interest, but alienation may be a more accurate descriptor of the conditions that plague us. From the perspective of relational theory, we are caught in webs of connectedness on which we depend, from which we benefit—or from which some few of us think we benefit—but which, in a profound sense, have a debilitating, deleterious effect on the delicate structures of life.

4. An Ecological Crisis

In the next three sections of this chapter, I shall delineate three crises, one in each of the three theaters of life: an ecological crisis, a social crisis, and an economic crisis.

Whether and in what sense there is an ecological crisis depends, I have asserted, on the theory or vision that informs one's thinking about the world and about one's self. Ecology, broadly understood, means the pattern of relationships between an organism and its environment or between self and nature. But, what is nature? That word and its counterparts in other languages have been used in widely diverse ways throughout the history of human consciousness.

Nature, from the standpoint of a narrowly construed rights theory, is that stuff around and about one with which one's labor may be mixed and which one thereby appropriates for the extension of one's self. Nature has no dignity of its own. It is infused with dignity as it is transformed through labor for the sustenance of human life and the delectation of the human spirit. Foodstuffs and pharmaceuticals, satellites and symphonies—all are intricate admixtures of human labor and natural resource. So heavily has the human hand been imprinted on the world of nature, the eye cannot easily discern the boundary between them. The constructs of technology are so pervasive, we are led to speak of a *second* nature, an environment born of the conjunction between human enterprise and natural forces.

From this severely anthropocentric perspective, can there be an ecological crisis? Perhaps. First, Locke places all actions, therefore all property, under the strictures of the no harm principle. Thus where our creations threaten harm to others, directly or indirectly, a kind of ecological crisis may result. Consider such cases as pesticides and acid rain. We may have, in no small measure, conquered the first nature that surrounds us, but we have created a second nature that portends a dire fate. Moreover, Locke's doctrine of property contains a proviso. One may claim that to which one's labor is joined, but only "where there is enough, and as good left in common for others."[23] The implications of the proviso are far-reaching. Where resources, especially those needed for life and liberty, are scarce, we may encounter an ecological crisis even if induced not by nature itself, but by the maldistribution and monopolization of nature's goods. What is the availability to all the world's population of the four classic elements: arable land, clean air, energy resources, potable water? Is there enough and as good left in common for all? Where there is not, we face a crisis.

Thus, within a narrowly construed rights theory, impingement on the life and liberty of our fellows through our appropriation of the stuff of nature indicates an ecological crisis. In consequence, William T. Blackstone, a rights theorist, formulated the human right—which, he argues, should become a legal right—to a livable environment.[24]

Interest theory is far more generous than a narrowly construed rights theory in extending to nature a moral status independent of human concerns. The utility principle is not, to Bentham, anthropocentric. In a famed footnote pertaining to laws prohibiting cruelty to animals, Bentham asks why we should bother about horses and dogs. Because, he responds, they suffer. They, too, experience pleasure and pain.[25] On this ground, Peter Singer would distinguish amongst species according to sensitivities.[26] It is not morally the same to kill or to coddle a ladybug and a Labrador, a copperhead and a chimpazee. Nature is not a uniformly neutral stuff to be appropriated to human design. The felicific calculus, however, must enter even lower forms of reality on its ledger. It must consider what happens to ladybugs and copperheads, even trees and rocks. But it must consider them if not for their own sake, then for the sake of those whose feelings are affected by them. An organism's environment may enhance pleasure or cause pain. Where an environmental configuration threatens survival or induces deep suffering—think of the poisoned soils of Love Canal or the parched lands of Ethiopia—one may, with cause, speak of an ecological crisis.

However, rights theory and interest theory, with all their merits, are stretched to a breaking point when confronted with the full depth and complexity of the ecological problem. This is true even where rights theory is broadened to incorporate rights of animals and trees.[27] Thus, in inquiries about the ecological problem, many commentators are pressed toward a shift in theoretical framework: from exclusionism to inclusionism,[28] exemptionalism to environmentalism,[29] atomism to holism.[30]

The shift, I would contend, is toward relational theory, toward a communal view of the bond between self and nature. To Aldo Leopold, a renowned exponent of conservationism and proponent of a land ethic: "We abuse land because we regard it as a commodity belonging to us. When we see land as a community to which we belong, we may begin to use it with love and respect."[31]

Leopold would have us view land in a new way.

> [Land] is not merely soil; it is a fountain of energy flowing through
> a circuit of soils, plants, and animals. Food chains are the living
> channels which conduct energy upward; death and decay return it
> to the soil. The circuit is not closed; some energy is dissipated in
> decay, some is added by absorption from the air, some is stored in
> soils, peats, and long-lived forests; but it is a sustained circuit, like a
> slowly augmented revolving fund of life.[32]

The premise of all ethics, Leopold writes, is "that the individual is
a member of a community of interdependent parts."[33] We may be
impelled to seek our own within that community, but we are
constrained as well to cooperate for the sake of the whole. How
widely we cooperate depends on the boundaries of inclusion. The
land ethic extends the perimeters to embrace the entire ecosphere.

> The land ethic . . . enlarges the boundaries of the community to
> include soils, waters, plants, and animals, or collectively: the
> land. . . . a land ethic changes the role of *Homo sapiens* from con-
> queror of the land community to plain member and citizen of it. It
> implies respect for his fellow members, and also respect for the
> community as such.[34]

The central principle of the land ethic is simply put, if not simply
applied: "A thing is right when it tends to preserve the integrity,
stability, and beauty of the biotic community. It is wrong when it
tends otherwise."[35]

At stake in the ecological crisis are not just the rights of
people or the interests of sentient creatures, but the texture of the
whole community of being from which we benefit and to which
we are indebted. William Pollard has stated this sentiment in elegant fashion assuming one can forgive the sexist imagery in which
it is cast:

> the Earth is a rare gem of fantastic beauty, and . . . its desecration
> . . . by any being is an act of awful sacrilege against which the heart
> of all meaning and purpose in the entire universe must cry out in
> anguish . . . A full appreciation of not only the beauty but of the
> holiness of the Earth and of the immense creative investment that
> has gone into procuring it, including as an integral component man
> himself, is essential to man's continued occupation of this planet.

> With such an appreciation man will know how to love the Earth as
> she is indeed worthy of love, to woo her into ever greater and more
> wonderful creative achievements, to celebrate the wonder of the
> achievements already realized, and to have a holy fear of desecrat-
> ing her.[36]

Desecrating the earth is an act of alienation. To desecrate the
earth, however much it may seem to be one's right or to redound
to one's benefit, economic or otherwise, is to distort the deepest
meaning of the self as belonging interactively to the world of
nature.

5. A SOCIAL CRISIS

Alienation also marks the inner character of the social crisis
in the theater of relations between self and other. I shall take the
feminist question—the question of the place of women in the social process—as a paradigm for conditions of all oppressed peoples. There are significant historical and cultural differences
among the realities of racism, anti-Semitism, sexism, ethnocentrism, but all are structures of domination and in all cases there is,
at the present, an intense struggle for liberation. However, the
feminist question is appropriately paradigmatic, for women have
suffered from subordination from time immemorial.

In the tradition of rights theory, John Locke does not serve
the cause of women's liberation terribly well. As Susan Moller
Okin notes, Locke equivocates.[37] In attacking Filmer's
patriarchalism, Locke muses that the paternal principle "seems to
place the Power of Parents over their Children wholly in the *Father*, as if the *Mother* had no share in it, whereas if we consult
Reason or Revelation, we shall find she hath an equal title."[38] On
the other hand, where husband and wife are at odds on matters of
household and property, "it therefore being necessary that the
last Determination, *i.e.* the Rule, should be placed somewhere, it
naturally falls to the Man's share, as the abler and the stronger."[39]

Moreover, the eloquent pronouncements of the Declaration
of Independence within their original context, despite subsequent
readings, applied to white males only. The self-evident truths
"that all men are created equal, that they are endowed by their

Creator with certain unalienable Rights, that among these are Life, Liberty and the Pursuit of Happiness" referred indeed to men alone.

But once stated, the idea of human rights stands available for all classes of people chafing under structures of oppressive domination. Hence in 1792, two years after chiding Edmund Burke for his broadside against the French Revolution with her *Vindication of the Rights of Men*, Mary Wollstonecraft published her widely touted *Vindication of the Rights of Woman.*[40] Whatever biological differences obtain between male and female, there are none, she insists, in rational power and ought therefore be none in fundamental duties or rights. Humanity, not sexuality, is one's species; in that man and woman are of like kind.

Later, in 1848, at a convention on women's rights held in Senaca Falls, New York, under the leadership of Elizabeth Cady Stanton and Lucretia Mott, a Declaration of Sentiments and Resolutions was promulgated following the exact form of Jefferson's Declaration of Independence, but centered on a new premise: "The history of mankind is a history of repeated injuries and usurpations on the part of man toward woman, having in direct object the establishment of an absolute tyranny over her." The convention resolved, among other things, "That woman is man's equal—was intended to be so by the Creator, and the highest good of the race demands that she should be recognized as such" and "That the equality of human rights results necessarily from the fact of the identity of the race in capabilities and responsibilities."[41]

In the tradition of interest theory, John Stuart Mill, prodded by his companion and collaborator, Harriet Taylor, is the most prominent early defender of the feminist cause. In Okin's assessment, Mill "is the only major liberal political philosopher to have set out explicitly to apply the principles of liberalism to women."[42] His essay on *The Subjection of Women* (1869) is an explication of his long-held opinion: "That the principle which regulates the existing social relations between the two sexes—the legal subordination of one sex to the other—is wrong in itself, and now one of the chief hindrances to human improvement; and that it ought to be replaced by a principle of perfect equality, admitting no power or privilege on the one side, nor disability on the other."[43] Against arguments about the inherent nature of women, Mill intones:

I deny that any one knows, or can know, the nature of the two sexes, as long as they have only been seen in their present relation to one another . . . . What is now called the nature of women is an eminently artificial thing—the result of forced repression in some directions, unnatural stimulation in others. . . . [Respecting the mental potentialities of women:] It is a subject on which nothing final can be known, so long as those who alone can really know it, women themselves, have given but little testimony, and that little, mostly suborned.[44]

Given their internal logic—not always fully comprehended or supported by their devotees—rights theory and interest theory are perspectives from which the constrictive domination of any class of people is morally reprehensible and thus a central problem of public life. What possibly can relational theory add to the justifiable drive, gradual and agonized though it has been, toward full parity of treatment between men and women? Following Carol Gould, I propose it can add a dimension of social particularity and solidarity.[45]

Gould observes that the feminist question tends to be answered in either of two ways, both of which she rejects. On one side, women, like men, are seen as essentially human; differences between them are merely cultural and therefore accidental. Alternatively, women are seen as one side of a sexual polarity which divides all persons into two distinct categories, male and female.

Gould offers a third prospect, captured in the concept of concrete universality. With this concept, she is asserting that we constantly are creating and recreating ourselves, in our humanity and in our sexuality, through interactions with one another and with the world of nature. History is a process of new formations. What we are and what we shall become are not givens. They are results of the many relations in which we are engaged and whose character we affect, in however small a degree, by the manner of our participation. Liberation is a breaking through inherited forms, releasing the possibility of determining afresh our identity and therefore the mode of our interaction with others. What it means, therefore, to be a woman and what it means to be a man are not matters to be defined a priori or out of past experience alone, but in practice, with, in the most favorable circumstances, each of us supporting and encouraging the other: equality of women and parity of treatment, of course, but as conditions for interactive mutuality and creative possibility.

Valerie Saiving voices a similar ideal in her two-fold assertion: that the proximate goal of feminism is "liberation of women to full participation in the life of the human species" and that the final goal, "provisionally symbolized as androgynous life," is "life no longer governed by the paradigm of dichotomy and domination."[46] Androgyny is a controversial concept.[47] It signifies the conjunction of maleness and femaleness. What Saiving intends, I believe, is to affirm two things by the concept, both of which are expressive of relational theory: first, that certain qualities, traditionally assigned respectively to men and to women, need to be fostered in all humans[48] and, second, that, whatever the precise form of our sexuality, we all belong together.[49] Thus to the degree that women are denigrated, all humanity suffers. The social crisis is more than a question of rights and interests. It is a question of alienation, of reproducing structures of relationship which fail to do justice to the meaning of our selves as interactive beings.

6. An Economic Crisis

I turn, finally, to the third theater of life, to the relation of self to one's own work and station. In this theater there are, as Roberto Unger remarks, two dimensions to one's self:

> As a being who participates potentially in the many-sidedness of the species, the person is an *abstract* self. As a being whose life is always finite and determinate and who is never in fact more than a small part of what he might be, the person is a *concrete* self. The relationship between the abstract and the concrete self is the psychological counterpart to the relationship between self and others. It is the problem of individuality and sociability reexamined from the perspective of the internal organization of personality.[50]

Among the more significant locations in which one's abstract self becomes concrete, in which a broad range of possibilities is narrowed down to specific action, is work.

Narrowly understood, work is making a living, earning one's keep, drawing an income to pay one's bills. But that is a short-sighted view of the meaning of work. Broadly understood, work is a process of forming and extending one's self. It is a shaping of one's identity through time. It is a creation of one's being. Through the expenditure of one's energies, it is the unfolding of a pattern of interaction in which the specific sense of one's life is at stake.

This broad construction in which work is not merely a production of external goods, but a production of one's self and of the concrete meaning of one's life, is characteristic of several Western traditions. *"Ora et labora"*—pray and work—has long been a motto of Roman Catholic monastic communities. The doctrine of vocation is an essential motif in classical Protestantism: work is a calling, a way of living one's life to the greater glory of God. Again, within the liberal tradition, work is the infusion of one's energies into the stuff of nature and is thereby an amplification of one's being. And to Karl Marx and Friedrich Engels, work is the distinctive activity of humankind.

Work, in short, is of deep significance in the living of one's life. But, within a highly organized economic system, the question of meaningful work is not a simple matter open to personal determination alone. That question is, at the moment, tied intimately to a development Barry Bluestone and Bennett Harrison call the "deindustrialization of America," that is, "a widespread, systematic disinvestment in the nation's basic productive capacity."[51] Deindustrialization is most evident in the relocation and closing of plants: the shifting of textile mills, for example, from New England to the South and subsequently to the Far East or the closings of steel mills in the Youngstown and Pittsburgh areas.

In what sense do such plant closings constitute a social and political problem? That people are left, at least momentarily, without work when a plant closes is among the tragic facts of economic life, but in what sense have they been done a wrong?

From the standpoint of rights theory, conflicting answers are possible. On the one hand, a corporation, long held as a possessor of rights by the Supreme Court, may do with its property what it will so long as it honors its contracts, obeys the law, and serves the imputed interests of its stockholders. As I may dispose of my house, barn, or garden as I wish, so may a corporation dispose of its plants. On the other hand, the employees of a corporation and the community in which they live may hold some kind of property right in the enterprise. That was the dilemma stated sharply by

Justice Lambros in the Youngstown Steel Mill case, *Local 1330 v. U.S. Steel.*

In a pretrial hearing, the judge announced that we "pride ourselves in the United States on the preservation of property rights" and that no one "can criticize United States Steel in making decisions which they feel are in their economic interests, because we truly need today an economy that is responsive to changing world demands." But then, in a manner pressing his thought toward relational theory, he mused that Youngstown had been

> built around this industry. Everything that has happened in the Mahoning Valley has been happening for many years because of steel. Schools have been built, roads have been built. Expansion that has taken place is because of steel. And to accomodate [sic] that industry lives and destinies of the inhabitants of that community were based and planned on the basis of that institution: Steel.[52]

Hence he concluded "that a property right has arisen from this lengthy, long-established relationship between United States Steel, the steel industry as an institution, the community in Youngstown, the people in Mahoning County and the Mahoning Valley in having given and devoted their lives to this industry."[53] Yet, Justice Lambros bemoaned in the court case itself, "Unfortunately, the mechanism to reach this ideal settlement, to recognize this new property right, is not now in existence in the code of laws of our nation."[54] Lambros, we might note, represents a shift that has occurred in rights theory, not without opposition, from exclusive focus on political and civil rights to concern for economic and cultural rights.[55] Recently, for instance, Martin Carnoy, Derek Shearer, and Russell Rumberger have proposed a "new social contract" to include an economic bill of rights, listing, among others, "the right to a decent job for all those willing to work" and "the right to a secure and stable community."[56]

From the perspective of interest theory, however, with its linkage to the capitalist tradition, deindustrialization may be an admirable, even healthy, albeit momentarily painful, development. This is the implication of Lester Thurow's encouragement of disinvestment:

> While there are many voices calling for more investment, the process of disinvestment is even more important. Eliminating a

low-productivity plant raises productivity just as much as opening a high-productivity plant. . . . To close a low-productivity plant . . . makes it possible to move workers and capital that have been tied up in this activity into new, high productivity activities. With more men and investment funds, new activities can grow more rapidly. . . .

This is one of the places where the mixed economy has not worked. Capitalism is, after all, a doctrine of failure. The inefficient (the majority) are to be driven out of business by the efficient (the minority), and in the process productivity rises. Yet we are extremely reluctant to practice this part of our economic religion.[57]

Thurow is not, we should note, allied with the neo-classical school of economics. He assigns government a key role in reindustrialization and in solving environmental problems. He announces "a moral responsibility to guarantee full employment." But on the question of deindustrialization as such, he is clear: we should not stand in the way of disinvestment. All the customary considerations of an economic utilitarianism—Peter F. Koslowski calls it "the ethics of capitalism"[259]—support the mandate: continued economic growth, the maximal satisfaction of interests, effective organization, efficiency in the allocation of resources. In the short run, there is pain. In the long run, everyone benefits. Deindustrialization manifests the process of "creative destruction" which, in Joseph A. Schumpeter's judgment, is "the essential fact about capitalism."[60]

Justice Lambros, in his sensitivity to the devastating consequences of deindustrialization in Youngstown, was pressed to move beyond rights theory in its traditional form. So also must one move beyond an interest theory limited to sheer economic calculus to comprehend the full meaning of plant closings.

The immediate loss of jobs is but a beginning. Significant percentages of persons remain unemployed for months, even years. The burden falls more heavily, in proportion, on women and blacks than on white males. Hospital and pension benefits are lost; family savings are depleted; homes are repossessed by financial institutions.

More profoundly, "acute economic distress associated with job loss causes a range of physical and mental health problems."[61] In cross-national studies spanning fifty years, Marie Jahoda uncovers the social psychological dimensions of unemployment: the crushing of self-esteem, loss of imagination, oftentimes a withdrawal from reality, boredom and deep frustration, aggression, even suicide—all causing stresses and strains in families and other relations.[62]

Disinvestment, moreover, has ripple effects, economic and otherwise, throughout an entire community. The economic multipliers are the easier to measure: retail stores, banks, supplier plants are affected. Tax revenues are diminished, having an impact on education, infrastructural facilities, public services. But demands on public services—unemployment compensation and welfare benefits—are increased.

The effects are more than economic; they are political and cultural. Voluntary associations suffer loss of revenue and loss of leadership. In sum, the whole texture of relationships that constitute a vibrant and meaningful community life is shredded. Referring to a plant closing in New York State, Bluestone and Harrison remark, "The state of 'anomie' described for Cortland County— evident in community disorientation, anxiety, and isolation—is found almost universally in case studies of plant closings."[63]

What, then, is the problem in cases of deindustrialization resulting in mass unemployment? In some sense, a violation of rights; certainly an increase in pain, momentary or long-lasting; but most fundamentally a disruption of those extensive and complicated forms of interaction that comprise the context of our lives. The curiosity is that we not only tolerate, we ofttimes celebrate, and in our everyday actions perpetuate, a system of work running contrary to our humanity.

Taken altogether, the three issues I have discussed—the degradation of the environment, the denigration of women, the deindustrialization of our communities—are forms of alienation. That is the character of our political problem in its deepest meaning. Alienation is a negative structure of belonging. In the institutions of our common life, as we reproduce patterns of living that harm others, we are, in effect, harming our selves as relational beings.

The obverse side of alienation in its political name is the common good or the public good. Given its religious name, it is love. Common good and love signify a fundamental reality of our lives: we live together; we belong together; we depend on each other; even in moments of solitariness, we bear one another's burdens. In exalting the common good, I do not intend the whole-sale rejection of rights theory or interest theory. Of course, we should resist the violation of rights; most assuredly, we must seek the mitigation of pain. While we must go beyond Locke and Bentham, we should heed the wisdom they have to offer. They would be protective of our individuality. But individuality can be had only in community. The tragedy is that, nowadays, our communities are deeply riven by forces of alienation. That is the true character of the problems of our public order.

4. ON MEANINGS OF PUBLIC GOOD

FOR MANY CENTURIES, during times ancient and medieval, the concept of public good (or common good, general welfare, public interest) was central in interpretations of public life. To Cicero, for instance, a republic was any large group of persons associated through some agreement on the character and content of justice and joined together to promote the public good. To Thomas Aquinas, the common good was the final and governing purpose of political and legal systems. But during much of the twentieth century, the term, "public good," has often been discerned cynically, yet accurately, as merely a rhetorical costume for special interest. The question I would pose is whether and in what sense public good or common good might become a meaningful concept for the interpretation and evaluation of public life or whether it is a curious anachronism dependent for its meaning on classical or medieval world views.

An underlying aspect of this question is the relation between God and the world. How God is related to the world and what difference that relation makes or ought to make in the diverse pursuits of human life is a central issue in theological inquiry. It is an issue in political theory as well. Glenn Tinder, for instance, was recently provoked to assert:

> The first task of social thought in our time is to regain the posture, if not of religious faith, at least of religious openness and inquiry. During most of Western history theology and political theory have, despite some exceptional periods and figures, been close allies. What seems called for by the present failure of political imagination is above all a restoration of this ancient coalition.[1]

One focus for the restoration of this ancient coalition is the meaning of public good.

Over recent decades a vigorous conversation has transpired in Anglo-American political thought bearing on the topic. I shall

75

review four schools of thought in the conversation—the behavioral, the linguistic, the pragmatic, the traditional—and then present a fifth alternative.[2] These schools of thought diverge on several issues: the scope of experience relevant to political understanding, the relation between interpretation and evaluation, and the principle by which to study political realities. On this last point, the behavioral and linguistic schools rely on an analytic principle; the pragmatic school relies on a pragmatic principle; the traditionalists rest their case on a form of totality or holistic principle. The alternative I shall present is based on a principle of internal relations. In presenting this alternative, which relies on Bernard Meland's concept of the "structure of experience," I shall contrast its political implications with those of classical liberalism in areas of property and civil liberties, illustrating the position with several Supreme Court decisions.

The behavioral school of thought intends to be realistic. What is considered realistic, of course, depends on some idea of the character of reality. Realism is a function of ontology. To the behavioralist, realism in political inquiry means to analyze the manifest behavior of persons and groups as they pursue their respective interests in politics. This is the dominant approach in American political science:

> For whatever reason, recent and contemporary political science has adopted an essentially unidimensional conception of politics. Specifically, politics is viewed as oriented toward the maximization of personal interests within the constraints imposed by organized society. Accordingly, the political process, at any level, becomes a matter of bargaining for policies designed to achieve this end.[3]

Given this perspective, there is no interest or good of the public as a whole, for it is not meaningful to speak of a public as a whole. There are many and diverse groups, each with its own particular set of interests and goals, values and purposes. Each group reaches for power and influence over others to protect its own interests, to pursue its own goals, to gain whatever advantage it can in the mad scramble for the resources and goods of human life. A society is "nothing other than the complex of the groups that compose it."[4] The assumption that there is an interest of the society as a totality, standing apart from and in judgment upon the particular interests of particular groups, goes contrary to all we know about the actual behavior of persons in public life.[5] From this standpoint, it is not even useful to designate moments of equilibrium in the political process as the public good, for such moments are rare, unstable, and, most importantly, themselves subject to contention. Nor is it useful to characterize the procedures by which group conflicts are resolved as the public interest, for procedures are also part of the stuff of political controversy. Groups diverge widely as to whether the results of political struggle or the procedures through which the struggle advances are good.

To be sure, the term, "public good," is widely employed in political rhetoric. It is used by some groups to declare their moral superiority over others. It is used by politicians to give an aura of respectability to their pet policies. It is incorporated in legislation to instruct regulatory agencies how to administer the laws. It is invoked in judicial bodies as an alleged reason for particular decisions. But, from a behavorialist standpoint, when these uses are taken altogether and examined critically, they are so contradictory, so imprecise, so muddled, so vague, that the term must be adjudged virtually meaningless.[6]

Thus the analytic principle applied to political behavior results in a descriptive pluralism in which public good is little more than a rhetorical flourish.

The analytic principle also underlies studies of public good by the linguistic school, but with a different focus, an enlarged understanding of what counts for political behavior, and a different result. The language analyst focuses on how the concept public good functions in political argument. As the analyst notes, normative discourse is an integral part of political behavior. Talk constitutes a large portion of political activity. In the study of politics, one should attend to the manner in which arguments are adduced and justifications formulated. One should identify particular forms of argument associated with different key terms of political judgment, e.g., national security, fairness, equality, welfare. Language may be misused and abused. But there are normal, conventional, ordinary uses and to identify such uses will contribute to an understanding of politics and may contribute to increased rationality in actual political discourse as well.

Where to the behavioralist, language is a function of nonlinguistic behavior, to the language analyst, behavior is intended to express what is said and thought. Thus the language analyst broadens the scope of what is accepted as meaningful political action to include conceptualization and rational communication. From this perspective, public good is not merely a rhetorical flourish. Rather, to Brian Barry, it is a kind of political principle.[7] To Richard Flathman, it designates a way of doing politics.[8] To Virginia Held, it indicates a form of political institution.[9] All three, however, are merely reporting on ways the concept of public good is used in conventional discourse. All three maintain a theoretical distance from political evaluation. All three purport only to be dissecting the language game in political argument to identify how in fact the term "public good" is employed.

To Brian Barry, for instance, people invoke a variety of principles in their political arguments with each other. In that variety, there are two basic kinds—want-regarding and ideal-regarding principles. Want-regarding principles address the question of whether and how the wants, wishes, desires of persons shall be satisfied. There are two subtypes of such principles—distributive and aggregative. Distributive want-regarding principles, such as equality and justice, indicate whose wants should be satisfied and to what degree. Aggregative want-regarding principles, on the other hand, including public interest and public good, pertain to the satisfaction of wants in a more general way, without specifying precisely which persons or groups are to be benefitted. Crime control, defense policies, parks and roads, programs for health care are in the domain of public interest in Barry's taxonomy of principles as they are ordinarily used in political argument.[10] Thus Barry's claim about public good is modest. It is that public good is among the conventional considerations involved in disputes over public policies.

Both the behavioral and the linguistic schools view politics as a struggle among contending groups. The difference is that where the behavioralist tends to dismiss public good as a meaningless concept in the interpretation of public life, the linguist discerns it as fulfilling a meaningful function in political discourse.

In contrast to both behavioralist and linguist, the pragmatist views the concept of public good as emerging out of a special problematic and as constituting the central core of political organization. To the pragmatist, thought is a function of action. Notions of public good are formulated in response to challenges and difficulties presented by the concrete world of human action. In Dewey's classic formulation, two different kinds of consequences result from transactions among persons: those affecting only persons engaged directly in a transaction and those affecting third parties.[11] This difference is the basis of the distinction between the private and the public. A public is formed whenever persons associate to gain some control over the impact on them of the consequences of transactions in which they are not directly engaged. Officials are those who act on behalf of a public. Their role is to protect and advance the interests of a public whose lives would otherwise be conditioned and whose capacities to pursue their own purposes would be restricted by forces beyond their control.[12]

The pragmatist's concept of public good thus provides a general criterion for evaluating political associations, namely, the degree to which a public is knowledgeable about, is organized to respond creatively to, and has officers constituted to deal effectively with all those social transactions within its historical situation that have an impact on its life. The actual and detailed content of public good is transitory, subject to change as the indirect consequences of social transactions vary in kind and scope and as remedies are tested for their relative satisfactoriness.

At first glance, there appears to be some similarity between the pragmatic formulation of public good and the behavioralist conception of public life as a struggle among contending groups or publics to gain sufficient power to control their several destinies or to fulfill their several interests. But Dewey, over fifty years ago, discerned the antipluralistic drive of modern technology. Modern technology has effected a social revolution of major proportions. The affairs of local communities are deeply affected by remote, invisible, massive, powerful organizations. A "new age of human relations" has emerged. We have been forced into a vast complicated social organism. But, in Dewey's words, the "Great Society" thus formed is not the "Great Community." The technologically created world order has resulted instead in an "Eclipse of the Public," a dramatic loss of control over indirect consequences, a disintegration of genuinely public life.[13] Within the circumstances of modern technological society, a radical change in the conditions of social life is required in order to enable persons to form a public, to communicate their concerns with each other, to shape plans for the future, to cooperate in the effectuation of those plans. The pragmatic conception of public good thus calls for the subordination of modern technology and technologically oriented organization to public inquiry and political control.

This means that, under conditions of modern social life, public good is more a distant aspiration than a present reality. But it is not merely a rhetorical flourish and it is more than a convention of linguistic usage. It is an experientially grounded, agonizingly complex problematic of public life. The problematic is how a diverse and diffuse people can become an active public whole in order to institute a process by which they can continuously create new futures that will or might be good for them.

From the traditionalist standpoint, the other three forms of thought about public good are deficient. They all avoid direct confrontation with the ethical question. Behavioralists and linguists only describe political behavior, although linguists approach the ethical question in their insistence that normative discourse is an integral dimension of political life. Yet to them, public good is only one among several alternative principles in political deliberation. Pragmatists more nearly approximate the ethical question in their understanding that public good constitutes the core of public life. However, the pragmatists' conception of public good is more procedural than substantive. It concerns more the way in which persons might gain control over their future than what the substance of that future ought to be. In the open-ended and experimental nature of the pragmatists' conception, the question of proper ends and prescribed destiny is avoided.

To the traditionalist, each society or political association is the postulation of a good. That is, every political community is a totality; it is a corporate entity; it is not merely a collection of individuals and groups. A political community persists while individuals are born and die and groups come and go. A political community is a whole with a status in reality independent of its members at any one time. Its wholeness is a good that it affirms and after which it aspires. The good constitutes both its identity and its measure, for in its existent state, it is always in need of correction and development.[14]

From this perspective, an adequate understanding of public life must move beyond an analytic interpretation of diverse groups contending for political power, a clarification of how political arguments are constructed, and an elucidation of the crises and challenges provoking political response. On a more fundamental level, political understanding must focus on what Edward Shils terms the "center and periphery" of political association.[15] The center of a political association consists in a valuational and institutional system. The institutional system embodies the beliefs and symbols, sensibilities and virtues that make up the valuational system. One's membership in the association is determined by one's relationship to this central zone. It may be more direct or more distant, more supportive or more antipathetic. While in every political association there is a periphery varying in degree of indifference to or active rejection of the central system, no political association could exist without a significant measure of consensus supporting the center. The central zone is closely related to the authority structure of the association, each reinforcing the other and both sharing in the quality of sacrality. Within this framework, the ground and most vital content of public good is the central value system of the political association, whatever its content happens to be.[16]

On an even more fundamental level, the traditionalist confronts the center of a political association with the critical ethical question of whether the resultant postulation of public good is truly human. Shils's sociological theory of center and periphery is given an ontological twist. The center then consists of those understandings and values that are humanistic in character. The central zone of an actual political association may be eccentric, resulting in a distortion of genuinely human existence. The public good on this level is the valuational and institutional system in which and through which people are enabled as fully and as readily as possible within given historical conditions to achieve their perfection. This is what Jacques Maritain, Yves Simon, and others term the "common good."[17] It embraces a wide range of features: provision for the health, safety, and economic welfare of all members of the political community; transmission of the community's cultural heritage through schools and other institutions; maintenance of a rich associational life including domestic, voluntary, and political groups; education of all persons intellectually, emotionally, and morally; encouragement of and support for the qualities of civic friendship, social justice, and creative freedom; subordination of the political to the spiritual realm. The public good is the proper good of the community as a whole whose purpose is to provide that societal context within which persons together and individually might perfect their created powers and fulfill their natural and supernatural destinies. In sum, to the traditionalist the public good is the political aspect of the human good. The human good depends on and is nurtured by, although it ultimately transcends, the political association. The public good, the good of the political association as a totality, is thus governed by a substantive understanding of what is required for the fulfillment of human nature.

In large part, the difference among the four schools of thought depends on what dimensions of human experience are admitted as relevant to political inquiry. This is the point of Dante Germino's radical distinction between a behavioral and a traditional approach to political thought:

> Man in the fullness of his experience is the proper focus of the political scientist's attention, and whole areas of that experience—labelled "ethical," "metaphysical," or "theological,"—may not arbitrarily be banished from the realm of science on the ground that they do not yield hypotheses testable by the precise canons of neopositivist methodology. . . . if the empirical fact of the existing human person cannot be investigated by means of the sensory observation of phenomenal regularities alone, then it must mean that these methods in themselves are inadequate.[18]

Others as well have distinguished a narrower and a broader empiricism and have argued that social inquiry must become more expansive than contemporary behavioralism in what modes of thought and experience are accepted as pertinent to the interpretation of human affairs.[19] In sum, within social and political inquiry there is need to reconsider the status and nature of experience. How one construes human experience bears on how one thinks about public life in general and public good in particular.

Following Bernard Meland's theological reconstructions, I suggest that a principle of internal relations provides a ground for reconsidering the character of human experience and for conceiving public good in a way that draws together the holism of the traditionalist conception with the dynamism of the pragmatist conception.

Various developments of thought and aspects of cultural experience witness to a profounder realism about the nature of things than the realism intended by the behavioral movement or language analysis. A major shift in imageries of thought has occurred in several areas of scientific and humanistic study, although that shift has only begun to have an impact on the mainstream of Anglo-American social thought. The shift is from an atomistic to a relational conception of reality. Field theory, organicism, holism are expressions of the emerging conception. In this change of thought, the imagery of a mechanistic world has given way to an acknowledgment of a "dimension of depth" in our lives. That is, the realities in our experience extend far beyond our powers of analytic observation and verbal description; there are structures of meaning and relationship impossible to discern fully; an adequate understanding of experience must include respect for mystery; life is living in a dynamic context whose complete character can never be totally comprehended. An acknowledgment of this "dimension of depth" means the analytic principle as a mode of interpreting reality is deficient. To abstract entities analytically from their full living context is not improper and may be useful, but it is to distort their character, for the relations within which they exist are part and parcel of their life.

Thus, in contrast to the individualism of the classical liberal tradition which is allied with the analytic principle in social theory, each person and association is understood as existing within a context of relationships which are constitutive of its meaning and being. This context of relationships is, in Meland's term, a "structure of experience,"[20] a unified and organic, formative but evolving burden of meanings and sensibilities that is present in and presses upon each moment of existence. It is an inheritance that derives from and connects one to times and places of which one may have no conscious awareness. The structure of experience

> is a depth in our natures that connects all that we are with all that has been within the context of actuality that defines our culture. It is a depth in our nature that relates us as events to all existent events. It is a depth that relates us to God, a sensitive nature within the vast context of nature, winning the creative passage for qualitative attainment.[21]

The structure of experience is borne through individual memories and sensibilities and through social customs and insti-

tutions. This means experience is never simply internal and subjective. It has a manifest and public character. Moreover, the
structure of experience consists not only of the transmission of
past attainments, but of openness to change and transformation
as well. The interplay between persistent past and open future is
the location of the creative working of God which "presses upon
every emergent event the possibilities of past attainment; or bends
the persisting valuations to the opportunity of creative emergence."[22] Thus the principle of internal relations must not be associated in any simple way with classical conservatism even though
it incorporates an analogous respect for the definitive and normative relevance of past attainments.[23]

Meland defines experience as "a bodily event which conveys
to the living organism, in a holistic way, its rapport [with] and
participation in the nexus of relationships which constitute its
existence."[24] But while experience so defined is the primary
source of all awareness, persons and associations may be more or
less receptive to its full burden, to their dependence on it, and to
their responsibility for the enrichment or impoverishment of its
evolving structure. And, as is all too evident, individuals and
institutions are prone to do violence in ways subtle and flagrant to
the network of relations on which they depend, within which they
find their meaning, and for which they bear responsibility.

Meland insists on differentiating the ultimate communal
ground of being indicated by this understanding of experience
from sociality in the more ordinary sense of the term. Nonetheless, I suggest there is a political ethic derivable from the principle
of internal relations and its associated understanding of experience. It is a political ethic in which "relationship is of the essence."[25] From this perspective, public life is viewed, not as an
artificial but necessary *modus vivendi*, but, at its profoundest, as an
expression of the relational character of reality. A political association is therefore perverse if it is arbitrarily exclusionary, rigidly
nationalistic, even narrowly humanistic, for a political ethic constructed on the basis of the principle of internal relations affirms
the goodness of the vast but ever-changing connections among
entities, human and nonhuman, that sustain the whole creation
and constitute the context of public life and political activity. In its
religious dimension, this political ethic is grounded in the idea of
God as the one in whom and for whom we live, as the one who

unifies and preserves the world but who calls the world forward to new creation and qualitative attainment.[26] In its social dimension, this political ethic holds out the vision of an open society, a society that is equally respectful of duration, communal intercommunication, and creativity.[27] That is, in an open society, traditions are received appreciatively although not uncritically as a vital resource of meanings and possibilities; participants are understood as members of each other, responsible to each other for what they are and for what they become; and moments of decision are cherished as critical for the molding and shaping of a new future for the entire community, indeed for the entire world.

Within this framework, public good is the good of the public. It is the good of the open society itself. It is the good of the relationships through which the members of the community sustain one another, contribute to one another, and constitute a creative center for the ongoing life of the community. To act in the public good is not to deny the individuality of persons or associations, but it is to reject the indifference to others of individualism. It is to accept the obligation of being a gift to the entire community of being. This means the public good as the good of the open society has reference that extends beyond the confines of municipalities, nation-states, and regional alliances. As Cicero wrote centuries ago, "we must now conceive this whole universe as one commonwealth of which both gods and men are members."[28]

Suppose one accepts the argument that public good is a central value in public life and that the relational conception of public good is persuasive, what difference would that make in the way one thinks about political issues or engages in political activity? How does a relational conception of public good bear on central political policies? Among fundamental public issues that might be used to draw out implications of meanings of public good are what Nicolas Berdyaev has called the problem of bread and the problem of freedom, or more narrowly, the problem of property and the problem of civil liberties. In modern times, these problems have been conceived as vital tests of classical liberalism. Property rights and civil liberties are the litmus paper of liberal political thought. It would be instructive to compare the orientations of classical liberalism and of the principle of internal relations to these problems.

To the classical liberal, an absolute right to property is an indispensable means of protection against tyranny. Property is an expression of individual personality. The right to use, to enjoy, and to dispose of one's property at will, unencumbered by external constraints and regulation, is the mark of the free person. This orientation pertains to both older, more tangible forms of property (such as land) and newer, more intangible forms (such as negotiable instruments, contractual and statutory rights, and other types of claim upon the economic order). From the same standpoint, an absolute right to freedom of expression and association is conceived as necessary if persons are to be respected as self-determining agents. To be responsible for one's own being and destiny, one must be free to speak one's own mind and to associate with whom one wishes without control or regulation. In sum, to the classical liberal, property rights and civil liberties are political means for individual self-expression and self-realization.

From a relational standpoint, on the other hand, property is a trust. To be sure, without property in its most elemental forms life itself would be impossible, and without property in a variety of forms the prospects of creative expression would be exceedingly delimited. But the classical liberal doctrine of property blunts two truths: first, that property has a communal ground and, second, that property has a public consequence. From the perspective of a political ethic constructed on the basis of a principle of internal relations, possession, control, and use of property of all forms, tangible and intangible, should be evaluated by their contribution to the formation, maintenance, and qualitative character of an open society. While this proposition applies to all levels of property, it is particularly pertinent to the highly concentrated, complex, extensive systems of property that have emerged in modern industrialized societies, namely, economic corporations. Out of a dominant concern for productivity, profit, organizational growth, or technical development, economic corporations have tended to ignore their larger impact on the structures of life, human and nonhuman. Because of that impact, however, they cannot and ought not be thought of as strictly private institutions. They are thoroughly public and are therefore subject to the obligations of public good.

Similarly, from a relational standpoint, civil liberties are a responsibility. One cannot ignore the fact that where civil liberties are totally absent, have been narrowed in scope, or remain unenforced, individual lives and fortunes suffer. Governments are not unlike all other forms of organized power in their propensity to overreach their proper jurisdiction and to ignore or to exploit those whom they are meant to serve. Civil liberties, therefore, are properly understood as a means of protecting individuals from despotic power and providing them with the social space needed for creative self-expression. But civil liberties do not fulfill a function only for the individual. In principle they fulfill a critical function for the political association as well, indeed for the entire community of being. Civil liberties are a means for effective participation in communal decisions. They are a means to press for reform and to introduce novel patterns of relationship. They constitute a structure within which and through which persons and groups may contribute alternative modes of thought and styles of life to the ongoing community. An enforced system of civil liberties is an institutional channel through which social judgment, political transformation, and cultural renewal are made possible. The character of a community is enriched and enlivened to the degree to which a system of civil liberties is sustained within the political process and is utilized by the citizenry to respond to the vision of an open society.

Thus, from a relational standpoint, public good mandates that property be understood and treated as a trust and that civil liberties be acknowledged and utilized as a responsibility. The implications of this position may be made more concrete by comparing it with certain strains of argument found in a set of Supreme Court decisions.

The nineteenth-century case of *Munn v. Illinois* (1877), for instance, dealt directly with the question of property rights.[29] The question was whether a private business may be required by law to secure a license and to limit its rates or whether such a requirement violated the owner's right of property. The court was split. At stake was the meaning of public good. In the majority opinion, Chief Justice Waite argued that the fundamental purpose of a body politic is the public good; that the police powers of a state, that is, its specifically political powers, include the authority to regulate the use of property when needed for the public good; and that, as Lord Chief Justice Hale had pronounced in the seventeenth century, when private property is "affected with a public interest, it ceases to be *juris privati* only." Thus the critical issue to be addressed was: When does private property become affected with a public interest? Waite's response was general and far-reaching: "[P]roperty does become clothed with a public interest when used in a manner to make it of public consequence, and affect the community at large. When, therefore, one devotes this property to a use in which the public has an interest, he, in effect, grants to the public an interest in that use, and must submit to be controlled by the public for the common good, to the extent of the interest he has thus created."[30]

Justice Field's sharp and detailed dissent charged that the majority opinion was subversive of the rights of private property. In Field's judgment, the principle of public good pertains only to property specifically dedicated to or granted for public use, as in the case of innkeepers and public ferries. Otherwise, one's use of one's property may be regulated only to prevent direct and explicit injury to others. The difference between these two justices was not merely a matter of degree. It was a matter of social and political perception about the character of economic conditions at the time, about the nature and purpose of political association, and about the meaning of public good. Field's more analytic, individualistic, classically liberal perception was outvoted in this case, but within a few years it became the orthodox view of the Supreme Court in property cases and remained such through the first third of the twentieth century.

Nebbia v. New York (1934) was among the earliest cases in the 1930s to adopt and thus to revitalize Justice Waite's doctrine in *Munn.*[31] Justice Roberts for the majority noted that in American constitutional tradition, the use of property and the making of contracts were normally matters of private concern, but he argued that the body politic always has a paramount duty to provide for the public good and that public good takes precedence over private rights of property and contract so long as methods of due process are not violated in doing so. There is, he asserted, no class or category of business that may not be affected with public interest under some circumstances. The *Nebbia* case, which pertained to the question whether New York State could legitimately set minimum prices for the sale of milk, is particularly instructive, for both the immediate seller and the immediate buyer had an interest in a price lower than that which the legislature established, but the legislature was concerned with the long-range and systemic impact of the price structure on the entire process of milk production, distribution, and availability to the public.

During the same year, the case of *Blaisdell v. Home Building and Loan Association* (1934) dealt with the right to contract.[32] A contract, in principle, is a social institution in which parties freely and voluntarily create their own system of rights and duties relative to each other. In the classical liberal dictum of Sir Henry Maine, the progress of civilization has been a development from status relations to relations of contract. The constitutional mandate that no state shall pass any law impairing the obligation of contracts expresses the same liberal doctrine. The *Blaisdell* case effected a radical modification of the contractual principle by appeal to public good. The background of the case was the Great Depression of the 1930s. Many persons were unable to maintain payments on home and farm mortgage contracts. If the explicit terms of the contracts had been enforced, these persons would have lost their homes and lands. The question was whether the state may legislate a moratorium on such contracts to extend the period during which mortgagors might complete their payments. The controlling principle in the majority decision was a citation from an earlier case. "Into all contracts . . . there enter conditions which arise not out of the literal terms of the contract itself; they are superinduced by the preexisting and higher authority of the laws of nature, of nations or of the community to which the parties belong; they are always presumed and must be presumed, to be known and recognized by all, are binding upon all, and need never, therefore, be carried into express stipulation, for this could add nothing to their force. Every contract is made in subordination to them."[33] In effect, Chief Justice Hughes, for the majority of the court, invoked the principle of public good to legitimate a modification of the mortgage contracts out of concern, not merely for the persons threatened with loss of their homes and lands, but also for the society as a whole. The durability and the character of the entire community depended on how the body politic responded to the critical events of the time. The minority of the court dissented, invoking the sanctity of contracts and the unequivocal clarity of the constitutional prohibition against the impairment of contracts. It matters not that the owners of the mortgages were predominantly corporations and the mortgagors were predominantly individuals or that widespread loss of homes and

farms might deepen the economic crisis confronting the entire
nation.

In the first of two civil liberties cases that dealt with compul-
sory flag salutes in the public schools, *Gobitis v. Minersville School
District* (1940), Justice Frankfurter presented an argument that
echoes the concerns of classical conservatism for social cohesion
and continuity.[34] The Gobitis children, as Jehovah's Witnesses,
refused to salute the flag on the grounds of a right to freedom of
religious belief and practice. In Frankfurter's mind, the exercise of
that right in this case conflicted with the highest of political and
legal values, namely, national unity. There can be no rights or
freedoms at all without a unified, organized society. "The ultimate
freedom of a free society is the binding tie of cohesive sentiment.
Such a sentiment is fostered by all those agencies of the mind and
spirit which may serve to gather up the traditions of a people,
transmit them from generation to generation, and thereby create
that continuity of a treasured common life which constitutes a
civilization. 'We live by the symbols.' The flag is the symbol of our
national unity, transcending all internal differences, however
large, within the framework of the Constitution."[35] Thus it is appropriate, according to Frankfurter, for a body politic to devise
ways to evoke the unifying sentiment without which civil and
religious liberties are impossible. A society dedicated to the values
of civilization "may in self-protection utilize the educational process for inculcating those almost unconscious feelings which bind
men together in a comprehending loyalty, whatever may be their
lesser difference and difficulties."[36] The conflict in this case between the civil liberties of the Gobitis children and the need for
social cohesion may be tragic, but to Frankfurter the resolution of
the dilemma was clear. Public good in the form of unity must
prevail.

From the standpoint of a relational conception of public
good, Frankfurter's argument has some force. There is indeed a
need for communal spirit. His error, however, was twofold. He
ignored the critical question of the character of the unity that
ought to prevail among a people, and he failed to consider alternative means more appropriate than compulsion to attain communal
feeling. The unity of an open society must include the freedom to
differ. As Justice Jackson wrote in *Barnette v. West Virginia State
Board of Education* (1943), which overruled *Gobitis*, "The test of its

[freedom's] substance is the right to differ as to things that touch the heart of the existing order. If there is any fixed star in our constitutional constellation, it is that no official, high or petty, can prescribe what shall be orthodox in politics, nationalism, religion, or other matters of opinion or force citizens to confess by word or act their faith therein."[37] Community and freedom, including the freedom to differ, are not inherently incompatible. Both are vital to public good.

In *Marsh v. Alabama* (1946), Justice Black construed civil liberties in an explicitly relational manner and affirmed the subordination of property rights to the interests of civil liberties as they pertain to the good of the common order.[38] The question in this case was whether a person may legitimately distribute religious literature on the property of a company town against the wishes of the town's management. Black's affirmative response was grounded, not on the right of the person distributing the literature to freedom of expression, but on the right of citizens to receive such literature, information, and arguments as they might want or need to make decisions. Whoever owns the property on which a town is situated is irrelevant. The public has a vital interest in open channels of communication. All members of the public, wherever they live, make decisions that bear on the welfare of the community. To decide wisely and for the good of the community, they must be informed, and the information they receive must be uncensored and unhindered. According to Black, this is the reason freedom of speech, press, and religion occupy a preferred position over the rights of property. The good of the public as a whole is served by civil liberties. Even Justice Reed in his dissent affirmed the moral duty of the body politic to provide opportunity for information, education, and religious enlightenment to all members of the public, only insisting that owners of private property should not be compelled unwillingly to cooperate in the fulfillment of that duty. What Reed disregarded was that in this case the property owner was a shipbuilding corporation whose size and impact on the society were of evident public consequence and whose operation, especially as it concerned the inhabitants of the town it owned and governed, was properly subject to the requisites of public good.

The final case I shall discuss, *Steele v. Louisville and Nashville Railroad Co. and others* (1944), contains an implication that bears on freedom of association.[39] In this case, one of the defendants, the Brotherhood of Locomotive Firemen and Engineers, had become the exclusive bargaining agent for firemen with the railroad company under the provisions of the Railway Labor Act. The Brotherhood, an unincorporated union, was a private organization. Blacks were excluded from its membership. In its position as exclusive bargaining agent, the union secured a series of agreements with the railroad company whose effect was to demote blacks to more arduous and less remunerative positions and, ultimately, to exclude them altogether from any possibility of working as firemen. Chief Justice Stone's position was that the Brotherhood, in its capacity as bargaining agent, was exercising a power granted by Congress to act on behalf of the entire union of firemen, whites and blacks, union members and nonunion members, and it was therefore obliged to act impartially and fairly for the good of them all. A more general proposition may be derived from that argument, namely, that voluntary associations and private organizations, authorized and protected by systems of civil liberties, have an obligation to act in conformity with the requisites of public good. They have a responsibility for the manner in which what they are and what they do bear on the quality of communal life.

In general, civil liberties constitute an institutional form for communal interchange and for novel thought and action. Within the political association, they secure the possibility of creative contribution to the growth of qualitative attainment. It is by that criterion that civil liberties are justified, and it is by that criterion their use should be judged.

A concluding word. There is a strong strain of political alienation in our society and throughout the world. Its causes are many. Its manifestations are diverse. But its results, whatever forms they assume, are dehumanizing, for politics is part and parcel of human life. Politics is the public dimension of our common existence. Politics, in the deepest and broadest sense, is the public side of the adventure in which the entire community of being is involved. The construction of public good which I have suggested is an effort to acknowledge this sense of politics, to articulate the aspiration that should guide the adventure, and to indicate a vision of possibility over against which the full depths of political alienation and tragedy can be comprehended. In this construction, public good is the good of the open society in which creative interrelationship is of the essence and in which there is an intimacy of connection between the political and the religious, for the religious is not merely what one does with one's solitariness. It is also how what one does with one's solitariness bears on the world's togetherness. If God is that "sensitive nature within the vast context of nature, winning the creative passage for qualitative attainment," the concern of God is not only with the interior disposition of one's psychic life. It is also with the forms and texture of communal life. Public good is thus a category at one and the same time of religious ethics and political ethics. It is thus also a possible focus for the restoration of the ancient coalition between theology and political theory.

5. ON MEANINGS OF JUSTICE

NEAR THE BEGINNING of the twentieth century, social critics wrote often of *"die soziale Frage"*—the social question. Influenced by the Marxist tradition of radical social thought and concerned about the impact of capitalist and industrial civilization on the condition of human life, they were moved by a prophetic passion to speak a word of judgment much like that of Amos.

What did they mean by *"die soziale Frage"*—the social problem? Ernst Troeltsch formulated it this way:

> The social problem is vast and complicated. It includes the problem of the capitalist economic period and of the industrial proletariat created by it; and of the growth of militaristic and bureaucratic giant states; of the enormous increase in population which affects colonial and world policy, of the mechanical technique, which produces enormous masses of material and links up and mobilizes the whole world for purposes of trade, but which also treats men and labour like machines.[1]

Capitalism, militarism, bureaucracy, demography, modern technology, the fetishism of commodities, and the dehumanizing effects of industrialism and commercialism—these constitute a striking list of our social ills even yet. Add to the list the current ecological crisis, the persistent virulency of institutionalized racism and sexism, the hegemony of developed countries over the Third World, and the constant threat of a nuclear holocaust, and one has a thorough, albeit depressing, indication of the current condition of our common life.

Is it any wonder that Simone Weil, near the end of her tragic life, wrote, "the social order, though necessary, is essentially evil, whatever it may be. You cannot reproach those whom it crushes for undermining it as much as they can."[2] Of course, during an earlier, more politically activist period of her life, Weil also asserted, "The purely negative idea of a lessening of social oppres-

94

sion cannot by itself provide an objective for people of good will. It is indispensable to form at any rate a vague mental picture of the sort of civilization one wishes humanity to reach."[3]

There are two shades of meaning one might derive from this latter statement. First, those who complain about the present are obliged to propose alternatives for a possible and more humane future. Second, there is a reverse side to social criticism. A sense of wrong presupposes a correlative sense of right, however dimly understood. Perhaps this is what José Miranda means when he insists that the word of God is revealed in the cry of the oppressed.[4] The word of God is that sense of right that enables one to discern a world out of joint. One of the burdens of the social critic is to give articulation to that sense of right, to formulate the principles that seem most congruent with it, and thus to give direction to persons of good will.

That burden is essentially political, for politics, in a classical sense of that word which should be reappropriated in an age of political alienation, is the master art of the public world. It is the art of organizing a people toward the realization of the common good. Politicking in the more popular Hobbesian sense is perverse politics, perverse because it substitutes expediency for right, self-aggrandizement for coordination, deviousness for straight-dealing. Rather, as Dante Germino insists, "political theory is an experiential science of right order in human society."[5] If the times are corrupt, that is an issue of political concern. If there is need for at least a "vague mental picture of the sort of civilization one wishes humanity to reach," that is a task of political reason.

According to John Rawls, a central focus, if not the central focus, of political reason is justice. Rawls suspects we share a common intuition, namely, that "justice is the first virtue of social institutions, as truth is of systems of thought. A theory however elegant and economical must be rejected or revised if it is untrue; likewise laws and institutions no matter how efficient and well-arranged must be reformed or abolished if they are unjust."[6] If that be the case, justice may constitute a fruitful point of connection between religious thought and political theory, for, at least within the Western religious tradition, justice has been a central concern. Amos's thundering judgment, "Let justice roll down like water and righteousness like a mighty stream," has been a constant theme in Hebraic and Christian communities.

But while the social problem, the "sense of injustice,"[7] may be in particular instances startlingly vivid, its reverse image, the sense of justice, may be woefully lacking in sharp edges. To alter the metaphor, justice, in current debates among political theorists, shows itself as many colors, some of which shade off into others, but not all of which seem consistent with each other. Justice appears as through a prism. I am taking this metaphorical cue from Dorothy Emmet:

> Ideally moral judgement might be a white light showing clearly what action would be best in any situation. But just as light coming through a prism is refracted into a spectrum of different colours, so our moral thinking shows us a range of different features, and attention can fasten now on one and now on another. And just as it is absurd to maintain that one colour in the spectrum is the only true, or even the truest form of light, so we must not make the mistake of assuming that one feature in the moral spectrum is the only true form of morality.[8]

The prism metaphor is a way of asserting that moral judgment is composed of multiple features, each of which is attractive, each of which sheds some light on circumstances, not all of which are exactly or fully compatible with all others, yet all of which may derive from the same source.

As the prism metaphor applies to morality in general, so it applies to political morality and to the principle of justice. There is a plurality of meanings of justice by which the social problem might be viewed. But a plurality is not necessarily pluralistic. At least on a formal level, these meanings of justice are related, for each is a particularization of the generic definition of justice phrased in the Justinian code—the constant and continuous intention to give everyone one's due—*suum cuique.*

There are four meanings of justice I shall entertain. The first is found in Robert Nozick and Richard Flathman: justice as liberty, the principle of classical liberalism. The second is present in A. M. Honoré and John Rawls: justice as equality, the principle of reformism. The third is argued by Carol Gould and Robert Johann: justice as community, which to Gould is the principle of socialism. The fourth is articulated by Leo Strauss and Eric Voegelin: justice as wisdom, the principle of aristocratic conservatism. With each of these meanings, there is a correlative way of categorizing the social problem. Thus authoritarianism is the bane of liberalism. Inequity is the enemy of reformism. Alienation is the *bete noire* of communalism. And provincialism, or in Voegelin's lexicon, gnosticism, is the antagonist of aristocratic conservatism. I would propose that each of these theories of justice and ways of giving formulation to the social problem has merit, although I would hold them all on my own terms.

1. JUSTICE AS LIBERTY

Justice as liberty: "He has sent me . . . to proclaim liberty to the captives."[9] From Hegel's brilliant analysis of the dialectical intricacies of the master-slave relationship to Camus' interpretation of the meaning and implications of rebellion, we are reminded of the surging drive for liberty in the modern world. Those who are enslaved and oppressed reach a point at which they cry out for release, and release seems the only just thing to be done. Liberty from external constraint has been the inspiration of the liberal tradition and its principle of justice.

Liberalism in its modern form has been associated with the bourgeois revolutions of the seventeenth and eighteenth centuries.[10] The bourgeois revolutions were an integral part of a radical transition from a mercantilist and monarchical order to a capitalist and constitutionalist system. Thus the bourgeois revolutions signaled a new epoch of economic and political liberty. Yet liberalism cannot be dismissed as merely a bourgeois ideology. Underlying the bourgeois ideology is a more profound principle which, to be sure, was not absent in the bourgeois revolutions, but which was not fully captured in them and which, over the years, has been blunted by their consequences.

The more profound principle is captured in Simone Weil's declaration that

> nothing on earth can stop man from feeling himself born for liberty. Never, whatever may happen, can he accept servitude; for he is a thinking creature. He has never ceased to dream of a boundless liberty whether as a past state of happiness of which a punishment has deprived him, or as a future state of happiness that is due to him by reason of a sort of pact with some mysterious providence.[11]

Despite the dream, boundless liberty is unattainable, even unimaginable. Yet liberty, if not boundless, does seem to belong to one. It is one's birthright. It is central to the meaning of human existence. But it is not simply a given. It must be intended even as it is a presupposition of all intentionality. This is the moral and political truth that underlies the liberal principle.

In Richard Flathman's defense of the "Great Rights" of liberal individualism—rights to freedom of speech and association, to habeas corpus and suffrage—he defines the liberal principle as meaning it is a good thing for individuals "to satisfy their desires, to serve their interests, and to achieve their purposes and objectives."[12] One must, that is, honor the subjective aim of individuals as something of intrinsic worth. The imposition of structures of action upon an individual without consent results in inevitable loss. The forced asylum, whether in the form of penitentiary, sanatorium, or bureaucracy, does violence to the human spirit. Indeed, the vitality of society depends on the strength of individuality. This is not to say that compulsion is always wrong or thoroughly unjust. But it is to say that resort to compulsion, even in the form of defensive counterviolence, cannot be accomplished without cost.

One of the historical roots of Western liberalism, according to William Ernest Hocking, is Christianity's stress on individual responsibility. In that root, of which modern liberalism is a mutation, the "essential freedom of the self" is "that it stands for a fateful moment outside of all belongings, and determines for itself alone whether its primary attachments shall be with actual earthly interests or with those of an ideal and potential 'Kingdom of God'. Individuality is . . . a continued living tension between various possibilities of belonging."[13]

Modern liberalism begins as protest, as criticism, as revolutionary reaction. As Leonard Hobhouse puts it, "Its business seems not so much to build up as to pull down. . . . It finds humanity oppressed and would set it free. It finds a people groaning under arbitrary rule, a nation in bondage to a conquering race, industrial enterprises obstructed by social privileges or crippled by taxation, and it offers relief."[14] Liberal protest, however, is both negative and positive. It stands against heteronomy, but it stands for autonomy. It opposes those who would enslave, but it honors the cry of the single soul—let me be what *I* shall be! Thus the liberal principle acknowledges what Nicolas Berdyaev calls the "ethics of creativity." It indicates the quality of adventure in high civilization. It is the genius of the voluntary association and a requirement of effective imagination. The liberal principle should be honored because, in Hocking's words, the meaning of human life is "the right and the duty of thought to get out into the open and work its way to power."[15]

Yet the liberal principle of justice is not without its difficulties. Consider Robert Nozick's formulation of that principle: "From each according to what he chooses to do, to each according to what he makes for himself (perhaps with the contracted aid of others) and what others choose to do for him and choose to give to him of what they've been given previously (under the maxim) and haven't yet expended or transferred." More succinctly (though ungrammatically): "From each as they choose, to each as they are chosen."[16] Nozick's formulation, which seems innocuous on the surface, is tied to an entitlement theory which, as it works out, is troubling. Given that theory, persons have a right to whatever holdings they have acquired or have been transferred to them in keeping with historically inherited legal principles. It would be utterly contrary to that theory to redistribute holdings according to some patterned or "end-state" principle (e.g., to each according to I.Q. or ethnic origin or need or strict equality). Nozick's entitlement theory means that however things work out in accordance with historically inherited legal principles is the way they ought to have worked out; only in that way can liberty be preserved.

The irony is that the liberal principle, so understood, subverts itself. In the economic realm, the liberal principle has led to massive concentrations of wealth; in the political realm, it has led to analogous concentrations of power; in the cultural realm, it has tended toward the strangulation of creativity and difference. The rhetoric of a free society is not matched by the reality of the social order. The name of liberty, once invoked to stall the forces of authoritarianism, has become an apology for inequity.

2. Justice as Equality

And so I am led to justice as equality: "There is neither Jew nor Greek; there is neither slave nor free; there is neither male nor

female; for you are all one in Christ Jesus."[17] Paul's message to the
Galatians, declares Sanford Lakoff, "must surely have been received as a doctrine of equality."[18] Independently of the Mosaic
law, Gentiles may become children of Abraham. The inheritance
of the dignity of a child of God is open to all by faith regardless of
ethnicity, social status, or sex. While Ernst Troeltsch insists that
primitive Christianity was far from presenting a program of social
reform, he noted that the "revolutionary power of the idea of
equality" inherent in the primitive Christian message has not been
without historical impact.[19] Moreover, Ferenc Feher and Agnes
Heller, both followers of the critical Marxism of Georg Lukacs,
have asserted that the

> concept of equality arose with the concept of humanity. In its origi-
> nal formulation, it is perhaps only the blurred reflex of the process
> by which mankind attains self-consciousness. In essence, it holds
> that we are all human beings and as such are equals. This idea first
> appeared in Christianity and was perfected with the proclamation
> of equality before the law. The basic principle here . . . is the ab-
> straction of person and deed from property and from social rank
> (from the place occupied in the division of labor).[20]

The principle of justice as equality has been the basis of various types of reformism, all of which retain their appeal. The most
modest type has been that of equality before the law. The impartiality of strict conformity to rule is, despite some criticisms to the
contrary, more than a merely formal principle. Anyone who has
been subjected to arbitrary or capricious action by parent or police,
bureaucrat or boss knows of the importance of the principle. The
files of Amnesty International are rife with cases where the principle has been violated with the ugliest of consequences. So elementary is the intuition of the principle of justice as impartiality, as
treating like cases alike, that it finds spontaneous expression
among young children in family and in school.

But the rule of law, despite its force as a principle of institutional justice, can not carry the full burden of the meaning of
justice as equality. While in some cases, if applied seriously, it
may mitigate the disadvantages of social division (even the indi-
gent shall have their day in court), its general tendency is to reinforce any system that embodies that division. To treat a slave with

impartiality, given the rules of the plantation system, is in itself just, but that does not mean the system as a whole is just.

Thus reformist movements have gone beyond appeal to justice as equality before law to justice as equality of opportunity, that is, equality in the distribution of things necessary and desirable for a humane life. "This," declares Feher and Heller, "is a relatively recent development and is connected with the increasing influence of pressure groups. This principle abstracts from the place occupied in the division of labour as well as from other factors, such as sex, race, or religion. A prime example of this is the demand for equal opportunities for men and women."[21] Equality of opportunity may be understood narrowly as involving "equal chances to get ahead in a meritocratic rat-race" or broadly as "an equal claim on the earth's natural resources" or as "the same abilities and efforts should reap the same rewards."[22] These phrases are those of Brian Barry whose concern is to develop a conception of equality to deal sensibly with justice between richer and poorer nations and with justice across generations: "The planet is the common heritage of all men at all times and any appropriation of its resources must be subject to appraisal from the point of view of justice."[23] At the moment, opportunities for the creative use of the earth's resources are inequitably skewed across peoples and, given the current profligacy of industrialized countries, across generations. While Julius Stone expresses grave reservations about whether the principle of justice as equality can be meaningfully employed as a guiding criterion in particular cases, he asserts that there is one "indubitable role" it can and should play, namely, it "requires that all human beings physically within, or within the sway of, the community be taken into account as members of the justice-constituency."[24]

Underlying drives toward justice as equality before the law and as equality of opportunity is a profound sense of human dignity. Apart from whatever differences—physical, psychological, cultural, even moral—there are among persons, there is an irreducible quality that attaches to everyone simply as human and that must be honored and respected. In the formation of communities that quality must be factored in as central to the meaning of justice. A. M. Honoré captures this in his formulation of a principle of social justice: "all men considered merely as men and apart from their conduct or choice have a claim to an equal share in all those things, here called advantages, which are generally desired and are in fact conducive to their well-being," that is, "conducive to human perfection and human happiness." "Advantages" include "such things as life, health, food, shelter, clothing, places to move in, opportunities for acquiring knowledge and skills, for sharing in the process of making decisions, for recreation, etc."[25] Honoré admits, as a secondary principle, that there are exceptions given such considerations as choice, need, desert, special relations, but they are clearly exceptions. Furthermore, Honoré is aware of the radical implications of the principle. It mandates universal education, medical care for all, global redistribution of natural resources, indemnification of injured persons, etc. But the argument is that each and every person has a proper claim to those advantages needful or desirable for the fulfillment of human life. Nozick's principle of justice as liberty cannot accommodate this concern.

Yet principles of liberty and equality are both deficient. They are centrifugal in character. They separate. They individuate. At least within our current social setting, they set claim over against claim. They pull apart. As Wieslaw Lang argues in a specially focused critique of these principles, they "do not consider the fundamental problem of social justice, which is the problem of the control of the means of production by the working classes of society."[26]

3. JUSTICE AS COMMUNITY

I am drawn therefore to a third alternative, justice as community, a point at which considerations of justice and common good merge: "For just as the body is one and has many members, and all the members of the body, though many, are one body, so it is with Christ. . . . Now you are the body of Christ and individually members of it."[27]

Atomism and organicism are polar metaphors employed in political theory. In their more simplified forms, they distort the full meaning of human interaction. Where atomism, with its analytic and individualistic orientation, neglects the participative dimension of interaction, organicism, with its systemic and functionalist approach, neglects the reality of the individual. Classical liberalism and reformism are reminders of the status of the individual in matters of justice, but they overlook the feature of solidarity in its ontological and ethical aspects.

The presence of solidarity assumes two forms in human experience: a negative form and a positive form. In its negative form, solidarity is alienation. In its positive form, it is community. Marxist socialism has been among the most influential movements in the modern world focused on the negative form of solidarity, that is, alienation. As Bertell Ollman summarizes the meaning of alienation under conditions of capitalism, it entails a four-fold separation of persons from their life-activity: they have no authority over their work; they have no control over the products of their work; they are set in competition with their fellow workers; in short, they are estranged from the context within which and through which their life is lived.[28] Alienation, from this perspective, means more than physical or psychological separation between person and person. It is not merely the break in relations that often characterizes, say, parent and child, friend and friend, employer and employee, even nation and nation. It is, more significantly, a kind of relationship in which, curiously, persons act against themselves. It is a kind of institutional arrangement in which persons cannot help but participate, but when they do so, the consequences have a debilitating, deleterious effect on their lives. It is a quality of social life in which one's most creative endeavors contribute to a structure of domination from which one suffers and over which one lacks control. Within Marxist interpretation, the classic expression of alienation is the relation between capital and labor. In this case, to use Carol Gould's phrasing,

> alienation does not simply refer to the separation of labor from its products and to labor's lack of control over its productive activity. . . . beyond this, alienation underlies the whole production process by capitalism. In this systemic sense, alienation refers to the process by which labor produces capital and also constantly reproduces its relation to capital, in which it is dominated by capital.[29]

As I have noted in earlier chapters, the dynamics of alienation extend beyond the relationship between capital and labor, at least as that is understood in a narrow sense. Women in a patriarchal society, Jews in a Christian culture, developing nations in a world capitalist system are all profoundly entangled in structures of alienation.

There is a reverse side to alienation which, in Carol Gould's innovative interpretation of Marx's social ontology, is a principle of justice.[30] While Gould recognizes that Marx did not himself provide an explicit discussion of justice, she argues that he does provide a basis for the construction of such a conception. In its deepest sense, justice, within a Marxian framework, "consists . . . in mutuality in social relations"; it "designates social relations in which agents mutually enhance each other"; it "may be characterized as the most developed form of reciprocity." In short, a just society would be a communal society in which the primary form of relation between people would be not economic but social and in which "the activity of production itself becomes the activity of a community, as the differentiated, creative activity of its members in which they jointly determine the purposes of productive activity and the form of the distribution of its products."[31] Thus the principle of justice as community mandates the transformation of the social order in such a way that a people will gain control of its own life and will engage in continuously creative activity as a people.

In a critique of John Rawls's rejection of any theory of *summum bonum* or final end, Robert Johann presents an alternative, but similar version of the principle of justice as community. Each person, as subject, argues Johann,

> is essentially involved in a communicative process. . . . his life is essentially a shared undertaking in a shared world; it is a life in response to meanings which arise through communication and articulate the desires and expectations of others in his regard. It is this common life which alone provides the context in which the self-disposition implied in any deliberate act first becomes meaningful. And it is the maintenance of that life which he necessarily intends, whatever else he intends.[32]

Given the meaning of one's humanity, one is obliged to form one's purposes in keeping with the requirements of community life. These requirements "come down essentially to a certain respect for, and responsiveness to, the other as you, i.e., as an equal partner with me in the joint enterprise which is our common life. Not to do so, to pursue my objectives without regard for you, and in ways, therefore, which are inconsistent with the requirements of the communicative process, is not only to be at odds with myself (with my essential reality as subject), but, also insofar as it means subordinating the comprehensive reality of our common life to something which ultimately has meaning only in terms of it, to be doing something which is rationally indefensible."[33] Justice, concludes Johann, is a matter of regulating the patterns of human interaction to realize and to sustain the communicative process in as deep and as full a manner as is possible.

Johann might well agree with Jürgen Habermas that, under current social conditions, the communicative process is severely distorted and will remain so as long as any class of persons, deliberately or unwittingly, exercises hegemonic control of the conditions of social life. Systematically distorted communication which pervades the rhetoric and reality of our common life is the reverse of justice as community.[34]

Yet even justice as community is not without its potentially dark side. A community is too often an association that, while self-confident and comfortable, is smug, stagnant, and bent in upon itself. Within the framework of modern life, a commune has a strong appeal. But it may be an escape from the structural problems of the economic and political order. A commune easily becomes a new kind of tribalism. While it may be genuinely cooperative internally, it may also be a closed society whose horizons of thought and life are severely inflexible and limited. Moreover it may be, despite Marx's projection of a classless society, that the "dilemmas of communitarian politics," to use Roberto Unger's felicitious phrase, are ultimately insoluble.[35]

4. JUSTICE AS WISDOM

I am therefore led to a fourth prospect—justice as wisdom: "Do not be conformed to this world but be transformed by the renewal of your mind, that you may prove what is the will of God, what is good and acceptable and perfect."[36] Wisdom is an old-fashioned term that tends not to be used in modern essays on moral or political theory. The tendency not to use the term may be a mark of humility: Who is so impudent as to pretend to wisdom? It is also a mark of skepticism: Who is to say there is such a thing as wisdom? The corrosive acid of the modern skepticism has had a deep effect on our speaking and thinking about matters of truth, beauty, and goodness. And no wonder. All too often high-sounding appeals have been used to cloak low-level operations. All too often the invocation of principles of justice—as liberty, equality, or community—have served to rationalize self-interest. From widely divergent perspectives, Karl Marx, Sigmund Freud, and Reinhold Niebuhr have all taught us that elegant principles unmasked manifest inelegant if not disreputable motivations. There is, if I may put this way, some wisdom in our skepticism about appeals to wisdom. But to put it this way is to begin to make the point I intend to make: The point is that what is just is what is wise, but knowing what is wise is no simple matter. Furthermore, while seeking to know what is wise may be of direct political pertinence, it may, paradoxically, lead one beyond the world of politics.

This is the complexion of justice that has been represented so powerfully in efforts by Leo Strauss and Eric Voegelin to recall us to the roots of political philosophy in classical antiquity.[37]

Strauss argues, convincingly, that political thinking is fundamentally philosophical and essentially ethical. He insists that political action is aimed either to preserve or to change given circumstances. In the former case, one presumes to avoid what is worse. In the latter case, one seeks to achieve what is better. In both cases one is guided by some thought of what is good. The thought may be a matter of opinion. But, upon reflection, one might admit that one's opinion is questionable. If one admits that it is questionable, one is then directed toward the thought of a good that is not questionable even though one may not, at the moment, know what that good is. Nonetheless one is led to the idea of a good that is not a matter of opinion but a matter of knowledge.[38]

In another version of the same reasoning, Strauss suggests that the concern of classical political thought is the regime, that is, the fundamental form of a society, its manner of life, its symbiotic structure, its quality as a whole. But regimes, each oriented toward some purpose as its good, vary; in their variance they clash and conflict with each other. Each regime is, by virtue of its being, a claim on behalf of its purpose and its way of life. But the conflicting claims give rise to the question of the best regime which is the definitive question of political philosophy.[39]

Political life thus involves conflicts among persons and groups asserting opposing claims in the name of justice. Such conflicts call for arbitration, "for an intelligent decision that will give each party what it truly deserves. . . . The umpire par excellence is the political philosopher."[40] The point is that justice is giving to each one's due according to the nature of things; it means doing what is good for persons given what they are and who they are as humans within the order of the cosmos; but to know justice requires wisdom: "only the wise man truly knows what is good in each case for the soul. This being the case, there cannot be justice, i.e., giving to everyone what is by nature good for him, except in a society in which wise men are in absolute control."[41]

This argument leads to an intriguing curiosity, for political philosophy as all philosophy is essentially a *quest* for wisdom; it is not the *possession* of wisdom. The philosopher is the one with "insight into our ignorance concerning the most important things."[42] Even so, philosophy enables us at least to clarify the questions posed in and through our conflicting political claims and to keep us from the parochialism that tempts us to impose our favored systems and opinionated ideologies on the rest of humanity. That in itself is no mean service.

The curiosity is that political philosophy prods us toward philosophy proper. It presses us to transcend the political life for the contemplative life. It subordinates the realm of praxis for the realm of theory. It reminds us that in the quest for justice as wisdom we seek for a peace that goes beyond any possible creation of political peace. We are forced "to seek beyond the political sphere for perfect justice or, more generally, for the life that is truly according to nature."[43] To acknowledge justice as wisdom is, at least, to acknowledge the limitations of all structures of justice within the world of human interaction. It is to take seriously the finiteness of the human mind, the boundedness of our social orders, the circumscribed horizons of our common life. The principle of justice as wisdom enables us to lift our sights from the created good to the creative good and thus provokes openness to new possibilities of a cosmic justice in response to the calling of God.[44]

Yet, the principle of justice as wisdom is not without its flaw. It can be and has been employed to justify the status quo as the best that can be accomplished under given conditions of political action. It can be and has been employed to promote escapism for, in its Straussian form, it favors philosophic contemplation over

political action. It can be and has been employed to support elit-
ism, for it suggests that those who are cultured, who are of a
higher class, best rule over those not so advantaged. Taken as
such, it is a doctrine of *noblesse oblige*. It assumes that those with
knowledge of the whole best occupy positions of authority over
those who are narrow-minded and provincial.

5. JUSTICE AND HUMAN NATURE

In response to the social problem, four alternative principles
of justice have been asserted—liberty, equality, community, wisdom. They seem incompatible with each other. How can one at
the very same moment be a liberal, reformist, socialist, and aristocratic conservative?

Yet each principle seems to have some merit. Indeed I am
convinced that hegemony, inequity, alienation, and provinciality
are all facets of the social problem that confronts us and are all
properly condemned as unjust. Perhaps the four principles hang
together as deriving from and referring to the same source,
namely, our experience as humans and what we might reasonably
take as the normative implication of that experience. Here I take a
cue from Paul Tillich:

> The roots of political thought must be sought in human being itself.
> Without some notion of human nature, of its powers and tensions,
> one cannot make any statements about the foundations of political
> existence and thought. Without a doctrine of human nature, there
> can be no theory of political tendencies that is more than a depic-
> tion of their external form.[45]

Without pretending to a complete doctrine of human nature,
I would nonetheless suggest the following. Justice as liberty, the
principle of classical liberalism, articulates the experience of self as
individual, as a solitary one, as creative agent. Justice as equality,
the principle of reformism, expresses the experience of self as
relational, as engaged in a give-and-take with others, all of whom,
as human, have the same right to the fulfillment of their humanity. Justice as community, the principle of socialism, is derived
from the experience of self as communal, as belonging to and with
others, as engaged in a shared existence from which one cannot in

any simple or complete way be separated. Justice as wisdom, the principle of aristocratic conservatism, is rooted in the experience of self as transcendence, as openness to the beyond, as responsible to a higher order of goodness. Taken altogether, these four principles of justice constitute a sketch of "at any rate a vague mental picture of the sort of civilization one wishes humanity to reach."[46] The complexity of their relationship with each other is, most likely, a reflection of the complexity of the social problem. I would not want to give up any one of the principles totally, for each complements the others and is expressive of a vital dimension of moral experience.

The tragedy of the moral life in its political setting is that these principles clash at the point of decision and action. A policy to redistribute wealth through taxation might honor the principle of justice as equality, but it would violate Nozick's rendition of justice as liberty. The socialist principle—from each according to ability, to each according to need—might be expressive of community, but it transgresses considerations of simple equality. An educational program directed by concern for the contemplative life and the search for wisdom seems inconsistent with the view of education as a medium of social mobility and the equalization of social classes.

Yet tensions among these principles in political policy should not blind us to the prospect of synthesizing them in important ways in our political life. That is, if I am correct about their rootedness in our experience as human, they may hold together in the form of a moral possibility open to us if not burden upon us as individuals. They may, together, constitute the moral substance of what has traditionally been called civility, the personal counterpart of civilization. Justice is not only a virtue of social institutions, though it is that. It is as well a primary virtue of personal character. One may translate the four principles of justice into attributes of character.

Liberty means self-possession, independence of judgment and action, integrity, creativity in thought and conduct. Equality is manifest in respect for others, acknowledgment of their being as human, recognition of their potentialities and needs, and an active effort to enhance their lives. Community is evidenced in empathy in the strict sense of that word as "suffering in," that, the bodily apprehension of the feelings of others as if they were one's own.

Wisdom is present in humility, receptivity, the continuous probing for deeper and wider understanding, an openness to new
insight and responsiveness to new times.

These attributes—creativity, respect, empathy, humility—
the attributes of civility, compose a way of being and acting in the
world. Even as present in a single soul, they articulate a political
statement. They exemplify the meaning of a genuinely human
civilization. As attributes of character, they possess social significance, for they make a difference in whatever sphere of influence
is open to one and they point a direction for the more encompassing public order.

On its active side, civility is an exercise in both intolerance
and tolerance. The intolerance of civility is its discord with practices marked by the signs of injustice—tyranny, inequity, alienation, narrow-mindedness—even when those practices may seem
impervious to transformation. Indeed, the presence of civility is
by itself an indication that such practices, at least in some small
measure, are not wholly impervious to change. That is the tolerance of civility, for tolerance, in one of its possible etymological
roots, is not grudging acceptance of that which one does not like,
nor is it sheer indifferentism. Tolerance is rather to lift up, to
empower, to exalt. Civility as the embodiment of justice in the
world is, in itself, a moment of moral exaltation. It at least initiates
a constructive response to the social problem of our times.

APPENDIX TO CHAPTER FIVE
Meanings of Justice: Summary of Types

political ideology	classical liberalism	reformism	socialism	aristocratic conservatism
central political category	justice as liberty	justice as equality	justice as community	justice as wisdom
social-political problem	authoritarianism hegemony	inequity	alienation	provincialism gnosticism
experience of self	self as individual, agent	self as relational	self as communal	self as transcedent, openness
status of self	ego	ego-other	individuation-(societal) participation	individuation-(world) participation
interpretive method	analytic/ atomistic	analytic/ relational	dialectic/ societal	dialectic/ cosmic (hierarchical or progressive)

	individualistic		holistic	
scriptural reference	Luke 4:18	Gal. 3:28	1 Cor. 12: 12, 27	Rom. 12:2
representative political theorists	R. Nozick R. Flathman	A. M. Honoré S. Lakoff J. Rawls B. Barry	C. Gould R. Johann M. Sibley	L. Strauss E. Voegelin

6. CORPORATIONS, CONSTITUTIONS, COVENANTS:
THE PROBLEM OF LEGITIMACY

THE DOMINANT SUBJECT OF this chapter is the legitimacy of the modern corporation as a form of human relation. I conceive this subject as possessing not only legal, social, and political dimensions, but a religious dimension as well. Legitimacy is a concept of many meanings. In a *strictly legal sense*, it means conformity to prevailing positive law. In a *consensual* sense, it means social acceptability. In an *ontological* sense, it means conformity to a higher law, natural and/or divine.

The modern corporation is of critical importance in contemporary times. My argument is that a fully adequate legitimation of the modern corporation would require its transformation. While it may be legitimate in the strictly legal sense, its legitimation in the consensual and ontological senses would entail a radical alteration of its basic character and institutional structure. I maintain that constitutionalism as a form of human relation is an effort to fulfill the consensual sense of legitimacy and that the convenantal form of human relation is intended to fulfill the ontological sense of legitimacy. Within this framework, the full legitimation of the modern corporation would entail both its constitutionalization and its convenantalization.

Thus while the dominant focus of this chapter is on the legitimacy of the modern corporation, it involves as well a comparative interpretation of three forms of human relation: the modern corporation, the constitutional polity, and the covenantal community. Each form will be represented in typological manner. In the construction of each type, the effort is to capture the central direction of a reality that is more complex and variegated in its existent forms than the typological interpretation would have it appear. But the variations and violations of the type do not detract from the central principles of the type itself.[1]

In my conception, the central purpose of the modern corporation is growth and productivity. The fundamental concern of the constitutional polity is liberty understood negatively as freedom from interference and positively as freedom to participate in policy decisions. The basic intention of the covenantal community is the formation of a people who embody the qualities of life itself, the qualities of peace, righteousness, and loving kindness. The central issue, however, is that of legitimacy. Where the corporation is internally understood as autonomous, the constitutional polity is grounded in consensus, and the covenantal community intends conformity with the law of ultimate reality.

1. Centrality and Character of the Modern Corporation

The modern corporation is not merely one form of human relation among many in the modern period. It is the "characteristic institution of our age."[2] Its influence has extended throughout the world and into the most intimate aspects of the lives of people in virtually every country of the world. Without denying the continued importance of the nation-state, one can nonetheless discern the force of William T. Gossett's judgment that "America today is an industrial society, dominated not by agriculture, the church, or the state, but largely by the activities, the standards, the pace of corporate activities."[3] The same author has asserted that

> The modern stock corporation is a social and economic institution that touches every aspect of our lives; in many ways it is an institutionalized expression of our way of life. During the past 50 years, industry in corporate form has moved from the periphery to the very center of our social and economic existence. Indeed, it is not inaccurate to say that we live in a corporate society.[4]

While the notion of corporation had antecedents in ancient Greece and Rome, the modern corporation is the last of a four-stage development in Euro-American history. In the medieval stage, the notion of corporation was applied to boroughs, guilds, and ecclesiastical units. In the mercantilist stage, particularly in sixteenth- and seventeenth-century England, the corporation was the form through which trading companies and joint stock companies organized to pool capital, distribute losses, minimize risks, and, from the king's standpoint, contribute to a favorable balance of trade.

The liberal stage in the development of the corporation occurred in the nineteenth century when laws of incorporation were liberalized, government restrictions on corporate organizations decreased, and government protection of corporate enterprises increased. Increasingly the belief took hold that all matters pertaining to the organization and conduct of the corporation are properly left to managerial discretion. The corporation was conceived as a being unto itself, an autonomous entity, a self-determinative association.

The latter part of the nineteenth century marks the beginning of the modern stage of the corporation. During this period,

> The corporation matured, ceased to be the medium of personal ambition, and became instead the primary instrument for the government of industry. The owner-managers like Carnegie, Rockefeller, and Ford disappeared and were replaced by the professional manager or administration whose ownership interest, if any, was irrelevant. . . . It [this basic change] marks the advent of the "modern" corporation.[5]

One of the most significant definitions of the corporation, formulated during the liberal stage, but applicable as well to the modern stage, is found in Chief Justice John Marshall's opinion in the case of *Dartmouth College v. Woodward.* In this case, the corporation was conceived as contractual and thus protected under the constitutional principle prohibiting states from legislation impairing the obligation of contracts. Marshall writes

> A corporation is an artificial being, invisible, intangible, and existing only in contemplation of law. But the mere creature of law, it possesses only those properties which the charter of its creation confers upon it, either expressly or as incidental to its very existence. These are such as are supposed best calculated to effect the object for which it was created. Among the most important are immortality, and. . . . individuality; properties by which a perpetual succession of many persons are considered as the same, and may act as a single individual. They enable a corporation to manage its own affairs, and to hold property, without the perplexing intri-

cacies . . . of perpetual conveyances for the purpose of transmitting it from hand to hand. It is chiefly for the purpose of clothing bodies of men, in succession, with these qualities and capacities, that corporations were invented, and are in use. By these means, a perpetual succession of individuals are capable of acting for the promotion of the particular object, like an immortal being.[6]

The corporation is thus an autonomous being with a life of its own, a *persona ficta* that, despite its fictitiousness possesses rights and privileges at law originally instituted for natural persons. This legal judgment, combined with the increasing tendency of states throughout the nineteenth century to grant charters with virtually no restrictions, left corporations free to organize and to reorganize, to pursue interests, and to define objectives in whatever way those in control deemed fit and for whatever purposes they projected so long as they were not unlawful. The advantages of the corporate form of collaborative action were clear—limited liability, perpetual succession, accumulation of capital from diverse sources, protection of the common capital from private debts of owners, a standardized form of organization, and the possibility of extensive and long-term operations.

What began as a fairly simple and attractive form of organized action has over the years grown into a massive, complex, dynamic, powerful organism partly as a result of its own impetus and partly as a result of its interaction with technological developments and industrialization. There are, to be sure, even yet a great number of small, locally oriented corporations, but these are relatively insignificant given the economic and organizational power concentrated in the large modern corporation whose character, scope, and influence have had a revolutionary impact upon the common life of man.

The modern corporation is a form of association whose fundamental impetus is to grow. It shares with all associations the drive for survival. But the drive of those in control of corporate enterprise goes beyond sheer survival to increase unendingly. Growth is its basic orientation, continued growth without any purpose or end beyond sheer growth. John Kenneth Galbraith has noted other goals of the corporation—productivity, technological virtuosity, maintenance of earnings—but they are all oriented to growth. The association is propelled by an inner drive to expand, to become larger, to increase.[7]

In its drive to grow, the modern corporation is conceived to have a life of its own, relatively independent of the persons who are related to each other in it and by it. It is conceived to be properly autonomous, even though limited by environmental conditions, political and legal restraints, and other forces within its context.

The modern corporation is not in all respects monolithic. But all flexibility and variation in organizational pattern tend to be oriented to the same end—the life and growth of the corporation as an autonomous entity. I cite three examples.

First, General Motors Corporation, which long served as a model for corporate administration throughout the world, was organized in the 1920s according to a policy of decentralization. Divisional managers are given a high degree of autonomy to conduct their divisions as they themselves determine, such that, in Peter Drucker's interpretation, GMC "has become an essay in federalism."[8] But decentralization does not mean federalism in the political sense. It is promoted because it was found to contribute to the growth of the corporation as a whole. Central management remains in control, establishing basic objectives, defining limits, and maintaining constant check on divisional operations. Divisions are held to measurements of efficiency, productivity, market standing, growth.

As a second example, there are among corporations at least two significantly different types of management, labeled by Douglas MacGregor as "Theory X" and "Theory Y." Management by Theory X assumes that the average employee must be cajoled into productive behavior by threats and rewards, and that managers must demonstrate a heavy-handed and strict authority over their subordinates. Management by Theory Y assumes that most persons possess a capacity for imagination and creativity, and want responsibility. Every effort is made, through consultation and conference, to integrate personal aspirations, interests, and ideas with the objectives and organization of the corporation. One cannot deny that corporations organized along these two lines would be strikingly different in character and experience. But what must be noted is that Theory Y is promoted because thereby the individual "will continuously be encouraged to develop and utilize voluntarily his capacities, his knowledge, his skills, his ingenuity in ways *which contribute to the success of the enterprise.*"[9] It is assumed that Theory Y is more effective than Theory X in solidifying commitment to the objectives of the corporation itself.

Third, five years after the publication of William H. Whyte's thesis that the corporation is populated by "organization men,"[10] W. Lloyd Warner countered with the assertion that "to be successful and to meet the demands of the high position they occupy they [top executives] must be capable of autonomous decision-making."[11] The higher the position in the hierarchy, the more executives are required to project into an uncertain future, and the more they must attempt to construct the world to fit their objectives. Such decisions require not "organization men" but "autonomous men." However, Warner's thesis, interesting as it is, in no way qualifies the basic proposition that managers, whether autonomous in Warner's sense or organizationally minded in Whyte's sense are devoted in their respective roles to one thing and one alone—the enhancement and growth of the corporate enterprise. Autonomy in Warner's sense merely means creative decision making within the framework of the corporation and its needs and goals. The more genuine autonomy is that of the corporation itself to which the functionally required autonomy of the corporate manager is subordinated.

Thus even if a modern corporation is organized structurally according to the principle of decentralization, even if its managerial process embodies the qualities of Theory Y, even if its top managers are autonomous in Warner's sense, its basic impetus is toward its own growth.

The thesis that the governing purpose of the modern corporation is growth is supported by the fundamental trends of contemporary big business—merger, expansion, diversification and internationalization.

The merging of corporations is a process that has gone on for some time. But until the 1950s and 1960s, mergers were dominantly horizontal or vertical. That is, mergers were among corporations engaged in the same type of activity or were among companies involved in varying stages of the development of the same product. These two types of merger resulted in the oligopolistic structure of major industries in the United States.

In the 1960s, however, the merging of corporations intensified greatly in quantity and changed significantly in character. Mergers began to occur among the largest of corporations and with increasing frequency among totally unrelated industries. Thus, many corporations are no longer identifiable with a single product or family of products. They are conglomerates. One corporation may control and operate fifty different companies engaged in as many different forms of enterprise, each in itself of an appreciable size measured in assets or revenue.

The modern corporation is not only a conglomerate; it is also multinational. As in the late nineteenth and early twentieth centuries in the United States, the corporation became national in scope, making state boundaries virtually irrelevant in the economic realm and making the federal system almost an anachronism, so now the corporation is becoming global in scope. Most large corporations have engaged in foreign trade for many years. What is new is the explosive growth of corporations conducting complete business operations in more than one country. Three types of multinational corporations are distinguishable: *"ethnocentric* companies, run from their home country and sending management abroad, *polycentric* companies, having strong subsidiaries operated by local management but subject to firm central control, and *geocentric* companies that have stockholders throughout the world, find management anywhere, and have a global flexibility."[12] Currently most multinational firms are ethnocentric and only a small number are geocentric, but it is predicted that in time the bulk of multinational corporations will become polycentric and geocentric. Indeed, it is more appropriate to speak of the modern large corporation as transnational or anational than as multinational.

The economic size and the geographical scope of the modern corporation make many nation-states look puny. It is difficult to speculate what impact corporate growth will have on the nation-state system. Some suggest the multinational corporation is an instrument of regional cooperation and may become a means of peace and unity among the peoples of the world. However peace and unity are not the direct intentionality of the modern corporation even if they may, by some stretch of possibility, become a by-product of the development of world corporations. The basic impetus of the corporation is instead simply to grow, to expand, to extend itself as an intentionally autonomous body.

In interpreting the character of the modern corporation it is instructive to consider what constitutes a crisis in corporate enterprise. But crisis must be understood both internally and externally.

Some years ago, Richard Austin Smith published a series of studies in *Fortune* on corporations undergoing crises in the internal sense of the term.[13] In each case, crisis *meant* decreased standing in the market, falling profits, loss of sales revenue, an inability to sustain growth. The precise conditions of the crisis varied from case to case: wide-spread diversification without adequate expertise in the central staff; decentralization without sufficient centralized surveillance and control; overly centralized management lacking in channels of information or methods of accounting to be able to know what was occurring in all branches of the entire enterprise; antitrust actions resulting in loss of revenue and change in management; twists of fate such as the death of key personnel; erroneous judgments about trends in industry or developments in technology. But in every instance crisis meant an obstacle to future growth. The crisis was in the life of the corporation itself as an autonomous body. Its life was in jeopardy. And its life was defined not merely as its continuance, but as its expansion and growth.

2. The External View and the Problem of Legitimacy

However, from an external perspective, the crisis of the modern corporation is significantly different. It is a crisis engendered by the corporation's own being, its structure as a form of human relation, its impact on human life and the ecosphere.

The corporation has an ambiguous character within the modern world. On the one hand, the modern corporation seems to be a necessary form of association in an industrialized or an industrializing society.

> Given the technologically determined need for a large stock of capital, the managerial requirements set by the problem of administering the efforts of many men, and the area of discretion demanded for the effective conduct of an entrepreneurial function, the corporation, or a reasonable facsimile thereof, is the only answer.[14]

Among many countries of the world there is an intense drive for modernization and all that it means economically, politically, and culturally. For such countries, the modern corporation is a functionally useful form of relation, for it is the type of association that can realize the fruits of the modernizing process.

On the other hand, from a variety of perspectives, the corporation is alleged to be a corrupt form of human relation, an illegitimate mode of association precisely because it epitomizes all that the modern age stands for. There is, among significant segments of the world, a sense of revulsion against modernity with its core values of productivity, achievement, mobility, and technical rationality. According to Amitai Etzioni, "There is little doubt that the legitimacy of modernity, especially of the capitalist-industrial variety, is waning for more and more people in capitalist-industrial societies" and "it has been recognized that the erosion of legitimation and the loss of meaning are the twin sources of western civilization's deep crisis."[15] The crisis is compounded by negative reactions of Third World peoples to the imperialistic impositions of a global capitalist system.

The crisis of the corporation within this framework is a crisis of legitimation. Yet, as already indicated, legitimacy is not univocal in usage. Given its etymological origins as "lawfulness" or "according to law," one can correlate its possible meanings with various types of jurisprudence. On one level, that of positivistic jurisprudence, legitimacy means conformity with the statutes and decisional principles of a given legal order. Consequently, to the extent that the modern corporation is legally sanctioned through its charter and is operating within the framework of given legislative and relevant judicial opinion, it is obviously legitimate.

While this construction of legitimacy is not without its usefulness, this is not the manner in which the concept is applied in social scientific circles, or for that matter in ordinary language, where it is possible to speak of laws and legal establishments as illegitimate. Nor is it the manner intended by the judgment that the modern corporation is suffering a crisis in legitimacy. In these contexts, the concept of legitimacy is used in the manner of sociological jurisprudence. The law that legitimates is, in sociological jurisprudence, neither statutory principle nor judicial opinion. It is the living law of the people. The question of an association's legitimation is whether the people find the association useful or whether the people are provided opportunity to respond effectively to the association's policies and their impact upon them.

This is the meaning of legitimacy that prevails in social scientific usage. Seymour Lipset, for instance, in a study of democracy writes that "legitimacy involves the capacity of the system to engender and maintain the belief that the existing political institutions are the most appropriate ones for society."[16] A system is legitimate if the values it embodies conform to the values of the group engaged in the assessment. Thus legitimacy is a culturally and socially relative process of evaluation. Legitimacy is a matter of social acceptability. During a period of social transition, varying groups will differ in their assessments.

Within this framework, whether the modern corporation is legitimate is not simply a matter of legal judgment narrowly construed. It is a matter of the relative conformability of the values, the consequences, the form, the perceived meaning of the modern corporation with the interests and values of the larger society of which it is a part and of the various subgroups of that society.

This is the perspective that informs James Willard Hurst's lectures on the legitimacy of the business corporation in the history of American law. Hurst asserts that the two key components of legitimacy in American legal experience have been utility and responsibility. "Legitimacy means that no arrangement of relations or of power recognized in law should be treated as an end in itself or as autonomous."[17] An institution is legitimated (a) if it is *useful* for some end other than itself and/or (b) if it is held *accountable* to some judgment other than that of those holding power within the institution.

In this connection, there have been significant changes in the concerns expressed through corporate law. The tendency in the late nineteenth and early twentieth centuries was to stress *utility* in the legitimation of corporations. Acknowledging the usefulness of the corporate form for economic growth, the lawmakers not only liberalized the laws for incorporation but also provided constitutional protections for the corporation against governmental regulation and interference. The attitude seemed to be "if the law of corporate organization was legitimated by its utility to business enterprise, legitimacy would be most fully achieved if the law empowered businessmen to create whatever arrangements they found most serviceable."[18]

In time, however, concern for legitimacy shifted to the component of *responsibility*. Laws were created intending to increase the accountability of the corporation's operation to the public, in particular to stockholders. The corporation was subjected to a legitimating process through the market, through stockholders' votes, and through the possibility of stockholders' suits.

3. Constitutionalism and Procedures of Social Legitimation

The alleged lack of conformation between the values of society and the values of the modern corporation and, more particularly, the lack of adequate methods of social accountability have led some reformers to urge the constitutionalization of the corporation. The constitutionalization of the corporation would result in its legitimation in the sense indicated above, but at the same time it would require a radical alteration of the structure of relations both within the corporate body itself and between the corporate body and the larger society. This assertion raises the question of the meaning and implications of constitutionalism as a form of human relation.

Since constitutionalism is a theory about the proper form of government, at first blush it might seem inapplicable to the modern corporation which is intended to fulfill an economic function. However, the modern corporation is of such a size and has such a powerful impact upon the human community, it is virtually a form of government itself. Furthermore it is so tied in with actual governments through contractual relations and coordinate operations, it is difficult if not impossible to distinguish between political and economic aspects of the corporate enterprise. On the other hand, constitutionalist doctrines and institutions were formed because of the problem of power and of the abuse of power in the political sphere. But the problem of power is not unique to the political sphere; thus the tradition of constitutionalism may be a resource for the creation of a more responsible, and in that sense more legitimate, form of corporate relation.

Where the central purpose of the modern corporation is the growth of the association itself as an autonomous entity with a life of its own, the fundamental concern of constitutionalist polity is the liberty of individuals and their associations. The key objective of constitutionalism is to protect the members of the political community from the overbearing power of central authority. It is to maintain a significant arena of private action within which individuals and voluntary associations have the right to determine their own action and mode of being.

In seventeenth-century England, constitutionalists proclaimed their liberty against the King. The consequence of their struggle was effectively to reduce the power and authority of the monarch and to realize the supremacy of Parliament understood as an instrument of the people. This radical institutional change was construed as contributing to the actualization of the basic goal of constitutionalism—the liberty of the human person from overextended governmental action. Thus, in McIlwain's terms, the core or minimal meaning of constitutional polity is limited government, government restrained through various means.[19]

Despite significant differences among the interpreters of constitutionalism, it is commonly agreed that there are two essential and related dimensions to the tradition—the valuational and the institutional. Valuationally, as indicated, the fundamental concern is with the autonomy of individual persons and voluntary associations. Institutionally, the concern is to design and to implement various formal arrangements within the political system to secure that value. The tradition has tended to focus on the question of institutional arrangements, but it was never forgotten that the forms of constitutionalism were but ways and means to assure liberty.

Constitutionalists promoted a variety of types of institutional forms. *Double majesty* (in Fortesque's terms *dominum regale et politicum*) was an effort to acknowledge that while the king's authority was absolute over some matters of state, over other matters he must abide by the law of the land and the customs of the people, or else obtain the consent of the people. *Mixed government* was supported to provide a means whereby the interests of king, lords, and commoners would all receive an effective hearing within the political process. *Separation of powers* initially between functions of the legislature and the executive was pressed for a number of reasons, among them, to avoid arbitrariness of executive action, to assure rule of law in administration, and to provide a means of governmental accountability. *Republicanism* together with *extension of suffrage* was presented to guarantee the responsiveness of government to the people whose consent was required to legitimize the political process. *Bicameralism* was promoted as a means of limiting the amount of factional or partisan legislation. *Checks and balances* were constructed among the branches of government to provide each dominant political interest and social class with sufficient access to power that no other interest or class could totally subordinate it. *Bills of rights* were supported to guarantee limits on legislative and executive action. *Judicial review* was conceived as an instrument to assist in enforcing that guarantee and in maintaining proper procedures in legislation and administration. *Federalism* was understood as a means of conjoining effectively both the principles of centralism and pluralism in governmental form.

According to Francis Wormuth all of these institutional devices are efforts to secure rule of law. Thus in his interpretation the jurisprudential strain of the constitutionalist tradition is central.[20] That is, constitutionalism above all else means government according to fundamental law, according to regularized processes established by procedural rules that are general and prospective.

This conception of a political form of relation has both a negative and a positive side to it. Negatively, constitutionalism is a polity in which there are procedural and substantive boundaries established beyond which government may not permissibly act. Constitutionalism is a means of limiting and controlling institutionalized power, of keeping authority responsible, of holding accountable those who make and implement policies for the community. In this sense, constitutionalism through fundamental law, promotes the freedom of individuals and voluntary groups. But this is freedom in the negative sense of protection against improper external restraint. It is the freedom of privacy.

Constitutionalism, however, has a positive side as well. The same institutions that are designed to preserve a significant sphere of privacy provide a variety of modes of access to government. Through the constitutionalist form of political relation, the possibility of active participation in the process of communal decision making is made available. The fundamental concern of constitutionalism is not merely liberty in the negative sense. It is liberty in the positive sense of the possibility of participation in creative communal action.

Thus where the basic impetus of the modern corporation is toward *growth* and the corporation is conducted through *central management* even if qualified by some form of decentralization, the constitutional polity is oriented toward *liberty* understood negatively as *privacy* and positively as *participation* in the political process, and the polity is conducted through *fundamental law* that establishes procedures for and sets limits to political action. The constitutionalist form of human relation is always pressed back to a concern for consensus, or consent.[21]

The connection between constitutionalism and legitimacy as social acceptability is perhaps obvious. The constitutional form of human relation provides for participation and therefore citizen support. Support and participation, of course, may not be synonymous. Support may be granted through apathy, acquiescence, ignorance, or coercion. Moreover participation and the expectations aroused through participation often lead to dissidence rather than support. Nonetheless, from the constitutionalist perspective, the only support of government that is acceptable and compatible with liberty is support deriving from constituent participation in the policy-formation process.[22]

On a more general level, the legitimacy of any form of human relation is contingent on the possibility of the participation of the people involved in and affected by the relation in the processes through which the policies of that relation are formulated and implemented. This proposition is basically a formulation of the meaning of legitimacy within the logic of the constitutionalist tradition. As such legitimation in the constitutionalist form of relation is more a matter of procedures than a matter of substance.

Thus the constitutionalization of the corporation, promoted as a response to the crisis of legitimacy, would mean the establishment of procedures or the promotion of forces to render corporate enterprise acountable to persons who are members of corporations and persons affected by corporate action. Three types of proposals have been promoted in this connection.

First, some theorists argue that *cultural and psychological forces* constitute the most adequate check on concentration of corporate power. A. A. Berle, Jr., suggests that the impact of public consensus upon the practice of corporations is analogous to the operation of "king's conscience." "Corporate managements, like others, knowingly or unknowingly, are constrained to work within a frame of surrounding conceptions which in time impose themselves. The price of failure to understand and observe them is decay of the corporation itself."[23] John Courtney Murray and Henry Nelson Wieman have similarly argued that, in the final analysis, one of the most effective controls on the power of corporations is the mentality, the conscience, the character of the managers of the corporations.[24]

On the other hand there are those who argue that the constitutionalization and thus the legitimation of corporations require subjection to the *interplay of social forces*. This proposal may take the form of insisting that the functioning of an impersonal, free, competitive market is the most effective means of holding corporations responsive to the people.[25] Or it may take the form of arguing that big business, big government, big unions constitute modes of countervailing power, and, properly understood and manipulated, these forces help assure responsibility within the corporate realm.[26] In effect, according to this general proposal, there is a process of societal checks and balances that like Adam Smith's hidden hand assures that no one source of power will dominate economic policy.

But reliance on cultural influence and on the interplay of social forces is an indirect, inefficient, ineffective means of assuring the responsibility of the modern corporation to the needs and interests of the society. Thus some theorists insist on the necessity of *formal, institutionalized means* of participation in the processes of corporate decision making by persons within the corporation and from social groups affected by the corporation's activity. This position underlies efforts at stockholders' democracy, reforms of boards of directors to include union and public representatives, and proposals for new kinds of regulatory agencies. Abram Chayes, for instance, urges that the constitutionalist principle of federalism be used to transform the modern corporation. As Chayes employs the principle, it is a commixture of principles of mixed government, republicanism, and checks and balances. The principle of federalism would require the identification of all relevant subgroups within each corporation—e.g., workers, distributors, salesmen, junior executives—indeed including "all those having a relation of sufficient intimacy with the corporation or subject to its power in a sufficiently specialized way. Their rightful share in decisions on the exercise of corporate power would be exercised through an institutional arrangment appropriately designed to represent the interests of a constituency of members having a significant common relation to the corporation and its power."[27] To some extent, the Wagner Act provided this opportunity for workers. The formation of dealers' councils in the automobile industry is another instance of what Chayes is promoting. But "we should be sensitive to the emergence of other groups equally entitled to a voice. And we should be imaginatively seeking institutional arrangements appropriate to record that voice."[28]

Robert A. Dahl has urged essentially the same reorganization of the corporation by suggesting the application of two principles for the proper governance of the "corporate leviathan." The first principle, that of "self-management," he derives from the Yugoslavian practice of considering all persons working within an industry citizens of that industry with rights and opportunities of participating in the formation of the policies of that industry. The second principle is that of "interest group management," which extends the federalist concept to include associations of persons who are not directly in the industry but who have some substantial interest in its purposes and operations.[29]

To reconstruct the modern corporation in the manner proposed by Chayes and Dahl would result in a radical transformation of its character. But, in Chayes' terms, that is precisely what is needed to make the modern corporation conform to rule of law, to make it responsive to the needs, desires, and purposes of society. Such a transformation is what is required to secure the social legitimation of the corporation.

4. The Higher Law and Ontological Legitimation

The constitutionalist form of human relation provides an effective means of participation in processes of policy formation. In that sense it provides a method of consent and a procedure for consensual or social legitimation. However, there is a third meaning of legitimacy not satisfied by constitutionalist procedures. From its perspective, social-consensual legitimation is by itself deficient.

The deficiency can be illustrated by examining Henry Nelson Wieman's distinction among three levels of good—individual good, social good, and moral good. The individual good is that which any particular person enjoys or approves. The social good is that individual good which at the same time contributes to the good of other individuals.

The constitutionalist form of relation is a type of social good for it provides a set of procedures to assure that the good of no one individual or corporate body be realized to the detriment of the individual goods of other persons or groups that might be affected. Constitutionalism requires methods of consensus, participation, mutual give-and-take.

But, argues Wieman,

> Thousands of people might live together in a civilization that lasted for hundreds of years, the good [individual good] of each supporting that of others; yet the only moral persons might be those who fought the whole system. In such a case the moral persons would be obstructive and destructive to the social system in which thousands found support and enrichment in getting and holding what seemed good to them.[30]

The third level of good is the moral good whose actualization requires conformity to the moral law which is "imposed, prescriptive, implacable against any desire or ideal we may set up against it, sovereign over all that we love and seek, not servant but master of our hopes."[31] The moral law is the law of the Creator, of the creative process that is productive of that which is characteristically human. The command of the moral law is to act so as to meet the conditions under which we may become more fully human within the full context of our existence. It is to act so as to meet the conditions for the progressive creation of the world of humanity and of all being. Individual good and social good may, by themselves, not only fall short of the moral good, but even to some extent contradict the moral good, as the good that is specifically human or that is required by the world of being within which humankind exists.

Constitutionalist procedures may provide an effective means for ascertaining people's wants, desires, and interests, which in itself is no small advantage. But people's wants, desires, and interests may contradict their real good. On the assumption that there is a law of our real good, a law of our creation, then there is a third meaning of legitimacy, a meaning that transcends the strictly legal as well as the sociological. If so, then the full legitimation of the modern corporation requires more than the constitutionalization of its form by introducing procedures for participation and consensus. It requires in addition a substantive transformation of its character by the qualities of the moral law of life itself. These qualities, I suggest, are the characteristics of a third form of human relation, the covenantal community.

5. THE COVENANTAL COMMUNITY AND THE QUALITIES OF LIFE

The concept of covenant occupies a central position in Hebrew history, even though the covenantal motif is insufficient for interpreting the Hebrew tradition in its entirety, and even though a number of variant understandings of covenant have been distinguished in Hebrew scriptures.[32] The intention here is to isolate this one motif in its Sinaitic form and to examine its significance as representing a form of human relation. As such, the concept of covenant expresses the conviction that Israel as a people stands in a unique relationship with God. The term covenant refers to a dynamic process of interaction that began at a particular time and place and that constituted the people as a people.

There are, however, many moments in history marked by the making of covenants.[33] Covenantal notions were widespread throughout ancient times. In basic form, a covenant is "a solemn promise made binding by an oath, which may be either a verbal formula or a symbolic action."[34] It establishes obligations, regulates the behavior between parties, introduces a measure of trust and predictability into social and political life, and creates new bonds between peoples. Among one set of covenantal treaties there was a typical form which may have been appropriated by the Hebrews. The form contains several parts: preamble, historical prologue, stipulations, statement of place of deposit and times for public readings, list of witnesses, and statement of blessings and curses.

In the Sinaitic covenant, the historical prologue refers to the action of God on behalf of the people, more precisely the liberation of the people from oppression, the action of redeeming them from a dehumanizing master-slave relationship and leading them to the possibility of a new life. The stipulations of the covenantal relation are presented as a result of that action. Thus "the foundation of an enduring covenant order appears as the purpose and consummation of the mighty deliverance from Egypt; the power, the ready assistance, the faithfulness of Yahweh experienced thus far are offered to the people for their permanent enjoyment, while at the same time their behavior is subjected to definite standards."[35] The Decalogue and the Code of the Covenant, as the law of this covenant, are therefore but part, albeit an essential part, of a total event in which God discloses himself to the people, through which a relation between God and the people is effected, and by which a certain quality of communal life is projected.

To understand the law of the Sinaitic covenant, its context must be remembered and its distinctive character stressed. According to Eichrodt,

> If we are seeking to define the distinctive character of the Mosaic law when contrasted with the corresponding laws of other ancient peoples, then attention must first be drawn to *the emphasis with which the entire law is referred to God.* Not only the cultic law, but the secular law derives its validity from being a direct command of Yahweh. . . . The law thus acquires a majesty, which removes it from the sphere of human arbitrariness and relativism and bases it firmly on the metaphysical.[36]

The moral precepts are connected essentially with the basic religious command. Since the legal-moral-religious dicta of the Covenant are of a general character and their precise application left open for determination, they are more of an encompassing legal policy than detailed legal techniques.[37]

Thus the covenantal community is grounded in divine action, and the law of the community is divine law. The divine origin of the community is an indication that, in conception, the covenantal community is not merely the result of arbitrary construction. Its foundation is not contractural. It is not simply an interesting and functionally beneficial social invention. By claim, its ground is the source of all reality. Moreover the covenantal community is not intended to fulfill only some one particular function in human existence. It is holistic. Its concerns include all dimensions and areas of life, including political and economic, although the qualities that apply to all these spheres are grounded in, derived from, and find their validity on the basis of the creative and redemptive action of God.

The actual stipulations in the Decalogue seem modest and

minimal. "The prohibition of murder, adultery, theft, and the inculcation of respect for parents, comprise no more than the elementary bases of communal human life."[38] On the other hand, the significance of these precepts is precisely their non-arbitrary character, especially when viewed as expressing those qualities of divine action that constitute as well the qualities of the covenantal form of human relation. That is, the precepts particularize the qualities of peace, righteousness, justice, steadfastness, loving kindness. These are at one and the same time the qualities of divine action and the pattern for human community. As such, they are constitutive of the stuff of life itself. They are the qualities of the real world.

According to Johannes Pedersen's interpretation, peace (*shalom*) is a fundamental quality of the human soul and therefore of any specifically human community. Peace means unity, harmony, totality, agreement. Its antithesis includes strife, murder, mistrust, slander, all of which dissolve community.

The family, in principle, exemplifies the meaning of peace for, to paraphrase Pedersen, members of a family form a complete unity with the family as a whole: "Psychic community means, above all, a common will and a common responsibility." Each member is the center of this common will. Members do not act for themselves alone, but for the whole of the house. Whatever a member has done, "the house, the family has likewise done, for together they form an organism so closely knit that no single part thereof can be separated as something independent."[39] Each member of the family holds the destiny of the whole in his or her hands.

Yet the family does not stand alone. It and the individuals who compose it are also one with the people as a whole, and the unity of the people is, by intention, as intense and as strong as the unity of the family. The people are, in this sense, one being with common responsibility. "There can be no doubt that peace must normally extend to the whole of the people, and in this there is always a community of will, a strong fellow feeling, even if it cannot compare with the family feeling in intensity."[40]

The quality of peace (shalom) should extend universally throughout both time and space. Thus, on the one hand, the community is historical with both past and future. The identity and the responsibility that constitute peace relate to prior events and are projected to future events. On the other hand, all forms of human relation ought to conform to the qualities of peace (*shalom*) and berith (*covenant*). While the two words "peace" and "covenant" differ in origin, they designate essentially the same kind of relationship, which is understood as equally appropriate for international relations and friendships, for associations of complexity and extent and for relations of intimacy and brief duration. Indeed, the covenant of peace is what is required by the very nature of life.

> All life is common life and so peace and covenant are really denominations of life itself. One is born of a covenant and into a covenant, and wherever one moves in life, one makes a covenant or acts on the basis of the already existing covenant. If everything that comes under the term of covenant were dissolved, existence would fall to pieces, because no soul can live an isolated life. It not only means that it cannot get along without the assistance of others; it is in direct conflict with its essence to be something apart. It can only exist as a link of a whole, and it cannot work and act without working in connection with other souls and through them. Therefore the annihilation of the covenant would not be the ruin of society, but the dissolution of each individual soul.[41]

But there is no peace without righteousness (*sedaka*) and justice (*mishpat*). Righteousness is right disposition and right action. Right disposition is integrity, innocence, purity of heart. It is the propensity to act in accordance with what is expected to effect the covenantal community. As such, it is not a propensity to act in accord simply with rules imposed from without. It is instead a propensity to act in accord with the laws of one's being, for one has being as a member of the covenant. Thus in action, righteousness is a form of relation rather than merely a quality of the individual person in isolation.

Righteous action is action within the context of the whole covenantal community in which context it attends to the concrete requirements of its particular situation.

> Ancient Israel did not in fact measure a line of conduct as an act by an ideal norm, but by the specific relationship in which the partner had at the time to prove himself true. . . . To some extent, therefore, the specific relationship in which the agent finds himself is itself the norm: only, it must be borne in mind that people are

constantly moving in very many relationships, each one of which carries its own particular law within it.[42]

Each individual is involved in all sorts of relations—political, economic, familial, cultural, religious—none of which remain constant. The particular content of righteousness and justice depends upon the concrete rights, duties, and claims that arise out of the particular relation in which a person is acting at the moment, although the basic reference of righteousness is to the covenantal community as a whole.

The point is that "the covenant does not make mankind one homogenous man."[43] Each person has a particular place within the social whole, with its responsibilities and privileges. Righteousness means being disposed to do and doing what is objectively required to maintain peace, harmony, the life of the whole community given one's relative place within that community at any particular moment. The Decalogue contains some indication of what that means, including the disposition to respect the life, the house, the full being of the other. The laws of the covenant are expressions of the meaning of righteousness in various relations—to the servant, the widow, the stranger, the poor, the enemy, the weak. The duties of righteousness are quite specific in demanding that the stronger shall assist the weaker, the mighty shall lift up the low, the powerful shall raise up the powerless. As Yahweh in righteousness has liberated the people Israel, so Israel is to liberate the oppressed of the world. Indeed this is a law of the very nature of life itself.

The unrighteous are those who break the covenant, destroy peace, and constitute the way of death. Unrighteousness shatters the relations of the community. In such circumstances, "justice demands that equilibrium shall be re-established between the wronged and him who commits the breach, for thereby the covenant is healed. To re-establish this relation is to *justify* a man."[44]

A related quality of the covenantal form of relation is loving kindness or steadfastness (*hesed*). "Whenever a *berit* governs relations between human beings, the kind of behavior which is expected in the normal way of those so associated is already recognized as *hesed*."[45] A covenantal relation establishes a structure of mutual expectations which can be fulfilled only on the basis of loyalty, of a positive readiness to devote one's attention to the requirements of the relation. *Hesed* is the constancy with which one devotes oneself to the content of the covenant even in circumstances in which the other parties to the covenant have violated their part in the relation. Loving kindness is not a kind of pious sentimentality, but an unshakable and courageous continuity of devotion. It is entailed by the binding character of a covenant, for a covenant is not a casual or ephemeral relation. It is a relation in which the identity of the parties is involved. The covenant fixes obligations that are critical not because of altruistic considerations. They are critical because they are constitutive of the meaning of all the members of the covenantal community.

Thus, within the Hebrew tradition, peace, righteousness, and steadfastness are conceived to be qualities of divine action, and therefore the defining qualities of the law of the Sinaitic type of covenant. So construed, the covenantal form of human relation can be interpreted as expressive of what Wieman has called the moral good. It is a good that transcends merely human wants and desires either individually expressed or socially agreed upon. It is a good that is required by the nature of being human. It is a good whose possibility has been disclosed by claim in the objective processes of human history. It is a good whose source transcends our humanity, but whose purpose includes our fulfillment within the context of all creation. Thus Von Rad writes of righteousness:

> It is the standard not only for *man's relationship to God*, but also for *his relationship to his fellows*, reaching right down to the most petty wranglings—indeed, *it is even the standard for man's relationship to the animals and to his natural environment*. [*Sedaka*] can be described without more ado as the highest value in life, *that upon which all life rests when it is properly ordered.*[46]

Accepted as such, the covenantal form of human relation is presented as the law of life. It is the substance of the criterion of ontological legitimacy. From this perspective, the legitimacy of any particular form of relation depends upon its conformity to the qualities of peace, righteousness, and steadfastness understood as qualities of the structure of being.

From this perspective, associations are not and cannot properly be conceived to be autonomous. Their ontological legitimacy is contingent on the quality of their impact on their field of action, internal and external. To the degree to which they contribute to the enhancement of existence within that field, they are legitimate. To the degree to which they, deliberately or unwittingly, exploit the human and natural resources that constitute that context, they have broken the terms of the covenantal law. While granting the generality of these judgments, I would stress that they indicate a radical difference in orientation between the corporative and the covenantal forms of human relation. The corporative form, which has become dominant in industrialized societies, is oriented toward its own economic growth and increased productivity. The covenantal form, in its structure and character, is oriented toward the continued presence of sensitivity to the depth of relations that sustain and enhance the whole world of being.

At this point it might be suggested that there is a complementary relationship between consensual legitimacy and ontological legitimacy, and therefore between constitutional polity and covenantal community. On the one hand, a covenant must be freely entered into. Peace and righteousness in this sense depend upon liberty. Thus a covenantal association is not necessarily incompatible with social and cultural plurality. Indeed, in some circumstances, associations of dissent, protest, opposition, even revolution may be expressive of the covenantal law. On the other hand, a constitutional relation is constructed as a potential means of fulfillment. The purpose of liberty is to give effect to peace and righteousness in human and natural relations. In this connection it is significant to note Carl J. Friedrich's argument that the historical foundation of constitutionalism is the Hebraic-Christian notion of transcendent justice.[47]

The crisis of the modern corporation, externally understood, resides in the question of whether it can satisfy the requirements of consensual legitimacy and ontological legitimacy. Internally understood, the modern corporation is an autonomous being with its own impetus, its own norms, its own purpose. It is oriented toward sheer growth. It is directed by a central management. It subordinates its members to its own purposes. While it is regulated by laws and agencies external to itself, it tends to resist such control, preferring to determine its own responsibilities. But it has grown to such expanse, and has such an impact upon both human and non-human life throughout the world, the question of its legitimacy has become critical.

In order to satisfy the requirements of legitimacy the modern corporation must be radically transformed in two ways. First, it must incorporate the procedures of constitutionalism to secure the participation of all populations affected by its operation to satisfy the requirement of consensual legitimacy. Second, it must be qualified by the characteristics of covenantal community to assure its conformity to the peace, justice, and steadfastness of being itself to satisfy the requirement of ontological legitimacy. The former requirement may be the relatively easier to implement at least in its institutional dimensions although, given the increasingly multinational character of the modern corporation, an effective constitutionalization will require the construction of legal and political forms that transcend the boundaries of nation states and regional confederations, and that is a step that appears remote in current circumstances. The latter requirement mandates a quality of concern, care, and commitment that is less susceptible to realization through institutional means, even though it is no less vital. On both levels, however, legitimation would entail a profound transformation of the prevailing ethos of peoples in all nations. Relations of a constitutional and covenantal character are not matters of institutional form alone. They are as well and more profoundly matters of perception and sensibility. The full legitimation of the modern corporation calls for radical change in both the political-legal and the cultural-religious dimensions of human existence.

A more general formulation of the same argument is to say that an economic association cannot be legitimated on its own grounds alone. Legitimation is first of all a strictly legal process; but more profoundly it is a political process of ascertaining the acceptance, criticism, and direction of the people; and finally it is a religious and philosophical process of subjecting the economic association to the tests of some vision of the nature and destiny of humankind within the context of reality as a whole.

APPENDIX TO CHAPTER SIX

Three Forms of Human Relation
Table of Comparative Characteristics

	Modern Corporation (typification of associations of the modernizing process)	Constitutional Polity (typification of the subjective or consensual aspect of the legitimating process)	Covenantal Community (typification of the objective or ontological aspect of the legitimating process)
Purpose	*Growth* Organization and economic expansion, productivity, technical virtuosity	*Liberty* Limitation of and participation in power	*Peace and Righteousness* Formation of a people, fulfillment of quality of life
Function	*Economic: procedural* function in pursuit of objectives; solution of problem of development in face of want and need	*Political: procedural* function in formulation of objectives; solution of problem of liberty in face of tyranny	*Religious: substantive* function in constituting fundamental objective; solution of problem of liberation in face of enslavement; fulfillment
Structural principle	Unity of *central management* often conjoined with principle of decentralization	Unity of *fundamental law* which mandates principles of federalism, separation of powers, independent judiciary, etc.	Unity of *spirit and commitment* at times conjoined with tribal separation and differences (amphictyony)
Notion of the "person"	*Collectivist* notion: corporation as *persona ficta;* subordination of the individual	*Individualist* notion: centrality of the individual as person	*Communal* notion: person as relational; relations include horizontal, transcendental, historical

	MODERN CORPORATION (typification of associations of the modernizing process)	CONSTITUTIONAL POLITY (typification of the subjective or consensual aspect of the legitimating process)	COVENANTAL COMMUNITY (typification of the objective or ontological aspect of the legitimating process)
Notion of freedom	Freedom as *autonomy* of the corporation; free enterprise	Freedom as *privacy* of the individual and as *participation* in political process	Freedom as *liberation* and *fulfillment*
Relation to law	Corporation as originated, limited, regulated by external, *positive law*	Constitutional policy as expressive of *fundamental law* (Rule of Law)	Convenantal community as expressive of Torah, and thus *Law of God*
Psychological basis	*Rational* (technical)	*Volitional*	*Ontological*
Direction	*Unidirectional* in pursuit of given objectives	*Centrifugal* (dispersion of power)	*Centripetal*
Scope	Shift from local to national to *transnational*	Shift from national to *universal*	Shift from local to *universal*

7. CORPORATE CULTURE AND THE COMMON GOOD

> The Sabbath was made for man, not man for the Sabbath. Mark 2:29

> Human society is not merely a fact, or an event, in the external world to be studied by an observer like a natural phenomenon. Though it has externality as one of its important components, it is as a whole, a little world, a cosmion, illuminated with meaning from within by the human beings who continuously create and bear it as the mode and condition of their self-realization. Eric Voegelin[1]

> Twentieth-century capitalism will justify itself not only by its out-turn product, but by its content of life values. A. A. Berle[2]

THE CORPORATION, ALLEGEDLY, is the characteristic organizational form of modern industrial society in the capitalist world. It is, in Dow Votaw's words, "our way of life."[3] Clearly, in the economic sphere, the corporation is the dominant way of doing business. But, given the import of economic relations in the modern world, its reticulations reach out into all other spheres of our common life—political, familial, educational, even recreational and religious. The business corporation, in particular the big business corporation, occupies the central role in industrial society that the military organization or the religious community occupied at other times and in other places.

The culture of a corporation is its character. As we shall observe later, precisely what that means is a point of contention—methodological and substantive contention—between various schools of social thought. Interpretive theorists (e.g., Clifford Geertz) and critical theorists (e.g., Anthony Giddens) understand culture in significantly different ways. In some recent studies of corporate culture, this difference has been ignored. A corporation's culture has been defined in seemingly simple and straightforward terms as "the amalgam of beliefs, mythology, values and ritual that, even more than its products, differentiates it from other companies."[4] This definition of corporate culture, however, is not innocent. It represents serious intent: "Corporate culture is the magic phrase that management consultants are breathing into the ears of American executives." The intent is a promise, namely, that by reinforcing, manipulating, or transforming the culture of their corporations, executives might render the enterprise more effective. They might improve its performance and increase its productivity. They might, to put it bluntly, make it more profitable. In a statement reminiscent of Francis Bacon's dictum "Knowledge is Power," Terrence Deal and Allan Kennedy conclude the initial chapter of their book on corporate culture with the affirmation: "We hope to instill . . . a new law of business life: In Culture There Is Strength."[5]

As may be obvious, these recent studies of corporate culture have been undertaken with a limited if honorable purpose. Their focus is particular: it centers on what is distinctive about an individual company, what makes it unique. Their motivation is pragmatic: it is to enhance the success of the company's operation, to increase its wealth and ultimately the wealth of the nation.[6]

However, to do justice to the meaning and significance of corporate culture requires a more extensive and a more complicated view, a view from which at least some of these recent studies, while instructive for some purposes are, at best, limited and, at worst, suspect.

In what follows, I shall first present an analysis of the *Methodenstreit* between interpretive and critical theories as means of probing into the culture of the corporation. I shall then examine four roughly distinguishable levels of corporate culture: that of a corporation taken as a separable whole (the mesoscopic view); that of subgroups and individuals within a corporation (the microscopic view); that of the corporation as a participant in a larger social whole (the macroscopic view); and that of the corporation over the course of historical development (the chronoscopic view).

The entire exercise is informed by the perspective of a relational philosophy according to which there is a continuously creative communal ground out of which we, as individuals and in our various associations, emerge and to which we are responsible. We are, if you will, denizens of an unfinished world which is the condition of our individual and corporate existence and the inheritor of our practice. There is a cosmic significance to who we are and how we act. Economic growth is neither the sole nor the most important criterion of our life's activity. As a criterion, economic growth is superseded by justice, the respect of one entity for another, and the common good, a texture of relationships in which the identity of each participant is translated into the condition of the whole. Relational philosophy is that form of empirical realism in which, to use Bernard Meland's terms,

> the primacy of experience as lived is emphasized, giving to the notion of reality the connotation of a Creative Passage in which all life is lived. In this mode of thought, it is assumed that our immediacies occur and participate in a dimension of ultimacy, however vaguely attended or unattended. Ultimacy in this context is not a nebulous term. It connotes a continuous thrust of the Creative Passage, and is thus simultaneously the present, inclusive of the legacy of the past inherent in its structure of experience, together with what is prescient of its future range.[7]

1. Modes of Interpretation

James O'Toole at a culminating point of his shrewd study of the performance of corporate enterprise in America asserts, "The root causes of low productivity and declining innovation are to be found in our culture, and not in national economic policies."[8] The assertion, cogent as it may appear at first glance, conceals a controversy prominent in social theory, a controversy over definition (What constitutes culture?), method (What is the most appropriate manner in which to study culture?), and purpose (What is the impetus or intention that provokes the study of culture?)

Clifford Geertz, acknowledging his indebtedness to Max Weber's *verstehende Soziologie*, espouses a semiotic concept of culture. Humans are creatures "suspended in webs of significance" spun by themselves. "I take culture," he writes, "to be those webs, and the analysis of it to be therefore not an experimental science in search of law but an interpretive one in search of meaning."[9] Adopting the language of Gilbert Ryle, Geertz distinguishes between thin and thick descriptions of human behavior. A thin description merely reports observable movement. A thick description goes beyond observable movement to the meaning or significance of the movement to the actors. Two persons running through the woods may appear to be engaged in the same behavior, but one is eluding a sheriff's bloodhounds, while the other is training for a cross-country race. A thick description of behavior is the presentation of the framework of interpretation (or the multiple frameworks of interpretation) through which behavior makes sense. From this perspective behavior is not raw movement, but is symbolic action. Culture, in brief, consists in symbols of meaning, symbols that inform a people what they are doing as well as what they ought to be doing. "The whole point of a semiotic approach to culture is . . . to aid us in gaining access to the conceptual world in which our subjects live so that we can, in some extended sense of the term, converse with them."[10]

Given Geertz's interpretive theory, to study corporate culture one should ask people within the corporations what they think they are doing, how they understand what is happening to them, what the "web of significance" is that makes sense of the complex interactions that make up the institution. In the process, one will hear a babel of voices, for not everyone or every group discerns the seemingly same event in the same way. But the reality is that discernment. An adequate understanding of corporate culture must uncover its multiple dimensions and be respectful of the differences and tensions among them. The official story of the corporation as told by its executives and expressed in its annual reports, even if honest, may be deceptive, and will certainly be oversimple.

However thick and complex the descriptions of interpretive theory may be, they are, from the perspective of critical theory, limited. According to Anthony Giddens, action is not simply meaning. It is praxis. It entails the transformation of the environment, natural and social, in the realization of interests which may or may not be adequately articulated by the actors. Action is the expression of power and manifests the asymmetries of influence that typify a stratified social order. It is a manifestation of struggles between and among groups striving for positions of hegemony. Action contains an historical component and must be viewed along the axis of trends in broad social change.[11]

Marvin Harris, contrasting his own cultural materialism with Geertz's cultural idealism, suggests, "the intuition that thought determines behavior arises from the limited temporal and cultural perspective of ordinary experience."[12] But ordinary experience, Harris intimates, is superficial. In the evolution of cultures, thought is secondary to inherited institutional forms and durable contextual factors. It is constrained by the material foundations of human life. Structures of symbolic meaning are not wholly ineffective in conduct, but their role is subordinate and their form may camouflage actual forces determinative of behavioral patterns.

Giddens' critical theory and Harris's cultural materialism are not identical. Yet both accuse interpretive theory (Geertz) with failure to incorporate the full dialectical interplay of thought and action, symbolic meaning and institutional form constitutive of culture. However, Giddens, more appreciative of interpretive theory than Harris, is particularly sensitive to the interaction of multiple factors in social practice. Structures of meaning, forms of morality, and relations of power are all interactively present in the reproduction of cultural life.[13]

Critical theory thus complicates the task of interpreting corporate culture. An interpreter must look for both intended and unintended significance. An interpreter must be receptive as much to relations of power and domination as to symbolic expression and articulated meaning. An adequate interpretation of the character of the corporation—its cultural sense, its ethos—must attend to historical and contextual factors as well as to the sensibilities of actors in a particular corporation.

The ultimate question, which goes beyond critical theory as Giddens has formulated it, is what the corporation represents as a cultural whole and whether it is responsive to the deepest yearnings of humankind and instantiates that kind of relationship among persons and between persons and nature most conducive to the enhancement of life. That is an ethical and, most deeply, a theological question. To neglect that question is to be less than fully realistic, for it is to ignore the deepest profundities of our common life even in the economic realm.

In what follows, I examine four dimensions of the reality of modern corporate life: the corporation as an entity in itself; subgroups within the corporation; the corporation as an agent within a more encompassing social whole; and the corporation through the course of history. In each case, I mean to demonstrate inter-connections and tensions between symbolic structures and insti-tutional structures on the supposition that culture embraces both of these factors in their interaction. In Whitehead's language, the cultural process is moved by both "senseless agencies and formu-lated aspirations."[14] For data, I rely, in large part, on a study of a major oil company headquartered in the United States (associated names are fictionalized) but also on a variety of other studies and treatises dealing with corporate life in America.

2. THE MESOSCOPIC VIEW

In an important sense, all large modern business corpora-tions are the same. They are representative institutional expres-sions of industrial societies. They constitute organizational tran-scriptions of advanced technology. Hence they manifest features of bureaucracy. Corporate practice is formalized in rules and poli-cies even where networks of informal association emerge. Deci-sion making is centralized even though subunits may be delegated a measure of autonomy. Strata within the hierarchy are isolated from each other even when open lines of communication are sus-tained.[15] Bureaucracy is a specific kind of institutional structure. But it is also an ethos engendered by interests of efficiency and control and governed by the mythos of economic growth. Where bureaucracies are modified out of concern for the humanizing of work, bureaucratic principles remain effective. Formal rules, cen-tral authority, and division of labor may be qualified, but they are not undone by a more humane style.[16]

On the other hand, each corporation has an individual iden-tity. Each has its own peculiar style of life. Deal and Kennedy suggest that corporations with strong cultures have a core value often encapsulated in a slogan which states the essence of the corporation's intended philosophy. In Sears Roebuck, the slogan is "Quality at a Good Price." In Proctor and Gamble it is "Always Try to Do What's Right." The slogans are more aspirational than obligatory. They are regulative ideals, not categorical imperatives. But if Deal and Kennedy are correct, they have an inspirational effect on employees.

The Apollo Oil Company does not have a slogan, but it does have a history out of which it has built an identity. During the past decade, it has suffered a severe identity crisis, the character of which manifests the dialectical interdependency of institutional structure and symbolic meaning.

Apollo was founded in 1901. For seven decades it was dominated by a single family whose imprint on the ethos of the company remains strong. As we shall note, without that imprint, there would have been no identity crisis.

Throughout its history, the company has grown steadily but prudentially. In a recent ten-year period, for instance, its annual revenues increased from two to sixteen billion dollars. During the final four years of that period, the number of its employees increased from 34,000 to 45,000. Apollo has operations in all fifty states and in forty-one nations throughout the world.

In its annual reports, Apollo describes itself modestly as "an energy company and more. . . . [During the year, Apollo] provided seven billion gallons of gasoline and heating oil to American consumers, while actively developing new domestic energy resources and a carefully selected array of non-energy businesses." But Apollo does not have the same character as all other petroleum-energy corporations.

In the *Philadelphia Inquirer*, the Podion family, founders of Apollo, was recently compared with the Artemis brothers: "Both families made their money from oil, and both share a penchant for right-wing politics and fundamental Christian causes. Otherwise, the two families are as different as Dallas and Philadelphia." The Artemis brothers, like their father, live fast lives, speculate in investments, press their credit to the breaking point, but despite control over billions of dollars in assets, they have a net worth no more than the Podion family. In contrast, the Podion family is intensely pious, shuns speculation and credit, and plows its profits back into the company. Thus, during the Great Depression when much of the country was broke, Apollo had huge cash reserves. In brief, the Podions are paragons of the Puritan ethic in its capitalist version. Not surprisingly, their character has had an influence on the operation of the corporation.

A few years ago, *Business Week* acknowledging (but implicitly deploring) the unique managerial ethos of Apollo, compared its business strategy with the Atlantis Oil Company during the preceding fifteen years. The comparison was revealing, for in 1965 the two companies were virtually identical in size, operations, and style. Furthermore, at the time, "both managements came out of the Philadelphia Main Line conservative mode that produced paternalistic employers, slow change and unexciting results." But by 1980, Atlantis had surged ahead to place eighth in income among American oil companies, leaving Apollo behind at twelfth. Several variables entered into the difference, but the determinative one was the occupant of the chief executive office. Anders, a *nouveau entrepreneur extraordinaire*, commandeered the position in Atlantis in 1965 and by sheer force of personal character quashed the previous managerial orientation ("Don't make waves; find the easy time to do something") through a sequence of daring moves— mergers, new construction, reorganization, increased indebtedness.

Similarly, but in 1974, Apollo Oil Company confronted a radical change in its CEO, yet with a different outcome. Throughout the decades that the Podion family had direct control over Apollo, conservatism and paternalism were the central features of the corporation's culture—conservatism in its business strategy and paternalism in its organizational character. But in 1974, Sharpie succeeded to the position of CEO. It had been assumed that Sharpie, though young, had been carefully groomed for the office and would perpetuate the tradition. Instead, he adopted organizational principles from the teachings of modern management. The corporation was radically reorganized into a cluster of semiautonomous units, each with its own president and each placed into competition with the others. Personnel practices—placement, promotion, and pay—were rationalized. Some degree of diversification in holdings was introduced.

As should have been expected in that milieu, the change sent shock waves throughout all echelons of the corporation. On the surface, it was merely a structural alteration for purposes of modernization. But beneath the surface, it effected a transformation of power relations and it violated the cultural sensibilities and moral expectations of the employee. By dint of a ukase from the highest office, the central concept of the organization was transmuted from paternalism to managerialism. The corporation was converted from a familylike association in which the members were joined together in organic unity to a professionalized organization through which the members were expected to compete with each other for increased productivity and higher position.

There was strong resistance to the move. Sharpie met his Waterloo in an effort at a secretive, late-night, quick-move acquisition of a health products corporation. He was summarily removed as CEO and replaced by Tabur. Tabur, in office now for eight years, has retained, with continuing modifications, the organizational reforms of Sharpie, but returned to the conservative strategy of the Podions.

As a result of these moves over the past twelve years, the corporate culture of Apollo is in a state of tension. Paternalistic sensibilities are still cherished. Apollo is remembered as a caring institution. No one, it is affirmed with pride, was released during the Great Depression. Members of the Podion family are praised for their integrity and honesty. When their power was paramount in the corporation's governance, employees trusted they would be treated fairly and charitably. There was no need to clamor for rights, for *noblesse oblige* was the corporate rule.

To a degree the paternalistic ethos still prevails. But it is counterposed by the structure of competitive decentralization. As persons in the employ of the corporation for two or more decades note, the reorganization under Sharpie set persons and departments accustomed to working cooperatively over against each other. Principles of trust and openness, which had characterized working relationships, now clashed with the pressure for hard bargaining among profit centers. Employees have become uncertain about their identity. For whom are they working and to whom is their loyalty due—Apollo or the subsidiary? They are aware that the subsidiary might be divested at any time by the parent company. Some employees, of course, thrive under the new organization. They find paternalism an anachronism at best and press for a more thoroughgoing managerialism. But the net result of the tension in the corporation viewed as a whole is a state that borders on anomie which will not and cannot be resolved merely by the adoption of a slogan.

From a mesoscopic perspective, each corporation is viewed as an isolated whole, an entity unto itself. Each company—Procter and Gamble, CBS, General Motors—is discerned as having its own discrete identity. One may, as with Deal and Kennedy, construct a typology of kinds of corporate culture, demonstrating certain congruities among individual corporations.[17] But such a typology nonetheless supposes that each corporation is a distinct social totality with a pervasive cultural ethos. Granting this supposition (a point of contention in contemporary social theory), a mesoscopic perspective may be intelligible and useful, but taken by itself it is delimiting. It neglects the contextual embeddedness and internal plurality of the corporation.

3. The Microscopic View

From a microscopic perspective, the large modern business corporation is a complex association. In 1981, for example, Apollo Oil had 45,000 employees clustered into about a dozen subsidiaries scattered throughout the United States and abroad. One should not be surprised to discover diverse cultural orientations within the enterprise. The character of relationships in a gas and oil production division in Houston should not be expected to be the same as in corporate headquarters in Philadelphia or in a coal mining operation in Appalachia. Such regional differences are openly acknowledged and largely tolerated within the company even though they are, at times, sources of irritation. More critical are other kinds of cultural differentiation which result in experienced stress if not overt conflict. The dominant culture in Apollo is white, male, hierarchical, and utilitarian. But there are groups of persons within the corporation who represent the antitheses of these features and thus comprise a set of subordinate and often suppressed cultural orientations—blacks, women, blue-collar workers, lawyers.

In policy statements, Apollo affirms its intention to comply with all government regulations including those designed for equal employment opportunity and affirmative action. In directives to personnel officers, that intention is reinforced. But in the actual day-to-day life of the corporation, deep-seated variances of sensibility are palpable. The American dilemma persists.

There is an articulate and not inconsiderable contingent in the corporation claiming that affirmative action programs violate the inner principles of the business corporation—principles of utility and meritocracy. The underlying motivation of the claim may be suspect, but in any case, the claim contravenes James O'Toole's judgment that

Since meritocratic systems of hiring and promotion function as they should only in the absence of unfair discrimination, it would seem that blacks will not be treated fairly in those work place systems that are designed to reflect merit only. For as long as there is subtle racism at work that whites fail to recognize and overcome, it will be necessary to pursue affirmative action and other compensatory employment practices.[18]

Blacks in Apollo Oil seem to agree that, while the corporation is not flagrantly bigoted, it is unintentionally but nevertheless empirically racist. Blacks joining Apollo in entry-level positions suffer the trauma of passage into an alien world if they have been without any prior close-working relationship in the white community. The tension accompanies blacks throughout the course of their careers. As reported in a journalistic study of "Black Executives and Corporate Stress,"

Isolated from other blacks and alienated from whites, many managers straddle two worlds. They consciously choose their speech, their walk, their mode of dress and car; they trim their hair lest a mountainous Afro set them apart. They know they have a high visibility, and realize that their success depends not only on their abilities, but also on their white colleagues' feeling comfortable with them. Some whites admit that certain kinds of behavior make them nervous.[19]

Yet the contrast is more than a matter of hair style and speech: "some blacks assert that the superficial and intrinsic profit-oriented values of the corporation differ so vastly from the people-oriented world most of them grew up in that the result is culture shock."[20] In some units of Apollo, blacks have quietly created an informal network of communication for mutual support. They did so secretively, fearing that an open organization would not be tolerated by the higher executives.

Some women, on the other hand, have publicly organized in small groups throughout the corporation. Women's organizations, it seems, are seen as less threatening to corporate unity. Yet even those women with the company for over two decades are explicit and sometimes bitter about the cultural barriers and organizational obstacles they have encountered in their careers. They may be respected for what they do, but they are nonetheless subject to stereotyping; little provision has been made to assist them in their familial obligations; and the primary power and most prominent positions in the company are firmly in the grip of male hands. None of the presidents or vice presidents of the subsidiaries is female; except for secretaries and administrative assistants, none of the occupants of the executive floor of headquarters is female; only one director of the corporation is female. As a woman who is director of several major corporations has noted, informal patterns of association are also indicative of cultural tension.

> Men sit together for lunch in the company cafeteria. They talk about football and baseball scores. They also talk about what went wrong that morning or the latest gossip about what's going on in the company. Men stop for a drink together to relax about work. As they relax, they review the day's events. Are women welcome? Is *one* woman welcome? Young men tell me that if a woman joins them, it is a different kind of conversation. Should the men welcome the women? Should the women want to join? If not, how do they become part of that informal structure? How do the men's wives and the women's husbands react to these sessions?[21]

In an innovative study of *Men and Women of the Corporation*, Rosabeth Moss Kanter argues that the condition of minorities and women in corporate enterprise can be transformed only with a change in the numerical proportion of those groups in the company.[22] The key factor is not symbolic. It is not attitudinal. It is instead institutional. In particular, it is quantitative.

Kanter's argument does not seem to apply, however, to the case of nonexempt employees, wage earners, blue-collar workers. Only a minority of Apollo's personnel serve in managerial, supervisory, or professional capacity. Yet that minority understands itself to be superior in authority and control: "the culture of management dictates that the most important things to preserve are the 'prerogatives' that make managers accountable to no one on matters of corporate strategy, policy, planning, marketing, production, finance, technology choice, and on all matters relating to the structure of the organization and the structure of work tasks."[23] Nonexempt employees, on the other hand, are often uneasy with, if not resentful of, managerial authority. They may themselves possess technical skills, have had years of experience in the company, and be highly educated, yet they are treated as pawns. This clash of sensibilities is especially evident between the executive group and the unionized workers. Executives, given what they perceive as the wisdom and humanity of their policies, cannot comprehend why workers would want to unionize. Workers, however, feel it is only through unionization they might protect their personal dignity and gain some degree of power and position in the corporation. Whereas executives have an image of the corporation as fundamentally and properly hierarchical, many wage earners find that feature of the dominant corporate culture demeaning and antagonistic to their self-understanding.

The dominant culture of Apollo, as noted, is white, male, hierarchical, and utilitarian. Within a business context, the utilitarian question is: What policies and actions will result in a satisfactory return on investment? That consideration is paramount even when modified by other important concerns—paternalistic, moral, political. But the paramountcy of that consideration stands in tension with the felt obligations of some members of the corporation's legal staff. Principles of utility and rule of law are not wholly compatible with each other. Neither are principles of bureaucratic organization and professional autonomy. The traditional professions bring with them a culture that is not, without distortion, reducible to the utilitarian impulse of the modern corporation.

Thus, from microscopic perspective, corporate culture is not homogeneous. It is not uniform. It includes tensions and sometimes open conflict among multiple communities within the company—regional, racial, sexual, class, professional. Programs to manipulate corporate culture to increase efficiency and productivity may have the unintended consequence of exacerbating the tensions, for they may be perceived, quite properly, as an effort at hegemonic control by the dominant group in the corporation.

4. The Macroscopic View

Although a large business corporation is, by law, but a fictional person (*ficta persona*) it is, in fact, a real agent of no mean significance in modern society. The precise manner in which a corporation exercises agency is a considerable problem, both theoretical and practical. But however that problem is resolved, corporations, especially the "supercorporations"[24] or "megacorporations"[25] or "metrocorporations"[26] have a cultural significance far transcending their strictly internal dynamics, even if that significance is not fully comprehended by the actors within the corporate structure.

In its beginning in 1901, Apollo was exclusively a petroleum industry. Petroleum remains its predominant activity. Subsequent to World War II, Apollo followed the lead of other large corporations by introducing a degree of diversification in its holdings, but it has done so cautiously. That caution is itself an attribute of corporate identity, of its inner culture.[27] But of greater cultural importance, on the macroscopic level, is its primary product—petroleum.

The modern petroleum and automobile industries in the United States were launched within a very few decades of each other. In the same year Apollo was incorporated, two occurrences gave strong impetus to the convergence of these industries—a dramatic decrease in the price of oil and the introduction of techniques of mass production into the automotive factory. Through this convergence, a new culture was born. Its possibilities unseen at the time, ranged from suburban sprawl to "American Graffiti." Patterns of work and residency, consumption and entertainment, courtship and family relations, crime and war have changed radically given this development. While the neighborhood, with its ethic of *Gemeinschaft*, has not been wholly obliterated, its existence has been jeopardized. A society in which the automobile is a central symbolic reality introduces a new kind of personal identity.

Carol Gould takes special note of the dialectical character of human agency. The transformation of material resources to fulfill an immediate want or need has a reactively transformative effect on the agent. As a result of what one creates, one becomes a different sort of person.

> For example, suppose the purpose is to get from one place to another quickly; the creation of an automobile satisfies this purpose. In addition, it opens up new modes of action and new opportunities by extending the regional limits of one's world and thereby the range of one's social contact. It gives rise to the feeling of freedom and control over one's environment. It also creates the require-

ments for a new technology of road building, the problems of the destruction of the countryside and of pollution, and the ubiquitous problem of traffic congestion, in which the original aims are thwarted. The agent is also transformed in this process, as anyone who drives an automobile can attest. For better or worse, a new human character is created.[28]

On the level of qualitative meanings, the culture of the automobile has reinforced, yet has given a unique form to, American values of mobility, privacy, independence, potency. It has also been a force in the emergent tension in advanced capitalist societies between the ethos of production (the so-called Puritan ethic: work hard, do your duty) and the ethos of consumption (the hedonist ethic: play hard, do your own thing). Moreover, on the level of institutional structures, the culture of the automobile has effected a conjunction of interdependency among several industries—construction, steel, finance, as well as petroleum and automotive manufacture. Thus petroleum has been among factors promoting a social revolution in the United States and throughout the industrialized world.

Petroleum together with other industries also contributed, in a seemingly paradoxical way, to promoting a political revolution. Over the past century, a radical change has been effected in the form of political governance in this country, a change from a laissez-faire state to what has been called variously a "welfare state," an "industrial state,"[29] a "technocorporate state."[30]

In rhetoric and, with important qualifications to be noted later, in policy, the corporate sector, including petroleum, has resisted the change. The political culture of the seventeenth- and eighteenth-century bourgeois revolutions retains a strong hold on the mentality of those who speak for and are in control of large business corporations.[31] Economic freedom and limited government were the by-words of that culture. Among methods of social control, economism (the use of monetary incentives through the mechanism of the market) was favored over legalism (the use of legislative directives enforced through governmental agencies).[32] Politicians and government bureaucrats were viewed as inherently self-serving, unknowing, rigid, and inept. Business leaders and entrepreneurs were discerned as sensitive to the needs and wants of the people and responsive to demand registered in the marketplace. From this perspective, the common good is better served by the business system than by the political system.

Despite the rhetoric, however, which was strategically functional at the time of the bourgeois revolutions, a strong symbiotic relationship has evolved between corporation and government. In ways direct and indirect, government has been a facilitator of corporate growth and a champion of corporate interests. Oil depletion allowances, highway construction programs, developments in military technology, subsidies to airlines and to automotive manufacturers are among the means through which the federal government has contributed directly to the petroleum industry. The manipulation of monetary and fiscal policies to stabilize the economy and the introduction of labor and social legislation to placate the demands of the working class are among the indirect means whereby the survival of corporations has been assured. Throughout this evolution, while the written constitution of the U.S. has remained the same, the actual constitution of the nation has been transformed.[33] Political culture and corporate culture exist in a state of mutual dependency.

Thus government, perceived as enemy, is actually friend and companion of the modern business corporation. The intense distrust of governmental officials expressed by corporate leaders conceals what is more than merely a *modus vivendi* in the coexistence of private and public institutions. The inconsistency may not be consciously hypocritical, but it has provoked George Cabot Lodge to call for a rejection of the "Lockean paradigm" as now outdated and the formulation of a "new American ideology" to legitimize the deliberate coordination of corporation and government to serve the common good.[34]

A related inconsistency that characterizes the culture of corporations on the macroscopic level is between their national identity and their "global reach."[35] The Apollo Oil Company, for instance, is based in the United States. Moreover, in its annual reports, it is expressly patriotic. It is, by its own affirmation, committed to the American system. It prides itself on contributing to the drive, announced by the Carter and Reagan administrations, for national energy independence. On the other hand, although Apollo is not a major multinational corporation, the extent of its international operations is remarkable. It possesses units engaged in exploration, manufacturing, marketing, and marine chartering in Canada, Iberoamerica, Western Europe, Africa, Australia, and the Far East. For purposes of doing business, political boundaries constitute at best artificial but meaningless limitations, and at worst irritating and unnecessary obstacles. In principle, the entire world is within the corporation's sphere of interest.

These two orientations, toward the nation-state and toward the world as a whole, derive from different kinds of morality. Loyalty to the nation derives from a morality of communal identity from whose perspective boundaries, legal or psychological, play an essential role. Openness to the world as a potential resource and marketplace is rooted in a morality of technical rationality from whose perspective economic utility has priority over ethnic origin and the lines dividing the territories and peoples are arbitrary designations.

The tension between these two orientations is manifest in opposing judgments over the wisdom of the Foreign Corrupt Practices Act (1977). The official policy of Apollo is to adhere strictly to the letter and spirit of the Act out of respect for the United States law and inherited scruples against bribery and deception. However, some managers in international operations declare the policy is hypocritical and dysfunctional. It is hypocritical since there is no way to avoid payments to foreign officials. The policy merely compels a more convoluted procedure to satisfy the need. It is dysfunctional because it detracts from managerial discretion, which should be paramount in doing business. The only ultimately guiding rule in doing business should be what pays off on the ledger.

In brief, on the macroscopic level, the supercorporation is an agency of wide-ranging cultural significance. It has promoted the development of a consumer society even though the mores of consumerism are not wholly compatible with the discipline of the highly productive workplace. It has been a dominant factor in the formation of the technocorporate state even though it fosters, in rhetoric, an outdated theory of limited government. And it has created a thoroughly international economic system, whose power seems to defy control by any currently existent political organization, even though it professes loyalty to the nation of its origins. Consumerism, corporativism, and globalism are among dominant features of contemporary corporate culture.

5. THE CHRONOSCOPIC VIEW

Institutions, more than individuals, are repetitive, for institutions consist in routinized patterns of interaction. They are, by their nature, addicted to habit. Yet institutions, much like individuals, betray a dialectic between durability and change, form and dynamics. They resist change. Yet, in time resistance weakens and institutions are transformed. In some instances, change is deliberately engineered, for persons learned in the ways of history know that institutions often must change in some respects to endure in other, conceivably more important respects. On occasion, the impulse to survive so dominates an institution's life that it leads, paradoxically, to the neglect of the institution's original purpose. But institutions, despite their pretense, are not immortal.

Institutions, in short, are historical processes set within a more encompassing historical process. They have their beginnings; they live out their lives; and, one day, they come to an end. The culture of the modern corporation must be understood within the context of the development of that institutional form out of its given past and toward its possible future.

In a classic history of corporations published at the turn of the century, John P. Davis asserted that "Modern corporations are so called because they are an integral part of modern society, of the society that originated in the sixteenth and seventeenth centuries, distinguished by individualism in general, but more particularly by democracy in the state, and by the destruction of tradition and the elevation of reason in religion and science."[36]

If Davis is right, the large modern business corporation is the progeny of the bourgeois revolution. In political life, the bourgeois revolution represented the principle of limited government and intensified the bifurcation between public and private sectors. In intellectual life, the bourgeois revolution promoted the principle of critical rationality, which, in the course of decades, was transformed into the principle of technical rationality. In economic life, the bourgeois revolution signaled the end of mercantilism and strengthened the forces of unregulated enterprise. In all spheres, the predominant slogan of the bourgeois revolution was liberty, and its philosophy was individualistic. In general, the bourgeois revolution introduced a new historical epoch.

To assert that the large modern business corporation was engendered by the individualistic impulse of the bourgeois revolution may, upon initial reflection, appear strange. Certainly the likes of the Fortune 500 were not part of the deliberate design of those whose struggles for political, economic, and intellectual liberty promoted the onset of the modern age. On the contrary, opposition to the corporate form of doing business was widespread in eighteenth-century England. And Adam Smith, whose *Wealth of Nations* (1776) is still a handbook in classical economics, was not sanguine about the effect corporations might have in economic development. As Dow Votaw remarks, it is "a paradox of history" that Smith's apology for a free-market economy was invoked on behalf of corporate enterprise toward the end of the nineteenth and well into the twentieth century.[37]

Yet the connection is not unintelligible. Among critical factors linking the bourgeois revolution with the contemporary supracorporation were the industrial revolution, with its new technologies for the production of economic goods, and materialistic culture, with its intense demand for economic growth. These factors, combined with the bourgeois beliefs—in limited government, in critical and technical rationality, and in free enterprise—led to the transformation of American society in the nineteenth century from agrarian individualism to laissez-faire industrialism. The corporation was the institutional embodiment of that transformation. Curiously, as George Cabot Lodge has argued, despite the social and cultural transformation, the modern corporation tends to persist in promulgating the ideology of the earlier period as if that legitimized its existence.

Thus the Apollo Oil Company, for instance, in a creedal statement adopted by its executive office with utmost sincerity during the past decade affirms as two of its eight principles:

> We believe freedom of choice is the critical requisite of any form of social organization that effectively provides for self-determination. Competition both encourages and makes practical the exercise of that freedom. And competition is in turn encouraged when meritorious achievement is recognized by commensurate reward.
>
> We believe economic competition spurred by the profit motive gives unparalleled thrust to production, provides the material base

for superior living standards, and preserves the widest latitude for the exercise of individual preferences.

But, according to Lodge, the liberal bourgeois ideology is now historically outmoded and socially dysfunctional. Its principles of individualism, property rights, competitive markets, limited government, and technical specialization are anachronisms. They are reflective of and constitute a sensible standard for a social order that no longer exists. More significantly, taken together, they serve as a defense mechanism or, more accurately, an avoidance mechanism, serving vested interests and deflecting attention from current conditions of human existence.

We are, declares Lodge, in the throes of a set of interwoven historical crises that demand new modes of thought and new forms of organization. Internationally, we confront the threat of nuclear holocaust. Ecologically, we are in an era of serious environmental decay. Economically, major public institutions are suffering from severe fiscal crisis. Socially, whole classes of persons are subject to forms of structural discrimination and deprivation. Politically, the nation-state can no longer sustain its traditional functions of protection and welfare.

If these crises are to be resolved, they must be confronted deliberately and cooperatively. The individualism of the bourgeois ideology must be replaced with a communitarian orientation openly acknowledging the mutual interdependence of peoples and explicitly encouraging forms of institutional interaction directly responsive to human need. The creed of Apollo, "recognizing that business is among the institutions affecting the well-being of mankind," is not totally unmindful of the communitarian imperative, although its admission of the imperative is carefully limited and cautiously balanced:

> We believe that while business cannot survive if incapable of performing profitably, its sole obligation does not consist literally of producing profits. Instead, it must also nourish values cherished by the society of which it is a part.

> We believe we are obligated to be responsible in conducting the affairs of the company to the interests of its customers, employees and stockholders. Also, we must be responsive to the broader concerns of the public, including especially the general desire for im-

provement of the quality of life, equal opportunity for all, and the constructive use of natural resources.

We believe we must be sensitive to the need and aspirations of others, and that it is important we seek understanding in turn of the goals of the company, its policies and the manner in which it attempts to discharge its responsibilities. Consequently, we will strive to maintain open communications with all affected by or concerned with our company.

Given Lodge's construction of the needs of the newly emerging historical epoch, these creedal affirmations, while acknowledging some breadth of social responsibility, are woefully short-sighted. Yet Lodge holds open the prospect of a radical cultural transformation of the megacorporation.

In contrast to Lodge, Robert Heilbroner's prognosis for the future of the modern large business corporation is dire and foreboding. Both argue that we are in a period of transition. To both a new historical epoch is emerging. According to Lodge, the delineament of that new epoch is what calls forth and justifies the adoption of a new communitarian ideology for the business corporation. But to Heilbroner, there may not be a future at all for the business corporation, for "the civilization of business—the civilization to which we give the name capitalism—is slated to disappear, probably not within our lifetimes but in all likelihood within that of our grandchildren and great grandchildren";[38] "our business civilization is on the decline and will perish."[39]

Heilbroner conjectures that the very character and success of business civilization have produced conditions that make it virtually impossible for that civilization to continue. While that civilization has been a miracle in economic productivity and economic growth, it has, as well, taken its toll in costs. Its profligate use of the natural world has produced scarcities in key resources. Its unregulated disposal of wastes has brought about a rapidly deteriorating environment, making it virtually uninhabitable in some locations. Its internationalization of the economic system has led to shifts in the balance of political and economic power and has provoked armed conflict between classes and among nations. Its subjection of labor to a position of social dependency and functional role has created a widespread sense of alienation and effected cycles of unemployment. Its commercialization of life has provoked serious question about the hollowness of the values of business civilization. How long the institutional forms and cultural system of the business corporation can be sustained given the onslaught of these developments is unpredictable, but Heilbroner's forecast is that they will, over the course of decades, disappear. The long-range historical question that must be answered is what alternative institutional and valuational forms will then be possible and desirable.

6. Conclusion

At the conclusion of their massive study of multinational corporations, Richard Barnet and Ronald Muller address the question of the kind of cultural orientation that may be necessary in the gradually emerging epoch of the world's economic history.

> The search for a systemic alternative is intimately bound up with a change in the global value system. As Tawney and others have shown, the goal of infinite accumulation was not present in the Middle Ages. Greed is a special characteristic of our modern economic system, which depends upon it as a primary incentive of social organization. The market mentality which puts economic activity, irrespective of purpose, at the center of the universe is a product not of human instinct but of social organization. Competitive individualism, a system in which community develops from common consumption rather than shared feelings, is increasingly incompatible with survival of the species, but it too is socially conditioned, and hence new values can be learned to take its place. The values needed for survival, if one reflects on it, turn out to be the familiar democratic values preached by prophets and sages since the beginning of history—respect for human dignity, justice, frugality, honesty, moderation, and equality.
>
> These values will not come to replace the contemporary outmoded values—competitive individualism, comfort, waste, infinite growth, and security through accumulation—because human beings suddenly learn altruism. They will come to be the dominant values of the coming century, if at all, only if enough people are awakened to their necessity for the survival of the species.[40]

Granting the Barnet-Muller thesis of the historical relativity of cultural systems and the openness of history to new possibilities, one may doubt whether the survival of the human species is contingent in any simple way on the development of a thoroughly democratic-communitarian cultural system. To be sure, without some degree of love in human relationships, the persistence of the human enterprise is utterly unimaginable. But the whole course of history gives testimony to the durability of the human species under conditions that are degrading and heavily oppressive. Many of the crises we have cited may well be resolved and the human species may continue to endure in a postcorporate world that stands in stark contrast to the "values preached by prophets and sages since the beginning of history." Some social theorists project an emerging epoch that is highly authoritarian, centrally controlled, carefully planned, bureaucratically organized, and militarily constrained.

The primary ethical question, however, is not what is predictable. Nor is it what is possible. Nor is it what will enable the human species merely to survive. It is rather what will conduce to the common good. Human life is intrinsically relational. It is lived in a set of contexts—a biosphere (the relationship between self and nature), a sociosphere (the relationship between self and other), and a psychosphere (the relationship between self and self). The common good is that texture of relationships in which the life of all is enhanced by the actions and dispositions of each one. Its common name is sympathy. Its profound meaning is love. Its ordinary, everyday demand is justice. Its grounding is ultimately ontological. That is, the common good is not an abstract principle imposed upon the reality of the world. It is a quality that derives from the structure of experience. It is the deepest impulse and profoundest need of all being. The suffering and misery that result from its violation are themselves witness to its presence.

Thus, to assess the full significance of the culture of the corporation, to interpret the meaning of the world that it manifests within itself (the meso- and microscopic views), the world that it produces through its agency (the macroscopic view), and the world that it tends to promote for the future even if it should itself disappear (the chronoscopic view), it must be measured by its conformity to the common good. The ultimate judgment of the corporation and its culture, like the ultimate judgment of all life, is whether and to what degree within the ongoing passage of history, it bodies forth some creative advance within the community of being.

In sum, the corporation, like the Sabbath, was not made for its own survival. Its legitimacy depends on whether its meaning is truly representative of the meaning of life itself. This judgment derives from a version of "empirical realism" which supposes that the

> immediacies of concrete experience actually participate in the depth of the Creative Passage in which the human structure of sensory life is integrally related to other structures, and to what is genuinely ultimate as a dynamic of creativity. Each individuated human structure or personality is thought to prehend, with varying degrees of relevance as Whitehead has expressed it, what is ultimate in the reality of things.[41]

From this perspective, interest in corporate culture lies not in its contribution to productivity or survival, but its character as a location in which and through which persons engage in creative intercommunication with each other and with the universe about them.

8. A NEW SOCIAL COVENANT: *FROM DEMOCRATIC CAPITALISM TO SOCIAL DEMOCRACY*

> In each age of the world distinguished by high activity there will be found at its culmination, and among the agencies leading to that culmination, some profound cosmological outlook, implicitly accepted, impressing its own type upon the current springs of action. A. N. Whitehead[1]

> The essential point to grasp is that in dealing with capitalism we are dealing with an evolutionary process. J. A. Schumpeter[2]

IN THIS CHAPTER, I HAVE undertaken a three-fold task: to develop a critique of democratic capitalism from a theologically informed ethical perspective, to make explicit the grounds on which the critique is developed, and to point to an acceptable alternative.

The task is as important as it is formidable. It is formidable because of the complexities of meaning associated with democracy and capitalism and because of the intricacies entailed in theological method. But it is important if, as some interpreters would have us believe, we are at a critical turning point in human history and the fate of democracy and capitalism both hang in the balance. In considering this task, we must not forget our place in history. We are inheritors of modernity.

On its negative side, modernity began as a rejection of the central principles of medieval civilization. The ideal of Christendom came under severe attack. The age of faith was repudiated as a time of simple credulity and naive faith. Religion, at least in its traditional forms, has thus become a problem for the modern mind.

On its positive side, modernity affirms the principle of autonomy and has given rise to kinds of thought and practice that, it is alleged, honor that principle. In social practice, autonomy as the liberty of individuals to act as they please is the principle customarily invoked to justify capitalism and democracy. In intellectual pursuits, autonomy as the unfettering of the mind to see and to think for itself is the central interest underlying the inductive method in modern science and the development of empirical and rational methods in modern philosophy.

Given that simplified version of modernity, a religious critique of democratic capitalism may seem quaint, possessing the character of a belated counterreformation. But it may not be so quaint after all. It may be that a religious critique is a way of honoring modernity through the projection of the possibility, if not the need, for a new epoch in social and cultural history, a post-modern epoch whose forms of thought and practice will more fully realize the principle of autonomy than those of the past three hundred years. In this respect, we have much to learn from the impetus of liberation theologies, for they have been inspired, out of profoundly religious motivation, to uncover those hypocrisies of modern thought and practice which, claiming the principle of autonomy, perpetuate structures of domination.

Faith as untested belief and sheer confessionalism is at odds with the modern mind's commitment to autonomy and devotion to critical analysis. But faith as appreciative awareness, as openness of the human spirit to the most fundamental realities of experience, even to the life of God, deepens the probings of critique and lends to it the possibility of transformative insight. To paraphrase Bernard Meland, faith as appreciative awareness provides a condition of human response to the world in which something creative can happen to our total nature such that our habits of response can be transformed. Under these circumstances, even the criteria we envisage as being designative of the good may undergo radical change.[3]

Against that background, I intend to advance three theses for consideration: first, that, particularly at this point in the world's history, the common good is the first virtue of social institutions; second, that capitalism and democracy, although long associated historically, are in tension with each other; and third, that social democracy is an alternative institutional form more directly ordained to the common good than what has been traditionally called "democratic capitalism." In developing the first thesis, I shall suggest that social interpretation and social ethics are, in their deepest dimension, ontological or cosmological. That is, they at least presuppose and sometimes deliberately articulate a vision of the world and they portray human agency as an expression of that world. In presenting the second thesis, I shall distinguish two interpretations of capitalism, orthodox and heterodox, and two sides of democracy, protective and participative. The tension between capitalism and democracy is evident even in instances where they seem most compatible. In stating the third thesis, I shall urge the need for a new social covenant in which concern for economic growth and distribution, while not ignored, is subordinate to the interests of commonwealth.

1.

> God, desiring not only that the human race might be able by their similarity of nature to associate with one another, but also that they might be bound together in harmony and peace by the ties of relationship, was pleased to derive all persons from one individual. Augustine[4]

Franklin I. Gamwell asserts that "ethics is peculiarly religious when it seeks to defend on humanistic grounds a comprehensive principle of evaluation, where 'comprehensive' is used in the strictest sense to mean a principle in terms of which the worth and importance of all things may be assessed."[5] Two criteria seem to be indicated by this statement. First, comprehensiveness is a criterion specifying the religiousness of an ethics. Second, defense of an ethics on humanistic grounds is a criterion, though perhaps not the only criterion, of the adequacy of an ethics, whether religious or not.

While these criteria are onerous, I intend to suggest that the common good is a principle of religious ethics which, rooted deeply within the tradition of Christian faith, is justifiable on humanistic grounds. That is, the common good is a principle which, while applying with particular force to social practices, is a measure for assessing "the worth and importance of all things." Moreover, the common good is a humanistic principle because it is expressive of the meaning of being a self within the world.

We begin with an examination of the meaning of "social practice," remembering that our topic, democratic capitalism, is a kind of social practice. In ordinary life, we engage in many social practices ranging from conversation and litigation to economic exchange and war. Some social practices are occasional and casual, such as the greeting of a stranger. Others are periodic and, by intent, transformative, as religious ritual. Still others are constant in their presence and far-reaching in consequence, as in the political and technological systems of the modern world.

But the idea of a social practice, which may seem obvious on the surface, is a matter of controversy. On one level the issue is methodological. What, the question is asked, constitutes the fundamental unit of social analysis? But the controversy is more than methodological. Methodologies are not divorceable from other aspects of social analysis and interpretation. They bear with them normative implications and ontological presuppositions. Thus, at another level, the controversy bears on the subject of social ethics. How the methodological question is resolved sets the conditions for determining what kinds of ethical principles are appropriate. And at still another level, the controversy is cosmological; it is a contention over the character of the world within which practice takes place. Consider Aristotle, Hobbes, and Marx in a round-table discussion over the meaning of social practice. The interplay in social analysis of questions of method, ethics, and cosmology would, I suspect, be evident in the discussion.

Among parties to the controversy, three positions are dominant: organic, individualist, and relational. Each position conveys something of importance about the character of experience which explains its persuasiveness, but the third, I suggest, is the most adequate in its comprehension of the conditions as well as the problems of human existence.

Within the framework of the organic position, a social practice has the character of a whole, a totality. The social practice is itself the unit of social analysis. Those who enact the practice are its members. Their identity is a function of the inner world of the practice itself. From this perspective, loyalty as devotion to the group and as willingness to perform one's role in its life is a primary virtue. The bonds of kinship and the compulsions of family are evidence of the sense of this position. But class consciousness and the urge to press for class interests also manifest the strength of an organic understanding of social practice. So do the strong pull of ethnic and racial ties and the mysterious attractions of nationalism. We do seem, under certain circumstances, to give credence to the idea of social totalities.

The opposite to the organic approach is the individualistic. According to methodological individualism, only individuals think, feel, and act. Nations and states, classes and ethnic groups are but collective concepts or metaphorical constructs. Such normative ideas as the public interest, the general welfare, the common good are mystical nonsense. As Murray N. Rothbard remarks,

> All these concepts rest on the implicit premise that there exists, somewhere, a living organic entity known as "society," "the group," "the public," "the community," and that that entity has values and pursues ends. Not only are these terms held up as living entities; they are supposed to exist *more* fundamentally than do mere individuals.[6]

But, insists Rothbard, there are no such entities. The fundamental axiom of social analysis is that only individuals exist, only individuals possess consciousness, only individuals have values and desires. This axiom is not without roots in human experience, for indeed experience is always that of a subject, even if the fact of subjectivity cannot without further argument be transmuted into a theory of subjectivism. Individuals, not classes or groups, suffer and wonder why, have desires and yearn for their satisfaction. But individuals conflict with each other, creating a problem of adjudication. From this perspective, the task of ethics lies in the resolution of conflicts whether through principles of utility maximization or distributive justice.

The third position is more complex, but more complete in its reflection of the relational character of our experience. In social theory, the position is represented in Anthony Giddens's concept of structuration which he intends to articulate the point of creative integration between the agency of individuals and the structures of society.[7] Agents are individuals, but they are not individuals in total isolation from each other. They inherit and they enact social practices. In their identity, they are constituted out of long traditions of understanding and sensibility. In their actions, they reproduce, in some form, a world of social practices. A social practice is a complicated mixture of several structural features. It is a shared knowledge by means of which agents explain their actions to each other and to outsiders. It is a set of expectations, of principles and purposes, through which agents assess what is desirable and correct and justify their responses when forced to do so. It is a structure of power, which both constrains and facilitates. That is, given an asymmetry in the distribution of power throughout a practice, its organized resources are structures of domination and limitation. But, at the same time, they are structures of transformative possibility. Giddens's concept of structuration thus affirms that agents are individuals, but in their agency they draw together, more or less intentionally and creatively, understandings, norms, and resources of social structure. As they do so, they set the conditions for all future agency. The focus for social analysis, from this perspective, is not the social totality as such. Nor is it the individual as such. It is the manner in which agents can and do bear forward through their action the features of social structure.

On the ontological (and theological) level, this position is represented in Bernard Meland's principle of internal relations according to which there is a depth within our experience that connects all we are as unique individuals with all existent events and, ultimately, God, "that sensitive nature within the vast context of nature, winning the creative passage for qualitative attainment."[8] It is also represented in Philip Hefner's ontology of belonging according to which our individuality is infused with multiple dimensions of belonging: (1) to our fellow humans across all barriers and boundaries; (2) to the ecosystem which bore us and sustains us; and (3) to the vast evolutionary process from which the whole ecosystem emerged.[9]

In moral philosophy, the third position is stated in a limited way in Michael J. Sandel's critique of John Rawls's theory of justice as neglecting, save insofar as Rawls presupposes it unknowingly, an understanding of community as basically constitutive of the meaning of selfhood. We live, Sandel asserts, as encumbered selves. To be a self is to be in relation, to have loyalties and allegiances, responsibilities and associations which, taken altogether, enter into our individuality. This means that at least "to some I owe more than justice requires or even permits, not by reason of agreements I have made but instead in virtue of those more or less enduring attachments and commitments which taken together partly define the person I am."[10] Sandel invokes friendship as an elementary case of what he intends, but he refers as well to family, tribe, city, class, nation, people. If Sandel is correct, the first virtue of social institutions is not, as Rawls contends, distributive justice.[11] It is the good of the community. The good of the community is a version of what Alasdair MacIntyre calls an "internal good," that is, a good that is realized only in a practice but that is for all those who participate in that practice.[12] MacIntyre cites the instance of chess-playing.

Relying on Meland's principle of internal relations, I would violate the strictures MacIntyre has placed on the concept to suggest we consider our entire life a practice in which all entities are engaged. This is the sense of Roberto Unger's theory of the self as consisting in a wide-ranging set of relationships to nature, to other persons, and to one's own work and station.[13] The self is separate from these three worlds, yet engaged in them. The dynamic interplay between separation and engagement is, in effect, the generic practice of being human. The ethical problem is to determine what quality of relationship will redound to the good of all parties in it and therefore to the good of the self.

The traditional language for this ethical concern is the common good. The traditional locus of its responsibility is the political association, for the function of the political association is to concern itself directly and deliberately with the quality of relationships throughout the community as a whole. What I am proposing therefore is that a relational approach to social analysis conjoined with a principle of internal relations implies that the common good is the first virtue of social institutions and that the public-regarding association has priority over those which are private.

What, then, is the common good? *In focus*, it is the goodness *of* the community, but it is a goodness *for* all its participants. Thus it is common in a double sense. As Jacques Maritain expresses it,

> The common good of the city is neither the mere collection of private goods, nor the proper good of the whole which like . . . the

hive with respect to its bees, relates the parts to itself alone and sacrifices them to itself. It is the good *human* life of the multitude; . . . it is their communion in good living. It is therefore common to both *the whole and the parts* into which it flows back and which, in turn must benefit it.[14]

In scope, the common good is local and global. Again, in Maritain's words,

> The common good in our day is certainly not just the common good of the nation and has not yet succeeded in becoming the common good of the civilized world community. It tends, however, unmistakably towards the latter. For this reason, it would seem appropriate to consider the common good of a state or nation as merely an area, among many similar areas, in which the common good of the whole civilized society achieves greater density.[15]

In content, the common good is procedural and substantive. The *procedures* through which a community sets its policies and conducts its work are not merely instrumental. In a significant manner, they constitute the quality of the community. Procedures are ways of living together through time. As a community endures, but changes, its basic character is manifest in large part in the structure of its public forum. Procedures are marked by varying degrees of openness and exclusion, access and denial, participation and domination. Precisely because a common good is intended as common, its procedural features are those of openness, access, participation. Absent those features, the common good can be but deficiently present.

On its *substantive* side, the common good is more readily specifiable by negative instance than by affirmative criteria: the rapid deterioration of the environment, the depth and extent of poverty throughout the world, the persistence of discriminatory patterns against whole classes of persons, the escalating threat of nuclear holocaust, the stifling of free expression of the artistic impulse in ways direct and indirect. But negative instances are the reverse side of affirmative principles: in the material dimension, physical well-being; in the economic dimension, meaningful work; in the social dimension, civic friendship; in international relations, peaceful modes of conflict resolution; in the dimension of the human spirit, creative openness. I do not mean this as an exhaustive definition of the substantive content of the common good, but as an indication of its qualitative meaning.

Because of the nature of the self as relational, the common good, so construed, is not only the first virtue of social institutions. It is requisite to the flourishing of the individual and is an expression of the deepest meaning of freedom in its material sense.

2.

> A Great Society has nothing to do with, and is in fact irreconcilable with 'solidarity' in the true sense of unitedness in the pursuit of known common goals. F. A. Hayek[16]

> Democracy is not founded merely on the right or the private interest of the individual. This is only one side of the shield. It is founded equally on the function of the individual as a member of the community. It founds the common good upon the common will, in forming which it bids every grown-up, intelligent person to take a part. L. T. Hobhouse[17]

The second thesis I would advance is that capitalism and democracy are in tension with each other.

In their modern manifestations, capitalism and democracy have been associated together as part of the emergence of the modern world. As modern science and philosophy broke through the dogmatisms of medieval theology, so modern economic and political systems shattered the strictures of medieval society. All these movements bore the promise of a new age in which freedom—freedom of thought and freedom of action—was the centerpiece. Capitalism and democracy, in particular, even where these exact terms were not employed to refer to the movements, were expressions of a new class of persons, the bourgeoisie, coming into a place of prominence. Thus capitalism and democracy would seem to belong together as social practices promoted by the new class as instruments for the realization of liberty. That association of movements and ideals has long been a fixture, at least in the American mind. Joyce Appleby discerns it as central to the republican vision of the Jeffersonians in the late eighteenth century.[18] In a radically different version, Louis Hartz identifies it as underlying the interests of the New Whigs in the middle of the nineteenth century.[19] And it is a position espoused by Michael Novak[20] and Robert Benne[21] at the present time.

But however accurate the historical thesis in some sense or other, it begs an important but extraordinarily difficult question of interpretation. How are capitalism and democracy to be identified? The possibilities in the case of capitalism, for instance, range from the axiomatic approach of Ludwig von Mises[22] to the massive historical studies of Immanuel Wallerstein.[23] The resultant differences are striking.

For my purposes, I shall contrast two understandings of capitalism, one more orthodox, the other more heterodox. For the former, I rely on Adam Smith and Friedrich Hayek. Adam Smith, to my knowledge, never used the word, "capitalism," but his treatise on *The Wealth of Nations* is properly considered a classic statement of its meaning.[24] Smith was impressed by the emergence in the modern world of a new form of organizing human relations, the commercial society, a system, in his judgment, of perfect liberty. The central institution of commercial society is the market, the genius of which is that, if unconstrained, it will produce, out of the self-interested actions of myriad persons, a social order of benefit to all. Moreover, through it, the wealth of the nation, that is, the annual flow of its goods and services, will increase. As Hayek depicts the central idea of the system, "The chief cause of [its] wealth-creating character . . . is that the returns of the efforts of each player act as the signs which enable him to contribute to the satisfaction of needs of which he does not know, and to do so by taking advantage of conditions of which he also learns only indirectly through their being reflected in the prices of the factors of production which they use."[25] Resource allocation, capital investment, consignment and division of labor, distribution of products are all questions to be determined by the concerns and pressures of the marketplace. Political interference is held undesirable as infringing on the liberty of individuals to act as they please and as, most likely, resulting in an inefficient allocation of capital. Government is thus limited to a supportive and supplementary role, e.g., protecting infant industries and providing a national defense.

The idea of a self-regulative social mechanism possessed of an inherent drive toward economic growth and efficiency and oriented toward an equilibrium between supply and demand and between cost and price is an elegant conception, however faulty may be its realization in practice. At its heart, it is an individualistic conception in which questions of moral purpose and the exercise of social power are taken as essentially private. Capitalism is pluralistic or, more bluntly, agnostic about the ends of human life. Hayek states this with characteristic clarity.

> Many people regard it as revolting that the Great Society [i.e., the market society] has no common concrete purposes or, as we may say, that it is merely means-connected and not ends-connected. It is indeed true that the chief common purpose of all its members is the purely instrumental one of securing the formation of an abstract order which has no specific purposes but will enhance for all the prospects of achieving their respective purposes.[26]

From the standpoint of the market, depending on the structure of demands placed upon it at any given time, pushpin is as good as poetry (Jeremy Bentham) and cavier as tasty as carrion (Lionel Robbins). The market is in itself a neutral instrument whose sole governing function is the maximization of utility.

From a more heterodox perspective, however, capitalism, discerned historically and contextually, shows a distinctively different kind of face. It is not simply a benign mechanism for increasing the wealth of nations. To some, capitalism is a total culture—rationalistic, atomistic, ahistorical, quantitative in character—that comprises a threat to traditional societies and, more generally, to those ties of social cohesion that hold human civilization together: so observes Bruno Hildebrand in the nineteenth century[27] and George F. Will[28] in ours.

From a different angle, Joseph Schumpeter argues that capitalism is an evolutionary reality, expressive originally of the interests of the commercial and industrial bourgeoisie, but driven by the forces of its own success to its transformation and, ultimately, to its demise. The competitive market place has become an oligopolistic system. The entrepreneurial function has given way to the managerial role. Older meanings of property and contract, essential to the market system, have become essentially different kinds of legal relationships. The values and motivational drive of the early bourgeoisie are replaced by a consumer mentality.[29]

Within the Marxian tradition, as well, capitalism is viewed historically, but governed in its transmutations by internal tensions and contradictions. All history, at least heretofore, consists in class struggles. According to Marx, in capitalism as a form of production, the struggle is between those who control the means of production and those whose labor power, secured through contract, produce the results. Marx, particularly in his earlier writings, designated the structure of this relationship as alienation.[30]

Moreover, according to Immanuel Wallerstein, a contemporary socialist historian, capitalism is a movement driven toward self-expansion, toward the endless accumulation of wealth, resulting in the "commodification of everything."[31] The movement has become a global system, involving an intricate division of labor functionally and geographically. The consequence is a complex commodity chain in which not all exchanges are equal as between classes or geographical zones. In the struggle among groups for benefits, the state is, as it always has been, despite orthodox capitalist doctrine, a critical factor of control and distribution. Furthermore, capitalism is linked inextricably with a scientific and technological culture that it advances throughout the world.

We must acknowledge that both orthodox and heterodox interpretations purport to be describing the meaning of capitalism. They are both, by intention, concerned to specify its identity. But the differences are appreciable. At some points they are irreconcilable: the character of exchange relations (Are parties to exchange in a strictly capitalist system by definition equal or is there an inherent tendency toward patterns of domination?); the status of labor (Is labor genuinely free in its contractual relations or forced ineluctably into a condition of alienation?); the role of the state (Is the function of the state peripheral or critical?); the quality of capitalist culture (Is the market culturally neutral or does it propagate an instrumentalist, technologist morality?).

These variances are not merely empirical. They are rooted in divergent understandings of the world and methods of social analysis. But for immediate purposes, it is sufficient to note that at one important point, orthodox and heterodox perspectives seem to converge, a point at which capitalism is in tension with democracy. According to both, capitalism is a kind of social system in which the principle of private governance is preeminent. Capitalism is not simply a synonym for market. Markets of various sorts and sizes may exist, even be encouraged, in a wide range of social systems.[32] But, from the orthodox perspective, a capitalist society is governed dominantly (in the strictest sense of that term as *authoritatively*) by the interplay of private interests and the result, if there are no artificial constraints, is a spontaneous order which Hayek calls the "Great Society." The role of the political association is supportive (it enforces basic laws of the system) and supplementary (it remedies occasional defects and failures), but clearly secondary. From the heterodox perspective as well, capitalism is viewed as a social order governed by private interests, but in the sense that, at its foundation, capitalism rests on private control of the means of production. In a formulation by Marx and Engels, "modern bourgeois private property is the final and most complete expression of the system of producing and appropriating products, that is based on class antagonisms, on the exploitation of the many by the few."[33] Thus from both perspectives, capitalism intends a principle of private governance, which, in turn, means it intends that the political association shall not be supreme. On this issue, the central idea of democracy diverges. At stake is the question of authority. Most simply put, democracy means a people as such shall have authority for the quality of its own life as a people.

Within the history of political thought from ancient times to the present, there is an extensive range of theories of democracy. Even within the modern period, the spectrum runs from the direct congregationalist democracy of the "Puritans of the Left"[34] to Joseph Schumpeter's influential theory of democracy as competitive leadership[35] and Robert Dahl's polyarchy.[36] At times the theories are constructed out of special concern. Schumpeter, for instance, ponders whether democracy and socialism are compatible. And Dahl intends a theory susceptible to techniques of empirical research.

For my immediate purpose, I suggest that there are two sides to the meaning of democracy and that understandings of democracy differ according to which side is conceived as primary. The two sides are the protective and the participative. In protective democracy, participation is secondary to protection. In participative democracy, protection is secondary to participation.

Modern democracy, it is customarily argued, began with the bourgeois revolutions in England, America, and France. In each instance, tyranny was identified as the enemy and liberty exalted as the cause. The differences among these three revolutions and their resultant forms of democracy are of utmost significance and can be discerned even yet in their respective styles of political life. But in one pertinent respect at least they are alike. In Lindsay's words, "Democratic theory in its modern beginnings reflected a society in which men thought it more important to say what the state should not do than to say what it should do. The main emphasis of this early theory is negative."[37] Democracy was, in a sense, anti-governmental, but, in this context, government meant, first of all, the monarch and therefore the prospects of trampling on the rights and expectations of the people, or at least the class of people most interested at the time with acquiring the facilities and resources for pursuing their own life in their own way. At this juncture, the bourgeoisie, struggling against the constraints of mercantilism, found common interest with republicanism. New forms of political association were thus concocted for protective or defensive purposes.

In the tradition of John Locke, for instance, rights were annunciated, the rights of life, liberty, and property, or, in Jefferson's amended version, life, liberty, and the pursuit of happiness. Rights were understood as claims against a government. Congress shall make no law, it was declared, prohibiting freedom of speech or the right of the people peaceably to assemble. Rights constituted a preserve for the freedom of the citizenry. In the tradition of James Madison, on the other hand, institutional restraints were designed out of the shrewd observation that tyranny is a disease not reserved for monarchs. It may infect popular government as well. The remedy is structural: separation of powers, checks and balances, dispersal of rule throughout the governing system, a multiplicity of factions.

To comprehend the full implications of this version of democracy in principle (granting the miserable character of its historical record in practice), we must distinguish its purpose, procedures, and presupposition. Its purpose is protective, to negate whatever forces threaten the privately determined life activity of the citizenry. Its procedures—its legally defined rights and its institutional arrangements—are designed to promote that purpose.

At this point, democracy is individualistic. But the procedures have another, more positive side. They are means for participating in the public forum. Rights enable persons to speak and to act. Institutions, especially where their functions and powers are divided, facilitate access to the formulation of policy. Participation may be for purposes of protection, but at the procedural level it is, as well, a form of cooperation with others in the conduct of public business and, more importantly, it articulates a basic presupposition of the entire system: consent.

Procedures constitute a method of consent,[38] but consent itself is the primordial act of forming a public. It is the determination to live together, to share in a common destiny, to form a common life. Consent, however difficult it may be to construe what precisely that means theoretically or practically, is the beginning of a people. In that sense, it is the deepest authority of social existence. But what is authorized out of consent may be unauthorized. This is the reason for affirming that, within democracy, even of the protective kind, a people as such has authority for the quality of its own life as a people. What the people form for the sake of their living together, they may, with whatever wisdom they possess, reform or transform. There is thus a tension between democracy, which rests on a principle of consent, and capitalism, which intends a principle of private governance, even though, given the purpose of a protective democracy, a market system may be widely supported and encouraged within the economic realm.

The tension is more evident and more acute between capitalism and the version of democracy in which protection is secondary to participation. Where protective democracy, traditionally called "liberal democracy," serves a negative function, the role of participative democracy is affirmative. Moreover, where protective democracy is predominantly solicitous of the individual, participative democracy, more sensitive to the meaning of its grounding in consent, is concerned with the texture of relationship between personal and community life. This concern is the point of Eduard Heimann's affirmation that "The meaning of democracy lies in the liberty and dignity of the person and the community; or one may say that it lies in their dignity, which includes their liberty."[39] It is also the intent of Lindsay's statement that, "The function of the state . . . is to serve the community and in that service to make it more of a community."[40] But it is more amply depicted in John Dewey's formulation of "the nature of the democratic idea in its generic social sense":

> The idea of democracy is a wider and fuller idea than can be exemplified in the state even at its best. To be realized it must affect all modes of human association, the family, the school, industry, religion. . . . [1] From the standpoint of the individual, it consists [a] in having a responsible share according to capacity in forming and directing the activities of the groups to which one belongs and [b] in participating according to need in the values which the groups sustain. [2] From the standpoint of the groups, it demands liberation of the potentialities of members of a group in harmony with the interests and goods which are common.[41]

Participation, from this perspective, is not merely a procedure for conducting affairs or for protecting one's private interests. It is, more profoundly, expressive of the meaning of being a self within a community of selves. It is a good to be cherished, as exclusionary policies and practices demonstrate by contrast. But, the extension and deepening of democratic processes within a community require that the community through its public forum take deliberate control over its resources in a manner not to be expected in a system controlled by the capitalist principle.

The idea of participative democracy lies behind the complaint of those who insist that the traditional rights associated with democracy—rights of speaking, organizing, voting—are only formal without the economic and cultural conditions for their effective expression. As Joshua Cohen and Joel Rogers remark, "Both an unemployed worker and a millionaire owner of a major television station enjoy the same formal right of free speech, but their power to express and give expression to that right are radically different."[42] The idea of participative democracy also lies behind G. D. H. Cole's complaint that

> the answer that most people would give to the question 'what is the fundamental evil in our modern society?' would be the wrong one: 'they would answer POVERTY, when they ought to answer SLAVERY'. The millions who had been given the franchise, who had formally been given the means to self-government had in fact been 'trained to subservience' and this training had largely taken place during the

course of their daily occupation. Cole argued that 'the industrial system . . . is in great measure the key to the paradox of political democracy. Why are the many nominally supreme but actually powerless? Largely because the circumstances of their lives do not accustom or fit them for power or responsibility. A servile system in industry inevitably reflects itself in political servility'.[43]

In both its versions, democracy means a people as such has authority for the character of its own life as a people. On that point alone, there is tension between democracy and capitalism, for one is fundamentally a principle of public governance, while the other is a principle of private control. But the tension is exacerbated in participative democracy because, since the basic questions of economic life—the allocation of investment, the organization of production, the distribution of wealth—bear directly on the quality of the life of a people as a whole, such questions are considered matters appropriate for public determination.

3.

> This interrelation of agents, which makes the freedom of all members of a society depend upon the intentions of each, is the ground of morality. . . . If we call the harmonious interrelation of agents their 'community', we may say that a morally right action is an action which intends community. . . . If the world is one action, any particular action determines the future, within its own limits, for all agents. Every individual agent is therefore responsible to all other agents for his actions. John MacMurray[43]

To this point, I have proposed that the common good is the first virtue of social institutions and that capitalism and democracy as basic principles of social order are in tension with each other. The third thesis I would advance is that social democracy (an alternative expression for participative democracy) is more directly ordained to the common good than what has traditionally been called democratic capitalism.

Democracy (of the protective kind) and capitalism (understood in the orthodox way) are born in the modern world as parties of a general movement of liberation. The breakthrough of democracy is the effort of a people, or some classes of people, to gain control over their own lives. Civil liberty is among its primary concerns, the liberty to think, to speak, to act as one pleases. The emergence of capitalism is the effort to remove the limitations of restrictive legislation. Free contract is among its dominant interests, the right to associate, to negotiate, and to bargain as one wishes. Both are expressions in social practice of modernity's turn toward the subject. Sights are shifted from the heavens above to the earth beneath, from ultimate destiny to immediate circumstances, from final causes to what works. The shift is toward a world in which the solitary human agent, the subject, is central. Tradition is abjured as the dead hand of the past. Each of us, born as a *tabula rasa*, must ponder: what do *I* think, what shall *I* do, and what do *I* want? Democracy and capitalism are thus linked, granting the basic tension between them, in their avowed respect for individuality. Democracy promises an institutional context protective of open and free thought and action. Capitalism promises a system through which the wants of individuals, whatever they may be, can be satisfied.

The promises are attractive to anyone sensitive to the dignity of individual life. But for that very reason, the promises are easily transmuted into ideological explanations of practices that belie their stated intent, and appropriately provoke a hermeneutics of suspicion. It does not take a Marxist to discern that the language of modernity in general and of democratic capitalism in particular has been persistently used to justify institutions of domination. To cite but one example, racism, in its various versions, has accompanied modernity from its beginnings to the present and has been built into its institutional forms, all of which have been justified in the name of freedom. Significantly, the mitigation of racism, where it has occurred, is attributable neither to capitalism (within which, it has been argued, racism is functional)[45] nor to liberal democracy (which treats such matters with benign neglect), but to a political struggle in which democracy is transformed into an agent of and for participation.

While charges of ideological confusion may be dismissed with the maxim, *abusus non tollit usus* (abuse does not eliminate use), they must not be dismissed too quickly for the confusion may be symptomatic of a flaw in the practices themselves, their structure or their theory. Thus, for instance, liberal democracy may be unable to honor its ultimate intention of protecting the liberty of the individual without an affirmative move toward the extension and deepening of the rights it professes to honor, in which case liberal democracy must make a move on the way toward social democracy. On the other hand, capitalism may be unable to support a thoroughgoing market system without an aggressive means of assuring the equality of all parties to all contracts, in which case capitalism must engage in the kind of intervention into the distribution of power and resources it abhors. In sum, to honor its own promises, democratic capitalism, understood as the historical conjunction of liberal democracy and capitalism in its orthodox interpretation, must be prepared to transform itself in the direction of the common good but away from capitalism's principle of private governance and liberal democracy's negative orientation.

Moreover, we must pose, at this point, a question of historical interpretation. The structures of social life change over time. While change may be relatively imperceptible to those engaged in it, there are moments of radical transition, of passage from an old world to a new. It is a matter of settled judgment, for instance, that the forms of life we distinguish as medieval and modern are appreciably unlike each other though the transmutation may have been gradual. Now, during recent decades, some interpreters claim to discern signs of a new epoch, a post-modern age, emerging—though not all cherish what they discern.[46] Granting the methodological problem of determining the point at which an epochal change has been effected, the evidence of structural transformation in the life of peoples over the past two hundred years at least in the Western world is compelling.

The industrial revolution transformed methods of production and the social relations of those engaged in the productive process. The allied movement of urbanization shifted the center of life for most of the population from village to megalopolis. Continuous developments in technology introduced both gigantic alterations in means of production and shifts in the expectations and character of daily life. The automobile, for instance, completely altered residential patterns and cultural sensibilities. Furthermore, it simultaneously enhanced the private life of individuals and increased their dependency in extensive ways on the organized economic and political life of the nation.

The emergence of the large corporation in the nineteenth century and its developments in the twentieth century (the managerial revolution, diversification of holdings, globalization of operations) have, among other things, complicated structures in the division of labor, changed the distribution of organizational power in society, and completely reversed patterns of work from self-employment to employment in a productive process controlled by others. The effects of periodic business cycles, culminating dramatically in the Great Depression, demonstrated convincingly the national, if not the global, scope of economic interconnections. The nation-state system, with its militaristic propensities and its increasing reliance on developments in military technology particularly beginning with World War I, has promoted the formation of a military-industrial complex. Struggles by the working class during the nineteenth and twentieth centuries to improve working conditions led to organized labor as an important economic and political power in the social order.

In short, the actual structure of economic production and distribution in the Western world, throughout the globe, is a far cry from Jefferson's "vision of a free society of independent men prospering through an expansive commerce in farm commodities"[47] or Adam Smith's pin factory.[48] We are enmeshed in a complicated "material web of interdependence."[49] Even if ours is not yet strictly a new epoch, it would seem an anachronism to equate the prevailing structure of our political economy with either Smith's capitalism or Jefferson's democracy.

More importantly, a range of public policies has been instituted in America over the past century which, taken together, manifest a move away from the capitalist principle of private governance toward social democracy. My concern is less with the detailed administrative arrangements of the policies which may be altered from time to time than with the principles they are intended to effect. Principles of public regulation (e.g., FDA, FTC), workmen's compensation, collective bargaining, public employment, social insurance, national economic accounting and control (e.g., Unemployment Act of 1946), equal employment opportunity, and environmental protection are all part of a limited but remarkable tradition demonstrating the felt need of a people through its public forum to gain some degree of deliberate control over the quality of its life as a people. They represent an affirmative effort to extend the rights of citizens beyond those of liberal democracy and to expand the participation of citizens in the control of their common life beyond the matter of voting in elections. Their overall concern, I would argue, is with the quality of the community as a whole, that is, with the common good. They represent the judgment that, at least in present social circumstances, democratic capitalism as traditionally understood is less able to secure the common good than social democracy.

However, at its deepest level, the difference between democratic capitalism (in its traditional sense) and social democracy lies in their respective understandings of self and world. That issue is at the heart of all social thought. In the relationship between self and world, there are three possibilities. First, the self exists for the sake of the world, whether the world of nation or race or class. This understanding is characteristic of political romanticism[50] and of the historical school of economics.[51]

Second, the world exists for the sake of the self. This position, I would contend, underlies liberal democracy, orthodox capitalism, and their historical conjunction. The intent of democratic capitalism is to construct institutional conditions conducive to satisfying the interests and life plans of separate selves. These interests and life plans may have nothing to do with each other, but that does not matter. What matters is to design arrangements enabling persons to get on with their lives, whatever they may be, with as little conflict as possible. Within this broad tradition, diverse principles have been constructed to deal with questions of resolving conflict: from Locke's natural rights theory and Bentham's concept of utility maximization to Rawls's two principles of justice and Nozick's entitlement theory. Differences among these principles should not be ignored, but neither should their convergence. All are anthropocentric; all are individualistic; all are agnostic about ends. Underlying all is a view of the world as resource, but as, in itself, purposeless and senseless.

In the third possibility, self and world exist for each other. The self is not first of all subject or consumer, but friend, neighbor, citizen. Friendship is, in the relation between persons, a goodness in itself: "It gives us an experiential taste of that wholeness to which as persons we are called."[52] Friendship is an analogue for neighborhood, civil society, even cosmopolis.[53] The ethical expression of this understanding of self and world is the common good. As we have already noted, the common good is a quality of community life composed of two interpenetrating dimensions. Procedurally, it means participating in the deliberations and decisions of a community by its members. Substantively, it embraces several qualities—in material life, physical well-being; in economic production, meaningful work; in social life, civic friendship; in group relation, peaceable means of interaction; in cultural life, an open spirit—whatever conduces to the enhancement of the life of its members. The reverse side of the common good is alienation. This is the sense of G. D. H. Cole's exclamation that the fundamental evil of modern society is not poverty as such, but slavery. It is also the sense of Gustavo Gutierrez's designation of dependency or domination as the primary social problem in the Third World and his projection of liberation as the immediate aim and solidarity as the governing purpose of political and economic action.[54]

The institutional implication of the common good, at least at this point in history, is, I would suggest, social democracy. Social democracy, as I have construed it, means the extension of the democratic principle, the principle of public determination, into all modes of social life, including the economic. It means therefore incorporating public determination into the functions of allocating investment, organizing production, and distributing wealth with the governing intention of enhancing the quality of relationships throughout the community of life. It does not mean that markets are inappropriate mechanisms within the economy or that no forms of administrative control are ever acceptable. But it does require explicit structures of public accountability and control. And it does require explicit attention to the governing intention and specific consequences of programs and policies. Among recent proposals for the transformation of the political economy which, while taking account of historical reality, its limitations and possibilities, at least approximate the idea of social democracy, I would cite Carole Pateman's participatory democracy, Daniel Bell's public household, Roberto Unger's theory of organic groups, Alec Nove's feasible socialism, Michael Harrington's democratic socialism, Martin Carnoy and Derek Shearer's economic democracy, and Robert Dahl's latest book, *A Preface of Economic Democracy*.[55] Once again, then, I am led to affirm the thesis that social democracy is more directly ordained to the common good, the first virtue of social institutions, than what has traditionally been meant by democratic capitalism.

Given the three theses I have advanced, I propose the need for a new social covenant. The language is intentional. At the beginning of the modern age, we were instructed to acknowledge a social contract as the foundation of our common life. The idea of a social contract bespeaks a world of individuals, a state of nature, out of which persons come to effect a *modus vivendi*—for they must live together even if they do not belong together. Each gains some benefit from the arrangement, else the bargain will not long be kept. The bottom line is commodity.

But the idea of social covenant invokes an alternative tradition of thought and action, religious in its expression but ontological in its claim. The idea of a social covenant bespeaks a world in which we already belong together but are called repeatedly to acknowledge that fact anew and to determine what the forms of our life together shall be. As Bernard Meland reminds us, the idea of covenant is a myth both of identity and of dissonance, for covenants are often broken. But even when broken, they remain covenants and compel us to their reaffirmation.[56] In its theological meaning, the idea of covenant is grounded in that God who intends a universal community of being and to whom each self is related in and through all other relationships.[57] In its meaning for social practice, the idea of covenant implies that what is most to be cherished in our associations is not the commodities that derive therefrom, but the commonwealth that is created therein.

9. AMERICAN LEGAL REALISM AND THE
COVENANTAL TRADITION

G. K. CHESTERTON IS SAID to have observed that the most important question to ask of a prospective landlady is not how often she changes the sheets but what is her world view.[1] What does she think the world is all about? That kind of question gets down to fundamentals. It underlies all other questions and gets at how the landlady will act and react in all kinds of circumstances.

What is true of a landlady is true of other kinds of people as well. In everyday activity, it is the world view that matters in the final analysis. Each person is a world of meaning. Each person participates in a world that locates personal identity and is constitutive of one's mode of perception, interpretation, and action. Each person is a microcosm. Landladies are, in this sense, no different from the rest of us; but then lawyers are, in this sense, no different from the rest of us either.

No one wants one's world view to be considered unrealistic, least of all practical people like landladies and lawyers. They have got to get things done. Who would rent from a landlady who neglected leaky roofs? Who would consult with a lawyer unable to draft a simple lease or unwilling to admit that one's legal rights might be viewed differently by different judges? Even lawyers and landladies with an idealistic streak want to be realistic, for realism is the effort to overcome deception. The reality principle is the hard rock that, sooner or later, shatters illusion.

The problem is that it is difficult to identify the hard rock of reality. The reality principle is more elusive than we sometimes think. Things are not always what they seem. What appears to be illusion may be vision. What seems at first blush an hallucination may be on closer examination fresh insight. A dreamer of strange dreams may be probing more deeply into the actual conditions and possibilities of our human reality than one whose sights are delimited by the pressures and parameters of immediate affairs.

Thus, landladies and lawyers want to be realistic; they intend world views that are in touch with the world as it is; they are practical people. But therein lies a problem. What is it to be realistic? In particular, what does it mean for those engaged in the practice of law to be realistic? What is the sort of world view of law that should inform their thinking and acting in the legal process?

Talk about world views is philosophical talk; to some, it is religious talk; in law, it is jurisprudential talk. Few lawyers are concerned about jurisprudence these days. It seems impractical and unrealistic. But jurisprudence is unavoidable in legal practice. One may not be an economic theorist in the technical sense, but one nonetheless enacts a theory of economics in one's participation in the economic life of the nation. Similarly, one's jurisprudence, however unsophisticated or ill-formed, is nonetheless played out in one's conduct at law.

Some years ago, a movement in American jurisprudence so prided itself on its realism, it adopted the term in its name. Even yet, legal realism is alleged to be the living jurisprudence of the average lawyer in American society. Legal realism is not dead; it is the dominant world view of legal practice at the present time. I intend to dissect the character of this movement in practical jurisprudence, but then contrast it with another kind of realism, one that may be, in the final analysis, more encompassing and adequate than American legal realism. I am referring to the covenantal tradition out of ancient Israel and primitive Christianity, particularly as interpreted through the process thought of Bernard Meland. In brief, my thesis is that we should consider the meaning of Moses' action as legislator as expressive of a realistic world view for legal practice more profound than that of American legal realism. Moses, we should recall, acted like a lawyer in his role during the effectuation of a covenant between the God of Abraham, Isaac, and Jacob and the people of Israel. Covenant is a familiar legal term, but it bears a tradition of meaning that goes far beyond its current legal usage. It is itself a world view, a world view being rediscovered today. It might put us in touch with dimensions of our life that we have neglected and forgotten, but neglected and forgotten to our peril.

1. REALISM IN LEGAL PRACTICE: KARL LLEWELLYN

American legal realism was at its peak in the 1920s and 1930s. Its intent was to instruct judges, lawyers, and laity in a world view that was stark and candid. It was part of a larger movement among the social and political sciences away from descriptive institutional history toward empirical causal analysis. It was presented as a way of understanding the legal process and of controlling law for personal and social purposes. It was an attempt to get behind the rhetoric of law to the reality of law. As such, it instructed us to attend not to stated rules but to actual conduct. As George Christie notes, it was most instructive for the practising jurist: "There is no question that a realist philosophy is often most attractive to a lawyer who wants to win a close case, or who is called upon to counsel a businessman about to enter a complex commercial transaction."[2]

Why does the spirit of American legal realism persist? Why does it seem still useful in practice though its heyday in theory is past? What is its compelling character? Is it perhaps an expression of certain qualities and tensions more generally characteristic of American culture?

Skepticism is among key terms used to characterize the realists. Harry W. Jones writes of the various forms of legal realism: "The common feature that justifies bringing them all under one tent is a shared skeptical temper towards legal generalizations, a shared conviction that the processes of law administration involve operations far more complex than the search for and logical application of pre-existing doctrine."[3] Realists are skeptical about some traditional ways of understanding law. Their skepticism is well-placed. When, for instance, "Rule of Law" is honored on Law Day, it is a fiction that is exalted, a fiction that has little to do with actual legal processes in this country. The fiction presumes a clear distinction between societies governed strictly by rule application and societies governed by personal command and decision. But, realistically, that distinction is not clear-cut. Personal decision, with all its vagaries and biases, is an inescapable part of law.

In a more complex judgment, Karl Llewellyn summarizes the diverse forms of American legal realism as a perspective, a set of attitudes, a trend, present to some extent whenever realistic work is done: recognition of law as means; recognition of change in society that may call for change in law; interest in what happens; interest in effects; recognition of the need for effort toward keeping perception of the facts uncolored by one's views on Ought; a distrust of the received set of rules and concepts as adequate indications of what is happening in the courts; a drive toward narrowing the categories of description.[4]

Karl Llewellyn is among the leaders and foremost proponents of American legal realism. On the basis of his work, I shall cast the determining principles of the movement in a set of five statements. First, since the meaning of law is problematic, the effort of legal realism is to drive beyond law's superficial manifestations into its inner significance. Second, law is a process of interaction between officials and subjects in which the actions and attitudes of both parties are constitutive. Third, law, as a process, is open-textured[5] and open-ended. Fourth, law is instrumental. Finally, the relationship between law and morality is ambiguous, although, in its most fundamental aspect, the legal process is profoundly moral. I shall explore each of these statements in turn, the final statement, perhaps more characteristic of Llewellyn than of other legal realists, provoking a series of questions that force consideration of the deeper realism of religious sensibility.

In the world view of American legal realism, the meaning of law is problematic. It is not self-evident and not certain. Nor is it simple. Ordinarily, if asked what the law is in this nation, one would refer to the U.S. Code, to Supreme Court Reports, or to local city ordinances. But there is more to law than appears in codes and in judicial opinions. Indeed, it is misleading to point to them as law. The legal realist would have us go beyond these appearances of law to its reality.

The understanding of law as problematic is not unique to American legal realism. Prior to and concomitant with the development of American legal realism were several other movements of thought, breaking open hitherto suppressed, ignored, or forgotten levels of social reality and human behavior. From a Marxist perspective, for instance, laws and legal procedures are expressions of the history of class struggle. Law and government are evidences of conflicts between oppressors and oppressed, those in control of the basic means of production and those whose lives are shaped and determined by forces beyond their control. There is merit to this understanding. To simplify the point, a wealthy white business executive would most likely have a better day in court than an unemployed black man on welfare.[6]

Similarly, from a Freudian standpoint, to understand law one must look beyond rules and ordinances to the psychodynamics of judges and lawyers, police and commissioners. The trial lawyer knows this well in the selection of a jury. One no longer looks for "twelve good men and true." One looks for jurors whose social background and psychological disposition are favorably disposed to one's client.

Like the Marxist and the Freudian, the legal realism goes beyond the appearance of law to the reality of law. This move lies behind Karl Llewellyn's distinction between a more traditional and a more realistic approach to legal analysis. The distinction is between rules and actions, words and practices:

> The traditional approach is in terms of words; it centers on words; it has the utmost difficulty getting beyond words. If nothing be said about behavior, the *tacit* assumption is that the words do reflect behavior, and if they be the words of rules of law, do influence behavior, even influence behavior effectively and precisely to conform completely to those words.[7]

While it is common to view law as a set of rules laid down by state officials, enforced by sanctions, and addressed to the ordinary citizen,[8] it is deceptive to view law that way. Statutes in code books and rules in judicial opinions may assist one in guessing what law is, but they are not themselves law, at least not most basically so. Without ignoring the role words and rules play in the legal process, Llewellyn insists that the final meaning of law is found in behavior, action, praxis. Thus Llewellyn's most quoted sentence: "[What] officials do about disputes is, to my mind, the law itself."[9]

To know what law is, one should look not at rules on the books, but at actions by judges and other officials. To know how law will apply to a particular case, look not only for relevant statutes and judicial opinions, but more importantly at how officials might read to the case. Llewellyn thus distinguishes paper rules from "real rules." The latter he always couches in quotation marks for "real rules" are the actual practices of a court or administrative body. Paper rules are helpful only when and if they might influence officials: "rules take on meaning in life only as they aid one either to predict what officials will do, or to get them to do something. . . . [The] heart and core of living law is how disputes are in fact settled . . . rules take on live meaning only as they bear on that."[10]

The implications of this perspective for legal education are far-reaching, for the development of a realistic world view of law would include a study of methods of behavioral and social analysis. A study of law restricted to casebooks is not useless, but is limited and short-sighted.

A second feature of the world view of American legal realism is that there are two sides to the behavioral meaning of law. To see what law means, one should look not only at the actions of officials, but also at the effects of official action on the citizenry.

> *Law* without effect approaches zero in its meaning. To be ignorant of its effect is to be ignorant of its meaning. To know its effect without study of the persons whom it affects is impossible. . . . To know law, then . . . we must proceed into those areas which have traditionally been conceived . . . as not-law. Not only what courts do instead of what courts say, but also what difference it makes to anybody that they do it.[11]

More broadly, law is a process of interaction. Not only judges make law what it is; people as well make law what it is. In a sense, people make judges what they are. This point is critical for a realistic understanding of the dynamics of law. A judge, magistrate, president, representative, gendarme is designated to serve as an official by rules of appointment, election, or tradition. Yet traditions have been broken, elections have been nullified, and appointments have been rendered void. Efficacy of office depends to an extent on coercion or the threat of coercion; but the legitimacy of office depends on acknowledgment. Without acknowledgment, no office. Revolution is the extremity of non-acknowledgment. Hard cases may make bad law, but extreme circumstances such as revolution may reveal dimensions of social and legal reality glossed over in ordinary social routines.

Law rests in a significant sense on the consent of the people. Another way to phrase this insight is to say, law is inextricably located within a social and cultural matrix and cannot be apart from that matrix. The behavior of laity is therefore an integral part of law, for

> the word 'official' tacitly presupposes, connotes and reaches out to include, all those patterns of action (ordering, initiative) and obedience (including passivity) on the part both of the official and all laymen affected which *make up* the official's position and authority as such. . . . The official exists as such precisely *insofar* as such patterns of action and obedience prevail.[12]

The point is not sheer pedantry. Prohibition was a classic case. Was it a law or wasn't it? Certainly the eighteenth amendment to the United States Constitution never mustered the authority from citizens that the seventeenth amendment did. *Brown v. Board of Education of Topeka* is a second case in point.[13] The fact that an implementing order was delayed for almost a year following the basic decision is an acknowledgment that law is a process of interaction. *Engel v. Vitale*,[14] the school prayer case, is presumably the law of the land, but in more than a few communities this is not quite true. A lawyer with a realistic world view will know not only the needs and practices of the client, but also the expectations, interests, power structure of the community. All these features in a complex interactive relationship constitute law.

This brings us to a third part of the realists' credo, namely, that law is open-textured. Its meaning is not fixed absolutely in rules. It is constantly open to reinterpretation and reevaluation. Law is an open-ended process. Its future direction is not predetermined. Its forms and shapes are always subject to remolding. This is obviously true of congressional action. The legislative process is a complicated interplay of forces, some more powerful than others, none completely giving up the legislative struggle even following the enactment of a bill. But open-endedness is a quality not only of congressional bodies; it is also a quality of law enforcement and administrative agencies. Police and prosecutors, administrators and bureaucrats enjoy wide areas of discretion. Yet again, open-endedness is a quality of judicial decision as well. Even a "strict constructionist" has made a determination, namely, to be a "strict constructionist." Judicial creativity, however used, even if to maintain some *status quo ante*, is a fact of judicial life. The legal system cannot work without repeated acts of human judgment. At every level, persons are determining what shall or shall not be done, to whom, and how. As Lon Fuller puts it, "The complex undertaking we call 'law' requires at every turn the exercise of judgment, and that judgment must be exercised by human being for human beings. It cannot be built into a computer."[15]

The doctrine of precedent presumably limits the play of judicial discretion. It does to an extent, but Justice William Douglas took delight in pointing out how often the Supreme Court overrules itself.[16] Even when a justice presumes to follow a line of preceding opinions, there is an elegance in the manner in which precedents are shaped, formed, carefully distinguished toward the conclusion of the case at hand. That point is dramatically illustrated by Justice Benjamin Cardozo's creative genius in *MacPherson v. Buick*.[17] More generally, as Llewellyn argues, to adopt the doctrine of precedent as binding leaves ample room for judgment, for there are two distinctive views one may assume of a prior case—a strict, orthodox, restrictive view and a loose, open, inclusive view. The restrictive view confines the authority of the prior case to certain selected facts, which is a way to set an unwelcome rule aside. The inclusive view pulls out any and all features of the prior case, whatever seems useful to make a point.

> Indeed, this view carries often over into dicta, and even into dicta which are grandly obiter. . . . This is a device for *capitalizing welcome precedents*. And both the lawyers and the judges use it so. And judged by the *practice* of the most respected courts, as of the courts of ordinary stature, this doctrine of precedent is like the other, recognized, legitimate, honorable.[18]

Llewellyn discerns two period-styles in the history of American law—the Grand Style and the Formal Style. He favors the former for two reasons: it represents a more accurate understanding of the open possibilities of legal judgment and it provides a more reasonable method of approaching legal decisions. The Grand Style is "our rightful heritage." By contrast, the Formal Style, adopting the strict view of precedent, assumes that rules determine decisions and thereby ignores the open-textured reality of legal processes. But it does not, for it cannot, itself avoid judgment.[19]

Emphasis on the open-textured quality of law leads Llewellyn to his striking proposal that natural law jurisprudence (at least in a certain version of that tradition) and legal realism are compatible. According to him, through every person who wrestles with the intricacies and frustrations of issues at law, "there pulses an urge for right, or decency, or justice: a drive toward an ideal attribute which men may well conceive as a proper and indeed the proper ultimate objective of all law and all legal institutions. The concept of Natural Law seems to me an expression of this urge."[20] Both natural law jurist and realist labor

> for the utilization of the greater leeways afforded by legislation, and the lesser leeways afforded by . . . case-law system . . . to produce a finer and more effective set of guides for conduct and for judging. And it is difficult for me to conceive of the ultimate legal ideals of any of the writers who have been called realists in terms which do not resemble amazingly the type and even the content of the principles of a philosopher's Natural Law.[21]

Thus there are leeways in law within which one may chart a variety of courses. Law does not chart a course independent of human judgment and human action. Within a realistic world view, therefore, law is instrumental. The legal process may be manipulated, used, exploited, pushed, and pulled to serve a wide variety of purposes. Law is a means, a tool, a technology. It is part of a technologically oriented culture. Those who know the workings of the agencies and officials of law are most likely to get their way. The grand precept of the realist is: Study "how to make the official do what you would like to have him [do]."[22]

The realist is a utilitarian, even if not in the strictest philosophical sense of that term. A utilitarian weights benefits and costs, taking the path that seems, on balance, most beneficial or least costly. A utilitarian approaches law like Justice Holmes's famous "bad man."[23] The "bad man" does not look at law as announcing what is right and what is wrong. The "bad man" looks at law as simply part of the environment of doing business: one may break a contract, pay the assessed damages, and think little of it, so long as, on balance, one's self-defined welfare has been served. Some tort liability might not hurt too much so long as one has correctly calculated the benefits that might result. Even a criminal fine, especially if paid for by the corporation, can be accepted as part of the costs of doing business. Thus, even where law seems to be against one, it may work for one. Law is a neutral object to be used where it might benefit, to be avoided where it might hurt, and to be put into the balance of calculations as one plans policies for the future. That is realism and the sort of understanding of law a lawyer with a realistic world view serves. Such a lawyer is a technician, willing to assist anyone or any group with a problem in mind and retainer in hand.

In this connection, Llewellyn makes it clear that a conflict model of society is more realistic than a consensual model:

> Law in particular presents . . . the phenomenon of clashing interests of antagonistic persons or groups, with officials stepping in to favor some as against others. . . . Hence the eternal fight for the control of the machinery of law, and of law-making, whereby the highly interested *A*s can hope partially to force their will upon equally but adversely interested *B*s, and to put behind that control the passive approval and support of the great body of *C*s—who happen to be disinterested, or, what is equally to the point, uninterested.[24]

To be fair, we must note that Llewellyn qualifies this view of law as instrumental and society as conflictual with a wistful comment that appears in various forms here and there among his writings. Amidst the struggle among contending groups to turn their respective interests, whatever they are, into legal rights, there persists a haunting sense of and drive toward the common good. Indeed, without the presence to some degree of a quality of wholeness, there could be no society and no law in any intelligible sense of those terms.[25] "No man," he asserts, "sees law whole who forgets that one inherent drive which is a living part of even the most wrongheaded and arbitrary legal system is a drive . . . to make the system . . . realize an ideal of justice."[26] Throughout law there endures a yearning for civilization, an urge for human decency, a nisus toward justice and common good.

Is this wistful comment on Llewellyn's part sheer rhetoric? Is it merely a yearning that maybe through the complicated workings of law, justice and decency *might* be served? Or is it something that is and must be incorporated in any realistic world view? Is there, realistically speaking, a good for law and in law that goes beyond the "bad man's" utilitarian calculus and that lawyer, judge, and citizen *must* take into account as part of the real world in which they live and move and have their being?

This question presses us to the fifth statement about American legal realism: The relationship between law and morality is ambiguous. On the one hand, the realist urges that we not cloud our vision of what law is with our yearnings of what law ought to be. This is a helpful, though trivial methodological point: To act effectively we must understand accurately, and to understand accurately we must see the world for what it is apart from our wishes and dreams. Granting the complications of sociology of knowledge and phenomenology of interpretation, prudence aims to discount the distortions of historical location and personal desire. Objectivity, in an absolutist sense, is a will-o'-the-wisp, but objectivity in some sense is a licit mandate in the pursuit of understanding. This point underlies the realists' repeated insistence on disentangling "Is" from "Ought."

On the other hand, the lawyer cannot avoid moral decision. Beyond the methodological point, there are at least three senses in which morality is intrinsic to the practice and interpretation of law. On the professional level, it must be remembered that law is open-textured and open-ended. Human judgment is an intrinsic part of the process. Some sort of decision about what ought or ought not be done is being made at every point. In this sense, at least, as Harry Jones asserts:

> The legal *is* and the legal *ought to be* are . . . inseparable. The legal *is*, here, is not a command but an authorization of alternative decisions. The choice between or among alternatives—the selection of a path to be pursued—is controlled by the *ought to be*. This is not a matter of theory but of realist analysis.[27]

Professional decisions are never merely technical. Whether to litigate, how to argue a case, what sentence to mete, what damages to impose, whether to appeal, what fee to charge, whether to prosecute—these everyday matters are not without their moral dimension. On the professional level, value judgments are indispensable in the selection and formulation of problems for legal inquiry and in the determination of legal policy. However, as Llewellyn also insists, "as we move into these value judgments we desert entirely the solid sphere of objective observation, of possible agreement among all trained observers, and enter the airy sphere of individual ideals and subjectivity."[28] This assertion of the subjectivity of value judgments, characteristic of American legal realism, was never developed by Llewellyn and, in fact, seems inconsistent with the other senses in which legal processes are discerned as moral. The issue of the grounding of value judgment and moral principle is among the more critical and difficult tasks any genuinely realistic world view must undertake.

On the institutional level, law and morality are intermixed as well. There are certain basic institutional functions—Llewellyn calls them "law jobs"—that a legal process performs, certain contributions law makes to society, such that if a society is good, so also is law. Law resolves conflicts (adjudication); it invents means of cooperation (incorporation); it controls behavior of individuals and corporations (administration); it promotes basic principle of social organization (constitution). An enlightened jurist with a realistic world view will be aware of these social and political values of law which Llewellyn calls the "Good-in-law."[29] But an enlightened jurist will also know that, in some cases, the professional good—the good of the client or of the lawyer—may not conform exactly to the good of society. With sufficient resources, both corporation and criminal lawyer can find ways to circumvent the intention of law and to do so legally. Moreover, although law may fulfill diverse social functions, a society as a whole may be structurally unjust. A racist society may be served quite well with efficient and inventive legal machinery. All the "law jobs" the realist can list may contribute to a society that is oppressive and unjust. Rule of law on this level does not always serve the causes of liberty and justice.

In this light, we must recall Llewellyn's wistful comment suggesting there is, beyond the professional and institutional levels, a teleological level on which law and morality are conjoined. There is an inherent drive in law, he asserts, toward justice, human dignity, and civilization. He argues that the "idea of self-sanation" is part of law. Sanation is the act of making whole, the process of making healthy. Self-sanation is a process of self-correction, self-healing, self-purification. Law purifies itself: "[Law] by its own weight calls its own concept to its own perfection."[30] There is a drive, in and through law, toward the enrichment of the life of all. Llewellyn seems to affirm that this drive is part of the meaning of law *understood realistically*.

Is Llewellyn still a legal realist at this point? Where does he see the inner drive of law? We may grant, realistically speaking, (1) that the meaning of law is problematic, (2) that law is interactive, (3) that law is open-ended, (4) that law is instrumental, and (5) that law is ambiguously intertwined with moral considerations. But what can be made of this idea of self-sanation as part of law? Is the idea of self-sanation integral to any realistic interpretation or scientific description of law? How can the notion that inherent in law is a drive toward social justice possibly be grounded?

Llewellyn seems unsure, but, as the beginnings of an answer, he quotes Augustine: *"credo ut intelligam,"* which he translates as meaning: *"as a result* of my faith I grasp it with my mind."[31] In this affirmation, Llewellyn seems to have reached the end point of his realism; he may even have gone beyond his realism.

Or has he? Maybe he has an intimation of a profounder realism than most admit to in moments of skepticism. Maybe he has an intimation of a realism neglected in the ordinary practice of law. Maybe he has an apprehension of reality in the absence of which American legal realism, proclaimed as the prevailing jurisprudence of legal practitioners, results in a strictly technological, narrowly utilitarian approach to life and law according to which law is but a technique to be employed, manipulated, exploited, avoided, or controlled to serve solely one's subjective interests or principles. Maybe Llewellyn discerns through the eyes of faith a context of meaning which, realistically, we ignore to our detriment. Indeed, if Llewellyn's thesis that there is a *telos* of law that constitutes the basic dynamic and meaning of law itself can be supported, then one's understanding of and approach to legal process must assume a radical turn from what is ordinarily thought of as legal realism. Support for Llewellyn's thesis might conceivably be found in what Bernard Meland has called "the new realism in religious inquiry."[32]

2. REALISM IN RELIGIOUS INQUIRY: BERNARD MELAND

There is a new realism in certain strains of religious inquiry—a new realism that opens up the possibility of a critical perspective on the meaning of law in our common life. We are accustomed to think of law and religion as occupying different places in our lives. One may be law-abiding without having to be religious. One may be a good lawyer or expert judge without any particular religious affiliation or interest. Even if a jurist is religious, that has no necessary bearing on professional practice. Most of us would be incensed if there were some religious test required to pass the bar. Such a test would be a flagrant violation of constitutional principles if nothing else.

Yet, serious consideration must be given to the import of religious sensibility as represented by the religions of the world. Religious sensibility is holistic; it is encompassing; it includes within its frame of reference our whole life. It bears on all we are and do. The religious world cannot be divorced from other aspects of our life, personal or professional. The question of the relation between this affirmation and the principles of free exercise of religion and nonestablishment lies beyond the scope of this inquiry. Suffice it to say, there is no *inherent* contradiction between them.

Against that background, the new realism in religious inquiry as expressed in Meland's work, can be characterized in four statements. First, religious language is symbolic of the most elemental dimensions in human experience. Second, the myth of the covenant is a formative metaphor of Western religious traditions. Third, the covenantal myth discloses a relational understanding of human life. Finally, such an understanding of human life forms a critical and realistic ground for viewing the meaning of law.

The first statement—that religious language is symbolic—is analogous to the insistence of American legal realism that the meaning of law is problematic. To get at the meaning of law, one must probe beyond surface manifestations to a deeper sense of legal process. Legal realists are critical of the traditional view that law is a set of rules for conduct. They distinguish between rules and actions, words and behavior, precepts and processes. Rules, words, precepts are of some value; they are symbolic of happenings in the world of practice. But the words and the world of practice must be interpreted in light of each other.

This is a basic thesis of the new realism of religious inquiry. The new realism entails a turn toward lived-experience. To get at the meaning of religious language, one must go through and beyond the words of religious tradition. Language is a necessary means of thinking, inquiring, communicating, even acting. It is a resource for theoretical understanding, practical action, creative production. But language is limited. Its forms are abstract and fallible. Language is suggestive of experience that is always richer and more complex than the words through which it is expressed—although the words themselves are an essential dimension of human experience. Interpretation of the meaning of language is a difficult task, for meaning is seldom obvious or self-evident. But interpretation is a fruitful task; at best, it results in a disclosure of the wider context of lived experience out of which language emerges, to which it points, within which it participates. Furthermore, interpretation is a needed task lest words become, wittingly or unwittingly, deceptions, rationalizations, tools of false consciousness.

This insight is not new. One need only recall the dramatic outburst of Jeremiah at a point of crisis in the history of ancient Israel:

> Trust you not in lying words, saying, The temple of the Lord, The temple of the Lord, The temple of the Lord are these. For if you thoroughly amend your ways and your doings; if you thoroughly execute justice between a man and his neighbor; if you oppress not the stranger, the fatherless, and the widow, and shed not innocent blood in this place, nor walk after other gods to your hurt; then I will cause you to dwell in this place in the land I gave to your fathers, for ever and ever. You trust in lying words, that cannot profit.[33]

The people could speak the words, but did not know the meaning. The meaning was not in the speaking. The words were symbolic of deeper realities. The words indicated a mode of being in and relating to the world. To speak the words without embodying their meaning was, in effect, to lie.

As literalism in law is deceptive for it neglects the realities of legal processes, so literalism in religion is deceptive for it neglects the experiential ground to which religious language points. The question to ask of any religious symbol, story, ritual, act is: What does it signify about human experience? What does it communicate about the character of the world? What does it divulge about the nature and destiny of humankind? What is the structure of life it represents?

Religious language is mythic, but myth, in this context, does not mean illusion. A myth is a story about the gods, about the sacred. As Meland notes, "Myth is the elemental response of a people to what is ever present as an ultimate demand and measure upon human existence (sense of destiny, *sensus numinous*, idea of the holy, ultimate concern, etc.)."[34] Religious myth is two-sided: it is a representation of the real world and it is a judgment and demand on the existent world. Religious myth has a creative intent: it intends to shape both psyche and society. It frames a critical perspective from which to view, understand, interpret, and judge one's self, one's institutions, one's society, one's surroundings. "All human existence takes place within a particularized orbit of meaning."[35] The fundamental myths of a people articulate that orbit of meaning, its structure and direction.

A second point of the new realism of religious inquiry is that among the more durable myths of Western religious traditions is that of the covenant. The myth of the covenant has been invoked repeatedly throughout the religious and political history of the West. But what does the myth of the covenant mean? What is the reality it symbolizes? What modes of being and acting in the world does it indicate?

For an initial response to these questions, I would focus on one of the paradigmatic cases of the covenantal tradition in ancient Hebraic history: the Exodus story. In the Exodus story, the covenantal relationship was inaugurated by the liberating action of the Holy One. Beginnings, in a strict sense of the term, are fundamental in the formation of political communities and legal structures. Beginnings mark a turning point and constitute an authority. That is the ultimate sense of the doctrine of *stare decisis*. The beginnings of this covenantal relationship were initiated by the Holy One, creator and preserver of all life, and had the character of *liberation*. As Christian writers from the Third World, especially Latin America, remind us, liberation is a central quality of the myth of the covenant, a quality of profound political and legal significance.[36] But liberation, in an act originated by the Holy One, translates into obligation: wherever persons are enslaved and oppressed, as were the Hebrews in the land of Egypt, the mandate is to liberate.

In the Exodus story, the Hebrew people were gathered under the leadership of Moses and brought into a new land. In the midst of these dramatic events, a bond of mutual loyalty and trust—of *faithfulness*—was effected between the Holy One and the people and among the people themselves. They were formed into a people through the covenantal interchange. The covenant was a creation, a calling into being of new life, the life of this people. They were pledged to be faithful to one another, that is, to sustain one another, to care for one another, to serve one another. They were held together by promise. Thus faithfulness is added to liberation as a quality of covenantal existence.

This new community was obliged to be a people of justice and peace. To do *justice* is to honor the rights and to fulfill the needs of all members of the community, especially the widow, the fatherless, the stranger within the gates. A restrictive covenant is a contradiction in terms. *Peace* is the quality of cooperation, coordination, harmonious action. Where justice attends to the needs of each individual member of the community, peace is the quality of belongingness that holds them together as a whole. In sum, a covenanted community consists of four qualities: liberation, faithfulness, justice, peace.

All the law codes of the ancient Hebrews are cast within the framework of a covenant. Laws about crime, property, torts, family relations, judicial procedures, as well as laws about sacred days, priests, and religious rituals, are all located within a covenantal structure. Thus the meaning of the laws derives from the covenant; they are interpreted in light of the covenant; their violation is understood as a betrayal of the covenant; they are changed and amended as the covenanted people discern the shifting needs of changing times. What remains constant as the overarching reality and demand is the covenant itself and its fundamental qualities and obligations.

A covenant is honored even in its breach, for a broken covenant is just that, a broken *covenant*. The covenantal qualities of liberation, faithfulness, justice, peace persist as the basis for interpreting and judging the people's condition. A rift in a relationship does not totally destroy the relationship, otherwise it would not be a rift. Under conditions of a broken covenant, a people stands in contradiction to itself: its fundamental identity is a judgment against its existence.

The myth of the covenant is not merely a story about times past. That is the third point of the new realism in religious inquiry. The myth of the covenant is a statement of ontological and anthropological significance. The claim of a myth is that it divulges important truths about our life. A myth is a paradigmatic statement;

a mythic narrative is a representation about the structure and dynamics of the world; it is a world view.

The myth of the covenant pertains to the character of human relationships. Negatively, it is a rejection of both individualism and corporativism. That is, according to the myth of the covenant, we should not view ourselves as essentially isolated individuals who may make and break social relations at will. Nor should we view ourselves as simply members of corporate bodies that dictate our identities and destinies. Rather, we should understand ourselves as responsible participants in a whole host of relationships—natural, social, political, economic. These relationships constitute the inescapable context of our individual life; but they also bear the imprint of our personal creativity. Life is a constant give and take; we receive and we give. How we receive and how we give make all the difference in the world. Some ways of receiving and giving enhance life; other ways degrade, delimit, destroy. That is the narrative of human life. If in our receiving and giving we are constituted by the qualities of liberation, faithfulness, justice, and peace, then life is enhanced. If we are constituted by the qualities of oppression, disloyalty, injustice, and alienation, the result is the destruction and degradation of life.

Although the idea of the covenant is a fundamental motif in the mythos of Western culture and has been invoked repeatedly throughout Western religious, political, and legal history, its meaning has been subdued in the modern era. Individualism, utilitarianism, technical rationality, contractualism have become paramount in modern patterns of thought and action. American legal realism is, in large part, an expression of these patterns. Yet, according to Bernard Meland, the mode of thought represented in the covenantal world view has never been totally lost and has tended to come increasingly to the fore in diverse movements of thought in the twentieth century. Holism, Gestalt psychology, field theory, process philosophy, radical empiricism have, in Meland's terms, broken open a "new frontier of realism." The shift effected in these twentieth-century movements has been "from an atomistic conception of reality to the ontological notion of the individual in community."[37] Meland depicts the import of this new "realism of a relational sort" in this way:

> What separates the present generation of thought in the West from that of previous periods of the modern era is the realism with which

it views the nature of man. . . . Present-day thought upon the nature of man partakes of a depth of being which is comparable in its range to that of the imagery of classical Christianity, say in medieval realism. . . . That it is a new frontier of realism means simply that it has become alerted to realities outside of and other than self-experience, existing independently of it, though engaging it both continuously and in intermittent encounters. One insistent theme of our present way of thinking about man is that the breadth and depth of our ultimate meaning are immediately apprehended in the momentary events of day-to-day existence. I do not say that man consciously knows this in the detached way that we are accustomed to speak of the mind attending the object; but he knows he is aware of himself as existing in, participating in, and belonging to a cluster of interrelated events which make up his life and the lives about him, and which, at the level of creation itself, gathers in all lives that have ever existed. Here we begin to get a glimpse of the complexity of man's existence at its ultimate ground.[38]

In documenting the emergence of this relational mode of thought and action, Meland attends primarily to trends in modern physics, biology, psychology and philosophy. I would claim there is a counterpart in legal thought, in the recent jurisprudential work of Roberto Mangabeira Unger. Unger, reflecting about the current state of jurisprudence, was driven to a radical critique of its prevailing orientation, modern liberalism. He argues that liberalism in its psychological and political expressions is faulted by irresolvable antinomies. The alternative developed by Unger is a relational understanding of self and a communitarian doctrine of society.[39]

In Unger's alternative to liberalism, human life is intrinsically relational. It is lived in three intersecting arenas—the natural, the social, and the productive. We are constituted by our relations with nature, with other persons, and with our work. Each relation is a given; we cannot escape it; it is part and parcel of our being and our world; it is constitutive of our reality. But each relation is also a problem; it is a task to be taken up. A relational understanding of self and its constitutive relations is simultaneously descriptive and prescriptive. "Moral discourse," writes Unger, "always presupposes an acceptance of humanity and the authority of the striving to be and to become ever more fully human."[40] How we perceive, interpret, act, and react within these three arenas affects the texture and quality of those relationships and of our own identity. By virtue of what we are and do, the life of the self and of the world is either intensified or diminished. Each arena presents its own problem for resolution. In the ecological relation, the problem is how both to use and to respect nature. In the social relation, it is how to draw diverse persons and groups, both within our nation and throughout the whole community of nations, into an association of equity and shared ends. In the productive relation, the problem is how to provide for everyone forms of creative work that will give expression to one's individuality and contribute to the community. The technical resolution of these problems is complicated, laborious, unending. But Unger provides a general direction for their resolution. For our relations with nature, the direction is indicated by the norms of symbiosis and natural harmony. For our relations with other persons, our course is plotted by the need for sympathy and a sharing of ends. For our relation to work, the proper orientation is specified in the need to create for everyone a concrete and specialized role that at the same time will do justice to one's full humanity. Without symbiosis, either self or nature is destroyed; without sympathy and a sharing of ends, either self or other is degraded; without humane and creative work, one's role is demeaning.

The four qualities of covenantal community apply to each of these three arenas. Liberation is the struggle to overcome structures that diminish life. Justice is the precept mandating that the needs of all parties in these relationships be honored. Peace is the quality of cohesiveness binding the parties together in a community of belonging. Faithfulness is that loyalty which sustains the commitment of each party to the relationship even at times when the relationship is threatened and lines of connection are strained to the point of breaking. On some occasions, faithfulness drives one to a struggle for liberation and a revitalization of the mandates of justice and peace.

In sum, to the extent that the qualities of liberation, justice, peace, and faithfulness characterize our relations with nature, with other persons, and with work, human life is enhanced. To the extent that those qualities are profaned, human life is diminished and degraded. Covenantal obligations are realistic requirements of the kind of world in which we live. Our destinies and identities are caught up with those obligations. The myth of the covenant thus discloses a world—*our* world—that presents us with basic problems we must take up and fundamental directions we should undertake. If we would live in that world, we must, realistically, be responsive to the obligations of liberation, faithfulness, justice, and peace.

This comment introduces the fourth and final point. The world view symbolized by the myth of the covenant provides a critical perspective on the meaning of law. Recall that, according to American legal realism, the full meaning of law includes its effects. One must ascertain who is doing what to whom. Therein lies a difficulty. How are we to interpret effects? With what terms are we to describe and to evaluate what legal action does to people?

This is a central problem posed by John T. Noonan, Jr., in his provocative study of the "persons and masks of the law." Noonan is as skeptical as the American legal realists of interpreting law as simply a set of rules. To be sure, rules are an important part of law. "But the [legal] process consists in the interplay of the persons forming the rule with the persons applying it and the persons submitting to it."[41] The tragedy—perhaps the inevitable tragedy—of law is the distortion of reality by the use of rules. When distortion occurs, rules become masks: masks are "ways of classifying individual human beings so that their humanity is hidden and disavowed."[42] A mask disguises, deforms, and may ultimately destroy.

The paradigm of legal masking is the legal institution of slavery. To classify individuals as slaves, and therefore as property, is to falsify their reality. Similarly, to classify states as sovereign and corporations as persons has the same deceptive, often destructive effect. A profound realism, a realism that acknowledges the reality of persons as persons is thus a critical basis for the interpretation, evaluation, and transformation of law. But the principle of evaluation is a principle of reality. The principle of criticism is grounded in what is. Noonan's critical jurisprudence, constructed on a neo-Thomist base, would have us remove the masks from both those who make law and those affected by law. It would have us see both these classes of persons engaged in a complicated interchange in which the destinies of all are involved.

Likewise, the new realism of religious sensibility, which testifies to a depth in the structure of human experience often ignored though never wholly absent in everyday life, would have us discern legal processes within a wide-ranging relational context. Legal processes are not merely rules of law or judicial decisions. They find their meaning in their articulations of and contributions to those relations—natural, social and political, economic and productive—that constitute our lives and our destinies as persons. From its critical perspective, the new realism poses two questions. The interpretive question is: What do particular forms and actions of law manifest about the legal aspect of conditions within those relations? In the spirit of this question, Lois Forer, former Judge of the Court of Common Pleas in Philadelphia, drafted her indictment of the judicial process:

> [I] have written this book to help myself, after days in court in which I find myself a participant in a mindless, archaic system which produces results that have little to do with justice. I see that law as a principle by which people conduct their lives is dead, that the entire legal system corrodes any sense of trust or truth. It is a juggernaut laying waste lives, businesses and social order.[43]

On its directive side, the question is: What transformations in the process and practice of law would effectively enrich life in the arenas of human existence? What is required to bring the operations of law to manifest the qualities of liberation, justice, peace, faithfulness? This question is manifest in Judge Forer's affirmation that "Essential to the revitalization of the law is the recognition that the business and purpose of law is justice."[44]

George Christie says that American legal realism is the world view of the practicing lawyer. Maybe so. But how realistic is that form of realism? Does it result in a manipulative, technological, narrowly utilitarian approach to law? Or does it provide a grounding for what Llewellyn perceived within law as a dynamic toward self-sanation, a drive toward social justice and the enrichment of life?

What I am suggesting is that the new realism of religious inquiry, the realism expressed in the covenantal tradition, does provide such a grounding. The realistic question is not how law might be manipulated to allow persons and groups to get what they want. It is how law might be an instrument to liberate the oppressed, to do justice to the widow and fatherless, to realize peace for the community, and thus to be faithful to the demands of the covenant of life. Fidelity to law goes beyond keeping the rules; it requires we attend to the agonizing crises confronting us in the ecological, social, and economic arenas of our common life. Whatever our professional role, as lawyer or citizen, what we do has an effect on the quality of that life. A realistic world view would have us never forget that.

10. CONTEXT AND COVENANT:

SOCIAL THEORY AND THEOLOGY IN BIOETHICS

> Reason which is methodic is content to limit itself
> within the bound of a successful method. It works in
> the secure daylight of traditional practical activity. It
> is the discipline of shrewdness. Reason which is spec-
> ulative questions the methods, refusing to let them
> rest. The passionate demand for freedom of thought
> is a tribute to the deep connection of speculative Rea-
> son with religious intuition. A. N. Whitehead[1]

IN THE EXERCISE OF ANY discipline, methodological questions may
be ignored, but they do not disappear. The practitioners of the
discipline merely assume the questions have been answered, per-
mitting them to get on with the immediate tasks at hand. Yet it is
wise, now and then, to pose methodological questions deliberately with the prospect that new light will be shed on the discipline and its shape and direction modified or transformed in some
creative and fruitful manner.

In this chapter, I pose three methodological questions—questions of scope (What are the boundaries of the discipline?), focus
(What should be the point of concentration of the discipline?), and
grounding (What is the foundation of the discipline?). All three
questions bear on the general issue of the meaning and character
of bioethics. With respect to each question I shall present a claim.
In its scope, bioethics should become less strictly case-oriented
and more contextually oriented. In its focus, bioethics should be
linked with social theory—social interpretation and social ethics.
In its grounding, bioethics should be allied with theology.

My intention is not to prove these claims, whatever proof
might mean, but to make them intelligible. Overall, I shall suggest
the conjunction of a contextual bioethics, a critical social theory,
and a process theology. From a critical social theory, the principle

of structuration provides a means of understanding the intrinsic connection between individuality and sociality. Given that principle, bioethics must be a form of social ethics. From process theology, the reformed subjectivist principle provides a means of understanding the intrinsic connection between God and the world. Given that principle, bioethics must become a form of religious ethics.

There are two reasons I am brought to present these claims. One of them is practical. The second is theoretical.

On the practical side, the professions are under seige. Because of their special role within the social order, the professions have long claimed and been granted autonomy. The alleged aim of the professions, each with its own particular focus, is to serve the well-being of the human community. Under conditions of modern society, however, suspicions have been roused. It is not altogether clear the professions can be trusted. The crisis of confidence that is expressed generally in attitudes of skepticism about large organizations and about persons in high office is expressed more particularly in attitudes of doubt about the professions. Serious questions are raised about the motivations of professionals, about the actual beneficiaries of professional practice, and about the social and political implications of professional conduct. The overarching question is whether the professions, given their current form and character, genuinely serve the common good.

On the theoretical side, a distinction may be drawn between two principles of understanding, an analytic principle and a relational principle. Each promotes its own method of interpretation. The former is characteristic of the cosmology of scientific materialism. The latter is characteristic of the philosophy of organism. Analysis separates, distinguishes, isolates. An analytic principle presses one toward simplification and precision. It drives toward careful definition and the delineation of narrow boundaries. In its social model, it is atomistic and individualistic. A relational principle, on the other hand, leads one to discern connections, associations, relationships. A relational approach is less concerned with sharp definition than with potential relevance. It is open to new pursuits, new possibilities, and is tolerant of complexity. In its social model, it is holistic and communal. Each of these principles has merit, yet the employment of each also runs a risk. The merit of the analytic principle is precision; its risk is loss of realism. The merit of the relational principle is its attention to full-bodied context; its risk is vagueness and uncertainty. This chapter is dedicated to the promotion of the relational principle as the more appropriate in our time given trends in cosmological thought and social reality.

About a decade ago, Daniel Callahan, among the creative pioneers in modern developments in bioethics, confessed to the fluidity of the boundaries of the field.

> Bioethics is not yet a full discipline. Most of its practitioners have wandered into the field from somewhere else, more or less inventing it as they go. Its vague and problematic status in philosophy and theology is matched by its even more shaky standing in the life sciences. The lack of general acceptance, disciplinary standards, criteria of excellence and clear pedagogical and evaluative norms provides, however, some unparalleled opportunities. It is a discipline not yet burdened by encrusted traditions and domineering figures. Its saving grace is that it is not yet a genuine discipline as that concept is usually understood in the academic and scientific communities. One has always to explain oneself and that leaves room for creativity and constant re-definition; there are many advantages in being a moving target.[2]

Bioethics is thus in search of an identity although, in Callahan's judgment as expressed above, there is some virtue in that identity not being too carefully prescribed or rigidly defined. More recently, one of the practitioners of medical ethics (whose relation to bioethics is an unsettled question) asserted that medical ethics "has come of age once again."[3] Yet the place of bioethics (and medical ethics) in the organization of knowledge is a point of contention. Some claim it as a subfield of philosophical ethics, the application of general principles of rational morality to a particular subject matter.[4] Others would join it to the practice of medicine as an integral part of the healing professions.[5] Still others conceive it as a new multidisciplinary science grounded in biology and needed at the present time for the survival of the human species.[6]

In this search for an identity for bioethics, I would, given the claims already indicated, offer three suggestions.

First, among its current practitioners, bioethics tends toward one or the other of two approaches. For ease of reference, I shall designate these approaches "personalist" and "contextual." The personalist approach is the narrower and the contextual is the broader of the two. The virtue of the personalist approach is its seemingly immediate practicality. But it runs the risk of committing the "Fallacy of Misplaced Concreteness" (A. N. Whitehead). It attends so closely to the interaction between physician and patient, it neglects the institutional and cultural context within which the interactive process makes sense and finds its meaning. What a contextual approach may lose in immediate practicality, it gains in historical and social realism.

Second, a contextual bioethics, given its character, must be allied with social theory. It must deal with the fundamental problem of social theory, the relationship between individuality and sociality. In doing so, it must look to and take account of investigations in the history, sociology, and politics of medicine for, even in one's individuality, one is a historical, social, and political being. Health and well-being, disease and illness are experienced by individuals but they are, at the same time, expressive of the relational context of an individual's life. Critical social theory, moreover, is both interpretive and normative. In its concern with what is the case, it poses the question of what ought to be the case. Thus a contextual bioethics, in its alliance with social theory, must be a form of social ethics.

Third, a contextual bioethics must, at least implicitly, enter the "theological circle" (Paul Tillich). To be sure, theology in the modern world is very much in flux: "that the contemporary theological scene has become chaotic is evident to everyone who attempts to work in theology. There appears to be no consensus on what the task of theology is or how theology is to be pursued."[7] The chaos of the contemporary theological scene, however, may be no more characteristic of theology than it is of philosophy or the social sciences. These disciplines, too, are in flux. Besides, uniformity and single-mindedness are no assurance of profundity or validity. Yet theology, in and through its many forms, brings to the fore the issue of the nature and destiny of human life. In theological terms, this is the issue of the relation between God and the world, for God is the objective ground of confidence in the ultimate significance of the world and, in particular, of human activity. This is the elemental issue that resides at the foundation of all human practice, including the practice of medicine and of the life sciences. In Max Horkheimer's phrase, "behind all authentic human activity stands theology."[8] By theology, Horkheimer means the consciousness that the world as it exists is not the last word. Theology is expressive of the hope for well-being, the yearning for freedom, the aspiration for justice. Without that kind of consciousness as its grounding, it is difficult to conceive of a contextual bioethics.

1. BIOETHICS: PERSONALIST AND CONTEXTUAL

The question of the scope of bioethics may be posed various ways. What is bioethics for? What are its purposes? To whom is bioethics addressed? For whom are its principles, policies, and prescriptions meant? What kinds of issues are most central to its task? Is there a difference between medical ethics and bioethics? What is the source from which the principles and insights of bioethics derive? The question of scope is a function of one's perception of social reality and the level at which one interprets the meaning of the biomedical field.

In a remark made initially for another purpose, Paul U. Unschuld suggests a distinction that bears on this question: "Standards governing practice of private and public health care have arisen as a result of continued interaction on at least two distinct, but not exclusive, levels of cultural and social activity. These levels include (1) the perception and propagation of *world views* by groups in society intending to maintain or establish social order, and (2) the *interactions* between various medical practitioners and their clients."[9]

Both levels are present in the current literature of bioethics. Each promotes its own response to the question of the scope of the field. The former tends toward a more macrocosmic and the latter toward a more microcosmic form of bioethics. A macrocosmic bioethics places issues of private and public health care within a broad theoretical or practical (political and historical) context within which the practice of a physician or scientist is comprehended as manifesting meanings that transcend the practice itself. A microcosmic bioethics is more limited in its concern with individual cases and the relationship between particular persons, professionals and clients or subjects. The latter appears to be the more concrete of the two levels, but in reality, may be the more abstract and may, in certain circumstances, be deceptive.

In Daniel Callahan's sketch of "bioethics as a discipline" of about a decade ago, there are evidences of a more microcosmic approach. Among the central tasks of bioethics, Callahan specifies "that of helping scientists and physicians to make the right decisions; and that requires willingness to accept the realities of most medical and scientific life, that is, that at some discrete point in time all the talk has to end and a choice must be made, a choice which had best be right rather than wrong."[10] What Callahan means by choice is particularized by the criterion he presents to test any proposed method in bioethics: "that it enables those who employ it to reach reasonably specific, clear decisions in those instances which require them—in the case of what is to be done about Mrs. Jones by four o'clock tomorrow afternoon, after which she will either live or die depending upon the decision made."[11] More recently, Callahan has urged that the discipline adopt a somewhat broader scope in order to deal with emergent conflicts and tensions between its traditional patient-centered concern and legitimate interests of the public.[12]

Yet even Callahan's revised version of the scope of bioethics stands in sharp contrast with a proposal of Van Rensselaer Potter. Potter, a cancer research scientist, claims to have coined the term "bioethics" to designate a new discipline made necessary by the ecological crisis of our times.[13] Bioethics, in Potter's conception, is a multidisciplinary science formed to concern itself with the survival of the ecosystem. Biology is at its core, but a biology in collaboration with humanities and social sciences. We shall need such a corps of persons "who respect the fragile web of life and who can broaden their knowledge to include the nature of man and his relation to the biological and physical world. . . . who can tell us what we can and must do to survive and what we cannot and must not do if we hope to maintain and improve the quality of life during the next three decades."[14] Out of such a discipline would emerge prescriptions for individuals[15] and for public policy.[16]

At first blush, it appears that Callahan and Potter, despite the common rubric, bioethics, are concerned with wholly different disciplines. Yet both are concerned with the life sciences and both cite the issue of death and survival as paradigmatic. The difference is, in part, a matter of focus. But it is also a matter of perspective on the character of social and historical reality.

A comparison of the approaches of Paul Ramsey and Ivan Illich to the ethics of medical practice illustrates the point. Ramsey's is a more microcosmic approach. In his understanding, bioethics is casuistic. It should attend to particular cases of medical care. There is, however, nothing unique about bioethics: "The moral requirements governing the relations of physician to patient and researcher to subjects are only a special case of the moral requirements governing any relations between man and man."[17] Bioethics is addressed to professionals and patients simply as persons who are obligated to conduct themselves as persons in their mutual relations. To Ramsey, as a Christian ethicist, this means to honor the covenant that binds them to each other.

> We are born within covenants of life with life. By nature, choice, or need we live with our fellowmen in roles or relations. Therefore we must ask, what is the meaning of the *faithfulness* of one human being to another in every one of these relations? This is the ethical question.[18]

However compelling Ramsey's Christian personalism is in its application to particular cases of professional interaction with subjects, it is, from the perspective presented in Ivan Illich's controversial text, *Medical Nemesis*, woefully deficient. To Illich, the most crucial problems of health and illness in contemporary industrial civilization are systemic, not personal. Physicians and researchers, given their inherited professional mind-set, may be faithful to their clients but at the same time exacerbate patterns of ill-health and disease which, presumably, they are committed to combat. Illich's concern is iatrogenesis, illness induced by the medical professional itself, which, he argues, assumes three forms.

> Iatrogenesis is *clinical* when pain, sickness, and death result from medical care; it is *social* when health policies reinforce an industrial organization that generates ill-health; it is *cultural* and symbolic when medically sponsored behavior and delusions restrict the vital autonomy of people by undermining their competence in growing up, caring for each other, and aging, or when medical intervention cripples personal responses.[19]

Even Illich's critics at times accept his basic thesis, that "the medical establishment has become a major threat to health," without adopting the full measure of his radical anti-technological and anti-industrial populism.[20]

Other perspectives furnish illuminating angles of vision on the question of the scope and character of bioethics. Richard Zaner, from the perspective of the phenomenological tradition, insists that bioethical issues are "context-specific." They cannot be settled by the application of traditional principles. They concern the totality of life of both patient and practitioner. Zaner derives this conclusion from an exploration of the phenomenon of embodiment. One's body is one's place of being and center of action; it is expressive of who one is and what one intends. Medical practice and research are thus interventions into one's self which is why bioethical issues have such a special character. Each self is a gathering together of a unique set of values, commitments, and concerns. Each patient and each practitioner bring to their interaction some understanding of the world and some vision of the good. In effect, this means to Zaner that each issue must be settled in its own way.[21] As observed in a commentary on Zaner's work:

> Each choice that is made must attend to the values already found in the situation, values brought to the situation by the life-history of the patient and intertwined with the expressive character of the patient's body, and by the goals and purposes the doctor seeks to actualize in the practice of his or her profession. The values found in the situation as concretely lived must be recognized and described before discussion of ethical universals in abstract form can be at all useful or informative.[22]

Zaner's position signals, *inter alia*, potential conflicts in world view between practitioner and patient which, in instances of racial, sexual, and class differences between the parties, may be vividly present.

More generally, Zaner's principle of embodiment may be translated, *per analogiam*, into the sphere of sociality. Michael Gordy, for instance, has asserted "the majority of bioethical issues presuppose a social nexus and have to be discussed in terms of the real relations between people."[23] Gordy contrasts two views of sociality, the contractual and the non-contractual or organic. Each casts its own light on the character of issues in bioethics and establishes a setting for their resolution. In the former case, medical care is a commodity to be bought and sold in the market and is susceptible to the laws of exchange. In the latter case, however, medical care is a particular set of relationships established by a community to attend to the quality of life and to promote the well-being of its members. In a complex way, views of sociality may, of course, be related to and expressive of historical circumstance. So, it can be argued, the contractual view is more appropriate to a post-industrial or post-capitalist civilization. If this argument has merit, then bioethics must extend its scope and sights to incorporate considerations of social and historical analysis; it must concern itself with changing views of society and with historical circumstance.

Such an extension would be in keeping with René Dubos' insistence that

> Physicians must learn to work with engineers, architects, and general biologists, as well as with city planners, lawyers, and politicians responsible for the management of our social life. Only through such collaboration can they help society ward off, insofar as possible, dangers to physical and mental health inherent in all technological and social change, especially when these occur as rapidly as they do now. From urban renewal to safety measures in industry, from environmental pollution to the trial of new drugs and therapeutic procedures, the sociomedical problems are countless and require technical, legal, and ethical considerations.[24]

Each of the two general forms of bioethics distinguished above—the microcosmic and the macrocosmic, the personalist and the contextual—is appealing. Each has its own integrity. Some bioethicists have urged that the discipline as a whole should incorporate both forms.[25] But that begs the question of how the two forms should be related and which should be paramount. The two forms exist in some tension with each other. On the one hand, particular cases present clinician and researcher with ethical dilemmas that are urgent; their resolution cannot wait upon broad historical change or new directions in public policy. The day-to-day necessities of medical practice seem to dictate giving priority to the personalist form of bioethics. On the other hand, to deal exclusively or primarily with individual cases as they emerge in clinic or research would mean ignoring the structural conditions that gave rise to the cases in the first instance. More pointedly, it would mean ignoring a trend within the medical world. Recently,

Renée Fox, in a searching interpretation of the historical development of medicine through three stages—archaic, modern, and
post-modern—argued that the inner dynamics of the medical profession are moving toward a more contextual approach including
but going beyond the societal toward the religious.

> Not only has the development of a more sociologically oriented
> theory of health and illness increased social activism in this domain,
> but also age-old philosophical and religious questions are revital-
> ized by what is felt to be the mystery-laden relationship between
> what now seems to be alterable and what not. Who and what is
> man? What are the meaning and purpose of his existence? What is
> life, what is death, and wherein lies the essence of the distinction
> between them? Why do men fall ill and suffer and die? How should
> we understand these experiences and believe toward them? This
> sort of querying is characteristic of post-modern medicine and its
> practitioners, as well as of its patients. If one accepts the sociologi-
> cal view that preoccupation with such questions of meaning consti-
> tutes a religious act, then one might say that in this sense
> post-modern medicine is less secular and more sacred than modern
> medicine.[26]

2. SOCIAL THEORY: INDIVIDUALITY AND SOCIALITY

The question of the focus of bioethics is related to, yet distinguishable from, that of scope. The question of scope is a matter of
the range of issues appropriate to the discipline. Some issues are
seemingly not pertinent to the field, although one must be cau-
tious in fixing boundaries too absolutely for relevance has a sea-
sonable quality about it. The question of focus, on the other hand,
is a matter of concentration. It is a question of determining importance and centrality. It is concerned with defining priorities. The
focus of a discipline may change over time without necessarily
distorting its boundaries in any appreciable manner.

In a recent criticism of the prevailing concentration in
bioethics, Roy Branson argues that the discipline should have a
double focus.[27] The dominant tendency is to center on questions
of direct professional interaction because these constitute the kind
of question posed by medical practitioners. Such a focus, Branson

asserts, is too narrow. It ignores crucial dilemmas of an institutional character and neglects issues of public policy. He cites, as examples, the financing of medical services, the development of a nuclear-powered artificial heart, and the distribution of health care. He concludes that bioethics should be both individual *and* social in its focus.[28]

The proposal that bioethics have two branches, that it deal with issues of both personal-professional interaction *and* social-institutional policy is appealing. But it evades the question of the conjunctive, namely, of how individuality and sociality are related. It seems to assume that individuality and sociality, personal agency and social structure, are separate and distinct. But that assumption is currently under question in social theory. As a clue to the position I would propose, I take the following statement from Anthony Giddens: "just as every sentence in English expresses within itself the totality which is the 'language' as a whole, so every interaction bears the imprint of the global society."[29]

Giddens uses the term "structuration" to indicate the connectedness of agency and structure.[30] Structuration is the process of presentation (or, better, representation) of structural forms in cases of interaction. Society, or social structure, is only through an abstraction independent of individuals acting. The actuality, the embodiment of social structure is in and through the agency of particular persons engaged in interchange. There is, to be sure, a relative disjunction between social order and individual agency which accounts, in part, for the dynamics of social conflict and the possibility of social change. But social structure and personal agency presuppose each other. To distinguish too radically between individual ethics and social ethics or between questions of personal-professional interaction and social-institutional policy is to falsify the congruity or, more accurately, the relative coincidence of sociality and individuality in their concreteness. The radical disjunction between sociality and individuality is an inheritance from the liberal tradition and its rejection of the relational principle.

In the biomedical field as in other professional fields each instance of interaction is part of a practice, and each practice is part of a social order and a social history. In more active language, each case participates in and re-presents a practice, and each practice participates in and re-presents a social process. A practice is a specialized set of interactions governed more or less consistently by certain conventions or rules whether or not those conventions and rules are deliberately acknowledged.[31] Yet a practice, while specialized, produces and re-produces the more encompassing social totality in which it is located. It is engaged in the making of social history.

From this perspective, precisely as bioethics attends to particular cases of professional or personal interaction, it must, *to encompass the full significance of those cases*, be a form of social ethics. As such, bioethics must incorporate more directly than it has in the past, the insights, theories, principles, and problems of the sociology and history of biomedical practice, yet it must do so critically since forms of sociology and history are conditioned by theoretical and practical assumptions and presuppositions. Bioethics, in other words, must attend to the synchronic and diachronic dimensions of professional interaction with biomedical practice and within the whole social process in which the practice participates. The distinction between synchronic and diachronic dimensions, it should be noted, is only analytic and, in any adequate interpretation, will not hold. The theory of structuration is an effort to overcome the false dualisms of both individuality-sociality and statics-dynamics.

The focus I would propose is exactly at the conjunction of agency and structure in part because of its central importance given the theory of structuration, in part because a double focus tends to misrepresent the character of action, and in part to demonstrate the full burden of responsibility of professional practice.

There is a wide range of literature from the sociology and history of medicine and the life sciences pertinent to this focus for bioethics. The following survey is presented only as suggestive of the possibilities.

Dimensions of a Contextual Bioethics

	synchronic (structural context)	diachronic (historical context)
internal (practice)	1. Talcott Parsons Eliot Freidson John and Barbara Ehrenreich David Mechanic	3. John and Barbara Ehrenreich Tom Levin Renée Fox
external (social totality)	2. Elliott Krause	4. Henry Sigerist René Dubos

Sociological Interpretations of Biomedical Practice

Among the more significant contributions to the sociology of medicine are those of Talcott Parsons and Eliot Freidson. From a sociological perspective, medical practice is a set of interacting roles fulfilling a specialized function within an encompassing social system. Among other things, it is an instrument of social control. From the standpoint of a contextual bioethics, it would be important to determine who is being controlled, how, and for what purposes.

In Parsons' judgment, health and illness are not merely conditions of individuals. They are defined and institutionalized through the social structure since whether one is officially designated healthy or ill bears on the performance of social tasks: "Health may be defined as the state of optimum capacity of an individual for the effective performance of roles and tasks for which he has been socialized. It is thus defined with reference to the individual's participation in the social system."[32] This means physician and patient occupy special roles. That of physician is the more obvious. One of Parsons' unique contributions to the sociology of medicine is his construction of the "sick role." It is composed of four features. The sick are (1) exempt from normal social responsibilities, (2) understood to be subject to forces beyond personal control, hence exempt from responsibility for their condition, (3) obliged to consider their condition as undesirable, and (4) obliged to seek professional assistance and to cooperate in the process of recovery.[33] Where its exemptions make the sick role attractive as a form of social deviance, its obligations constitute a balancing factor. The sick role is a mechanism of social control intended to reintegrate those who are ill back into the normal operation of the social system. The meaning of the process is given a peculiar twist by Sigerist's quip: "To immunize colonial people against disease with the one hand and exploit them into starvation with the other is a grim joke." [34]

Eliot Freidson presents another sociological slant on medical practice. Given the Berger-Luckman thesis—"reality is socially defined"—Freidson is particularly concerned with the "social construction of illness."[35] Medicine, like law and religion, is a profession authorized to distinguish normal and abnormal, proper and improper. An illness may have roots in biological causes, but what gets labeled illness depends upon social perceptions or professional judgment and is susceptible to placement under forms of institutional control. Increasingly over the past several decades, the medical model has been employed to deal with perceived forms of deviancy: "In our day, what has been called crime, lunacy, degeneracy, sin, and even poverty in the past is now being called illness, and social policy has been moving toward adopting a perspective appropriate to the imputation of illness."[36] Some physicians assume the role of "moral entrepreneurs" in extending or altering the definition of what is considered illness. Once lay persons enter the domain of illness, they are subject to professional management; they are forced to serve the social identity implied by the diagnosed illness. Freidson himself poses one of the central ethical questions provoked by discernment of the consequence of illness as a construct of social meaning: "How desirable is that consequence? Is it in the public interest for society to allow the profession the autonomy to define both the need and problem and to control their management?"[37]

Barbara and John Ehrenreich interpret Parsons and Freidson as both construing medical practice as a form of social control, but in two seemingly contradictory ways—disciplinary (Parsons) and co-optative (Freidson). To Parsons, medical practice is exclusionary: it delimits those seeking the advantages of the social role and is oriented to return the ill as quickly as possible to normal occupations in the social order. To Freidson, medical practice is expansionist: it moves to extend the sick role to include ever more classes of people in order to manage their lives.

The Ehrenreichs resolve the seeming contradiction by suggesting the orientations pertain to different socio-economic classes. The co-optative orientation characterizes the relation of the medical system to the "medical poor"—the non-white and the elderly. The disciplinary orientation typifies treatment of the "medical middle class." Moreover, the forms are promoted by different ideological groups: liberals, out of humanitarian impulse, are expansionist; conservatives, out of desire to curb costs, are exclusionary.

The Ehrenreichs, dissatisfied with both forms, propose a new beginning:

> If the medical system is understood as something more than a system for distributing a 'commodity', if it is understood as a system of direct *social relationships*, then the question becomes: what kinds of social relationships do we want a medical system to foster? . . . The problems which our society relegates to the medical system—the care of the disabled and dependent, the management of reproduction, individual suffering, and death—are no less than some of the central problems which confront any human society. Medicine has allowed us to evade them too long.[38]

David Mechanic's studies present several points where the organized structure of modern medical practice militates against direct social relationships. There is, for instance, a tendency, especially in a hospital setting, to neglect the life circumstance of patients and how that circumstance bears on the patient's condition even though

> the physician must . . . be sensitive to patients as individuals within a family and community context, since life situations are a major source of ill health and may be a barrier to convalescence. If he treats the presentation of the patient solely at the manifest level, his treatment may be only symptomatic, and he frequently will fail to deal with the basic underlying difficulties that brought the patient to him.[39]

Such neglect leads to complaints that the medical profession is inhumane. But,

> the institutions and the personnel who carry out medical functions behave as they do not because they are more inhumane than others but rather because the pressures and constraints of work, the priori-

ties health personnel have been taught, and the reward structures of which they are a part direct their attention to other goals and needs.[40]

The problem is a matter of structural design, not personal attitude. It is, in part, a function of compensation structure[41] and, in part, an expression of the elitist organization[42] of medical practice.

Political-Economic Context of Biomedical Practice

The structural problems of health care are not limited to the internal organization of medical practice. It is virtually a truism, for example, that those living in poverty are more susceptible to disease and have less access to quality health care than those who are economically comfortable.[43] Environmental conditions, malnutrition, lack of income, cultural differences from medical personnel, geographic locations of hospitals, and priorities of the health system are all factors contributing to the equation.[44]

The practice of medicine does not and cannot exist independently of its cultural surroundings. Where there is racism,[45] sexism,[46] or imperialism,[47] cultural ethos will have its effect on the character of health care. One should not forget that the Tuskegee syphilis experiments on black males were concluded barely a decade ago.

Eliot Krause generalizes the point by insisting that "if those who study it [the health care system] refuse to explore systematically the myriad ways it is tied to power and control systems of the wider society, then a disservice is done to those whose basic interests are at stake."[48] Krause's basic thesis is that the health care system of the United States is part and parcel of a political and economic structure that is ridden with profound social inequalities and that is itself productive of disease.

A dominant theme in Krause's study is that the political and economic arrangements of modern society constitute a "sickening environment": "At present, for far too many people, home is a place that makes you ill, work is a place that maims your body and spirit, and the environment is a place that functions to finish the job started by home and work."[49] Malnutrition, crowded housing, unenforced building codes, occupational hazards, toxic wastes, automobile exhaust constitute a limited listing of the problem.

Among Krause's examples: "sulfur dioxide pollution . . . has caused the rate of lung cancer on that part of Staten Island downwind of the Jersey refineries to be thirty-three percent higher than that on other parts of the island."[50] In every instance of concerted effort to meliorate these conditions, political forces have been mobilized in opposition.

Historical Development of Biomedical Practice

The structure of the American health system has changed significantly over the past few decades. While family doctors are still to be found, the dominant form of medical practice is now highly institutionalized. Its features are those of modern organization: concentration, bureaucracy, specialization, and complex technology. The American health system has become, in effect, industrialized both internally and in its connection with the manufacturing and financial sectors of the economy. While the benefits of this historical development should not be discounted, neither should the problems it has introduced. The Ehrenreichs, for instance, studied the impact of this change in New York City and cite a range of problems that especially low-income groups in an urban setting began to confront as the new system emerged.[51]

Tom Levin, for purposes of reform, has formulated a systematic interpretation of the development of modern medicine. On the ideological level, "the image the present medical practitioner would like to project to the American health consumer today is that of the dedicated, horse and buggy country doctor, the family practitioner whose deep human investment in his patients and in his community has brought about a totally warranted loyalty and loving social acceptance from the community he serves."[52] But the actual structure of health care under conditions of advanced capitalism is an uneasy amalgamation of a long-time heritage with modern social trends.

> The social organization of medicine has its roots in the medieval and Renaissance guild structure that was organized around a hierarchy of skills and knowledge. Such organization is essentially a craft social structure in which position is determined by the 'possession' of skills and information. . . . The American health system combines the worst of both social organizations; it maintains the

elitist hierarchical feudal guild system of interpersonal social organization around a master craftsman while its economic, service, and technological base is more akin to General Motors than Marcus Welby.[53]

More precisely, the social organization of medicine consists of four principles, each of which, Levin argues, contributes to the pathology of the system: (1) service for profit (which leads to "the existence of pluralistic service systems with vast disparities and inequities of service quality and availability to the poor, rural populations, and ghetto residents"); (2) a symbiosis between vendor and provider (which results in "service delivery . . . determined by facility site rather than patient site"); (3) a guild caste system (which causes "the continued escalation of designated health specialties and overspecialization of skills both in medicine and in allied health occupations"); and (4) a distorted relationship between doctor and patient (which means "the suppression of self-help in health procedures in order to reinforce the hegemony of the professional").[54]

As Giddens comments in his theory of structuration, action is a continuous flow of conduct. It is a movement in the present from a past into a future. The historical development of a practice is always underway. That is the genius of Renée Fox's interpretation of the evolution of medical practice. As already mentioned, Fox discerns a movement through three phases, from the archaic, into the modern, and toward a post-modern. In her projection, two features are particularly characteristic of the emerging medical practice: a social orientation (the social order will be blamed for the genesis and persistence of certain kinds of illness and held responsible for their alleviation) and an existential awareness (there will be increased awareness of the mysteries of life and death and the limitations of the medical profession).[55]

Historical Development of the Social Totality

During the 1930s and 1940s, Henry E. Sigerist, the most prominent historian of medicine in the United States, brought to that discipline a broad perspective leading to investigations of virtually all aspects of civilization. Repeatedly he asserted that medicine was more a social science than a natural science.[56] To understand illness, its origins and treatment, one should focus not merely on biological and clinical research, but equally as much on the mundane features of every-day life: "Food, clothing, housing, occupations, social relations—these factors have always played a considerable role, both in health and disease."[57] More particularly, "In any given society the incidence of illness is largely determined by economic factors . . . A low living standard, lack of food, clothing and fuel, poor housing conditions and other symptoms of poverty, have always been major causes of disease."[58] Following a survey of housing conditions over several centuries, Sigerist pronounces

> If health is vital for human welfare, then housing is certainly an issue of major importance. And if this is the case, housing should not be the object of speculation or source of profit which it is today. Competitive business can neither honestly face nor properly solve the housing problem of contemporary society.[59]

At one juncture in his history of the connections between civilization and disease, Sigerist concludes on a point of social ethics and social ontology.

> In every country disease must be attacked with all available means and where it is most prevalent, in the low income groups. And since the world has become very small as a result of the present means of communication, we must think and plan not merely on a national but on an international scale. There is a human solidarity in health matters that cannot be disregarded with impunity.[60]

The interconnections between personal welfare and physical and social environments are also central in René Dubos' approach to the biomedical field: "Clinical and epidemiological studies show that the inextricably interrelated body, mind, and environment must be considered together in any medical situation whether it involves a single patient or a whole community. . . . Whatever the complaints of the patient and the signs or symptoms he manifests, whatever the medical problems of the community, disease cannot be understood or successfully controlled without considering man in his total environment."[61] This means attending to processes of social change, for attributes of body and mind appropriate to one age may be causative agents in illness in a subsequent age[62] and, moreover, times of social upheaval have an impact on patterns and intensity of disease.[63] While some diseases seem to recur throughout all periods of history, nonetheless, "each civilization, each type of culture, has its own particular illnesses."[64]

In summary, given the focus I have proposed, a central task of contextual bioethics is to demonstrate how particular cases of biomedical practice constitute conjunctions of social structure and historical process. They are, to be sure, instances of personal interaction and must be treated as such. But they are much more than that. They are, simultaneously, moments in the reproduction of social forms and in the passage of time.

3. THEOLOGY: GOD AND THE WORLD

Two questions in the methodology of bioethics have so far been raised—a question of scope and a question of focus. In response to the first question, I have suggested that, of two general tendencies in the field, personal and contextual, the latter approach manifests a profounder social and historical realism than the former. In response to the second question, I have suggested that a contextual bioethics, focusing on the conjunction of individuality and sociality and appropriating resources from the sociology and history of medical practice and its social setting should attend to synchronic and diachronic dimensions of the cases and subjects into which it inquires.

There remains a more difficult, yet more fundamental, methodological question, namely, a question of the grounding of bioethics. What are the foundations of bioethics? What basic understandings or beliefs underlie its working? Where there appear to be irreconcilable procedures or principles among different forms of bioethics, how might one adjudicate the conflict to determine the more justifiable alternative? Why should one engage in bioethics at all? What is its ultimate purpose and point? What in human experience constitutes the impetus behind bioethics? What gives warrant to its premises and first principles?

There are varying levels of approach to this set of issues. Adapting a distinction from Anthony Giddens, I would propose at least two levels: practical consciousness and discursive consciousness. In Giddens's usage, the former includes those "tacit stocks of knowledge which actors draw upon in the constitution of social activity," whereas the latter involves "knowledge which actors are able to express on the level of discourse."[65] I shall use them in this context to refer, respectively, to popular understanding and philosophical (and theological) reasoning.

According to William Glaser, "Since every society has the fundamental problems of explaining illness to the sick and their families and of guiding practical action, each society develops a body of medical theory from its basic ideas about the universe, life, and man."[66] Such ideas may, in David Mechanic's judgment, have an ideological cast.

> The character and distribution of health care, in many respects, reflects the ideological preferences of society. . . . A health care plan must encompass a particular political philosophy concerning both the patients' and the providers' roles and obligations. These philosophies usually arise from the political and economic orientations prevailing in the community.[67]

To illustrate his point, Mechanic contrasts health care in the United States and the U.S.S.R. In the former, health care is "a manifestation of a capitalist entrepreneurial viewpoint emphasizing self-help, the maintenance of the private sector, and a pluralist system. Barriers to access are prevalent and are legitimized on the basis that free goods are unappreciated and exploited." Contrariwise, the U.S.S.R. "conceives of the health of workers as an important economic resource and the health system as an aspect of the government structure concerned with the public welfare"; thus access to primary services is open and encouraged, and industrial medicine is stressed.[68]

The ideologies of political communities and socio-economic classes constitute an everyday justification for institutional forms and practice. They exercise a powerful influence in the continuous production and reproduction of patterns of social relationship. They serve, on a popular level, as a grounding for group interest and as an apparently sufficient reason for supporting (or criticizing) social policy. Yet in an age imbued with historical consciousness, cognizant of cultural and political difference, and suspicious of self-aggrandizing rationalization, ideologies are strongly discounted as well. When they are discounted, there is an impetus to move from practical consciousness to discursive consciousness, from popular morality to critical morality. This is the point at which an explicit move may be made to philosophy or theology. In a provocative "essay on theological method," Gordon Kaufman has asserted

> the ideas of God and the world are constructed by the human imagination for essentially practical purposes: in order to live and act it is necessary to have some conception or picture of the overall context, the fundamental order, within which human life falls. The ideas and images of God and the world supply this. Thus, they are created primarily to provide orientation in life.[69]

While accepting Kaufman's assertion that ideas of God and the world constitute a conception of the overall context within which human life is lived and in accordance with which the processes and forms of human existence are ultimately grounded, I shall not pursue the basic thesis of Kaufman's argument, that theology in the final analysis is nothing but an imaginative construction of the human mind. I shall instead pursue a clue taken from process thought, a clue which forms the basis of the philosophy of organism (A. N. Whitehead) and the metaphysics of internal relations (B. E. Meland). The clue is the reformed subjectivist principle: "The starting point for a genuinely new theistic conception is what Whitehead speaks of as 'the reformed subjectivist principle.'"[70]

The reformed subjectivist principle is to philosophy and theology what the theory of structuration is in social theory. The theory of structuration points to the conjunction of individuality and sociality and to the coincidence of structural forms and historical passage. The reformed subjectivist principle indicates the connection between self and world and between self and God. Moreover, the reformed subjectivist principle, I mean to suggest, gives rise to a cluster of principles of action that constitute a grounding for social ethics and thus also for bioethics.

Modern philosophy and modern theology are characterized, in large part, by a turn toward the subject. What can be known about the world, it is assumed, is constructed from subjective experience. There are two versions of the subjectivist principle. In an earlier version, it is individualistic and, in an extreme form, solipsistic. In a later reformed version, it is relational and processual. In Whitehead's formulation: "The way in which one actual entity is qualified by other actual entities is the 'experience' of the actual world enjoyed by that actual entity, as subject. The subjectivist principle is that the whole universe consists of elements disclosed in the analysis of the experiences of subjects."[71] More concisely, according to the philosophy of organism, "Each actual entity is a throb of experience including the actual world within its scope."[72] Self and world, from this perspective, are engaged in a continuous process of interaction. The world is the condition for the self's realization and the self, in turn, is a contribution to the on-going world. Each is important to the other. *Per analogiam*, God and the world are engaged in constant interchange. The world is the condition for God's activity and God's valuation of and intentionality for the world constitute the impetus for its next moment of becoming.

In this metaphysics of internal relations,

> Relationship is of the essence. It is not just a connecting link forming the parts into a mechanism; it is a live and serious confrontation of created centers of dignity pursuing the intentions and ends of self in and through the drama of communal existence.[73]

Religion, Whitehead has argued, lies at the heart of this philosophical understanding, a religion

> founded on the concurrence of three allied concepts in one moment of self-consciousness, concepts whose separate relationships to fact and whose mutual relations to each other are only to be settled jointly by some direct intuition into the ultimate character of the universe. These concepts are:
> 1. That of the value of an individual for itself.
> 2. That of the value of the diverse individuals of the world for each other.
> 3. That of the value of the objective world which is a community derivative from the interrelations of its component individuals, and also necessary for the existence of each of these individuals.[74]

The self thus exists within a matrix of relationships whose dominant member is God. What matters is the quality of those relationships. In Meland's terms, the self confronts,

> a threefold demand, which is what gives complexity to his existence. He is made for God, he is made for other people [and, I

would add, for other beings within the entire ecosphere], he is made for himself. The living out of these relationships becomes man's daily burden as well as his opportunity. And it is his ultimate hope.[75]

This threefold demand may be translated into three principles, each of which has its ethical import and each of which bears on bioethics: the principles of autonomy (the value of an individual for itself), relationality (the value of the diverse individuals of the world for each other), and community (the value of the objective world). These may be construed in traditional ethical language as principles of liberty, equality, and the common good.

The principle of liberty, which pertains to the self, honors the individuality of experience. The principle of equality, which belongs to relations between beings, promotes the contribution each life can make to all future lives. The principle of the common good, which, in its most encompassing form, rests in God's apprehension of the universe as a whole and becomes a condition for each instance of self-realization, respects the ever-evolving quality of the connectedness of life with life as drawn together in every new moment in the passage of time.

Self, world, and God are thus conjoined in what Meland has called the "structure of experience," that is,

> a depth in our natures that connects all that we are with all that has been within the context of actuality that defines our culture. It is a depth in our nature that relates us as events to all existent events. It is a depth in our nature that relates us to God, a sensitive nature within the vast context of nature, winning the creative passage for qualitative attainment.[76]

Out of that structure of experience are born the principles of liberty, equality, and the common good that, in turn, constitute a foundation for the assessment and direction of personal agency and social structure. They therefore constitute, in particular, a grounding for biomedical practice and bioethics. But I would add, out of the Hebraic-Christian traditions, the principle of covenant. On the one hand, the principle of covenant conveys a "myth of identity" between the world and God and, as such, it points to an ideal conformity of the principles of liberty, equality, and common good. It embraces them in a single vision. On the other hand, the

principle of covenant, in its presentation in the narrative of the
Hebraic-Christian traditions, conveys a "note of dissonance" in
relations between world and God and, thus, it points to tensions
and conflicts among considerations of liberty, equality, and common good.[77]

In the literature of bioethics and, more generally, of health
and disease, various forms of these four principles have been
invoked as fundamental. Selected instances are summarized in
the following table.

Fundamental Principles of Biomedical Practice
and Bioethics

1. Principle of Liberty	T. Engelhardt
	W. Reich
2. Principle of Equality	L. Kass
	H. Sigerist
3. Principle of Common Good	H. Sigerist
	T. Parsons
	V. R. Potter
	A. Hellegers and A. Jonsen
4. Principle of Covenant	P. Ramsey
	R. Veatch
	W. May

1. In a searching discussion of meanings of health and disease, Tristram Engelhardt ultimately defines health as "a state of
freedom from the compulsion of psychological and physiological
forces." Treatment, therefore, is to focus "on securing the autonomy of the individual from a particular class of restrictions."[78]
Throughout his wide-ranging discussion, Engelhardt debates several important issues of philosophical anthropology pertinent to
biomedical practice—e.g., the contention between dualists and
monists on the body-mind problem and the difference between
Platonic realism and contextualism on the etiology of disease. In its
final conclusion, however, his position is centered in a strong
affirmation of the liberty of the individual. That is the reason for
biomedical practice and, presumably, a governing principle of

bioethics (although he claims the principle is a non-moral regulative ideal): "While there are many diseases, there is in a sense only one health—a regulative ideal of autonomy directing the physician to the patient as person, the sufferer of the illness, and the reason for all the concern and activity."[79]

Warren Reich, acknowledging the central importance of the principle of autonomy in bioethics particularly as it applies to the matter of informed consent, argues that the principle tends to be construed much too narrowly as "non-interference." Respect for autonomy requires that persons be provided with those conditions—physical, mental, and social—that enable them authentically and positively to make determinations about their future. In some instances, therefore, active intervention by medical professionals even against the expressed wishes of the patient may be a means of honoring the principle of positive autonomy.[80]

2. In a now classic essay on the goal of medicine, Leon Kass argues that the governing purpose of medicine is not, as with Engelhardt, to free persons from restraints thus enhancing their autonomy. It is rather to promote the actualization of specifically human potentialities. The underlying anthropology is Aristotelian. It assumes a kind of equality that underlies all differences among human beings and it assumes equivalence of treatment relative to the standard of human need. Health, the goal of medicine, is grounded in the nature of being human. Thus, in a summary definition, health is "'the well-working of the organism as a whole' or, again, 'an activity of the living body in accordance with its specific excellences'."[81]

3. Versions of both equality and the common good are discernible in the writings of Henry E. Sigerist. As mentioned already, Sigerist attacks the unequal distribution of wealth as a dominant factor in the incidence and apportionment of disease. But Sigerist postulates, without argument, "The goal of medicine is not simply to cure diseases; it is rather to keep men adjusted to their environment as useful members of society, or to readjust them when illness has taken hold of them."[82] In short, the goal of medicine is the common good of society. Sigerist, however, would have society understood inclusively: "the health and welfare of every individual is the concern of society, and *human solidarity beyond the boundaries of nationality, race, and creed is a true criterion of civilization.*"[83]

Talcott Parsons's rendition of the common good as the central principle of medical practice is much narrower. He defines health "as the state of optimum capacity of an individual for the effective performance of the roles and tasks for which he has been socialized."[84] By contrast, Van Rensselaer Potter's approach to the field of bioethics is cosmic in scope, for, in his construction, the fundamental purpose of the field is the "survival of the total ecosystem."[85]

The position of Albert Jonsen and Andre Hellegers stands between the extremes of Parsons and Potter. Jonsen and Hellegers propose that an adequate ethics of health care would be comprised of three moral concerns: virtue, duty, and common good. Virtue pertains to the character of the practitioner. Duty pertains to the quality of particular actions in the relationship between professional and patient. Common good pertains to the structure of the institutions through which and in which health care occurs.

> A theory of the common good seeks to elucidate the nature of human communities. These are the institutional forms that human actions create and human virtues sustain and, in their turn, should become the objective conditions nurturing virtue and sustaining action. . . . Properly conceived, the theory of the common good is a third dimension in which virtues and actions take on depth and tone that they do not have in isolation. The very meaning of a virtue or an action depends on its social or institutional setting.[86]

By invoking the principle of the common good, Jonsen and Hellegers are calling for an institutional ethic, that is, a theory of how the institution of modern medicine should be formed to serve the general cause of social justice for the whole community of humankind.

4. Diverse understandings of the principle of covenant are manifest in the bioethics of Paul Ramsey, Robert Veatch, and William F. May. Ramsey's construction is *confessional* in its derivation and *personalistic* in its result. As a Christian ethicist in the Barthian tradition, Ramsey holds "that covenant-fidelity is the inner meaning and purpose of our creation as human beings." The basic requirement of fidelity for the medical practitioner as for anyone is to respect the sanctity of human life which, where effective,

> prevents ultimate trespass upon him even for the sake of treating his bodily life, or for the sake of others who are also only a sacred-

ness in their bodily lives. Only a being who is a sacredness in the social order can withstand complete dominion by "society" for the sake of engineering civilizational goals—withstand, in the sense that the engineering of civilizational goals cannot be accomplished without denying the sacredness of the human being. So also in the use of medical or scientific technics.[87]

Veatch, however, proposes a principle of covenant that is *contractualist* in its preferred origin for, with Rawls, Veatch believes that a form of contractualism accessible to all rational persons will more nearly satisfy the need for a universally acceptable basis for bioethics than a theologically based covenantalism. In result, the principle of covenant entails the rejection of utilitarianism and the adoption of a set of prima facie duties in human relationships (e.g., promise-keeping, truthfulness, respect for autonomy).[88]

William F. May's principle of covenant appears to be *ontological* in its derivation, although expressed in and through the religious traditions of Judaism and Christianity. In its results it enjoins a reciprocity of giving and receiving between medical professional and patient and also between the institution of medical practice and social order.[89]

Of these three understandings of the meaning of covenant, May's most closely approximates what I intend by the reformed subjectivist principle as a theological means of grounding the ethics of biomedical practice. Moreover, the reformed subjectivist principle constitutes a framework for incorporating the principles of liberty, equality, and common good into a single conception, a conception whose full methodological and institutional implications remain to be developed.

In sum, I have posed three questions about the meaning of bioethics—its scope, its focus, and its grounding. On the first question, I have proposed the need for a contextual bioethics. On the second, I have proposed the need to concentrate on the conjunction between sociality and individuality in bioethics. And on the third, I have proposed the reformed subjectivist principle as a theological means for grounding bioethics and for developing principles for its practice.

NOTES

INTRODUCTION

1. John Locke, *Two Treatises of Government* II.ix.124.
2. Bernard Eugene Meland, *Faith and Culture* (New York: Oxford University Press, 1953), p. 133.
3. Ibid., p. 134.
4. Bernard Eugene Meland, *The Realities of Faith* (New York: Oxford University Press, 1962), p. 201.
5. Richard L. Rubenstein, *The Age of Triage* (Boston: Beacon Press, 1983).
6. Henry Nelson Wieman, *Man's Ultimate Commitment* (Carbondale, Ill.: Southern Illinois University Press, 1958). See also Henry Nelson Wieman, *The Source of Human Good* (Chicago: University of Chicago Press, 1947).
7. Daniel Day Williams, *God's Grace and Man's Hope* (New York: Harper & Brothers, 1949), p. 151.
8. Alfred North Whitehead, *Adventures of Ideas* (New York: The Free Press, 1961), Part IV.
9. Meland, *Faith and Culture*, pp. 172–175.
10. Bernard Eugene Meland, *Fallible Forms and Symbols* (Philadelphia: Fortress Press, 1976), pp. 96–101.
11. Wieman, *Source of Human Good*, chapter 5.
12. Meland, *Faith and Culture*, p. 147.
13. Roberto Mangabeira Unger, *Knowledge and Politics* (New York: The Free Press, 1975), pp. 199–231.
14. Ibid, p. 188.

1. ON THE RECONSTRUCTION OF PUBLIC LIFE IN AMERICA: AN AGENDA

1. Quoted in Sidney Mead, "Religious Pluralism and the Character of the Republic," *Soundings* 61 (Fall 1978): 313.
2. Roberto Mangabeira Unger, *Knowledge and Politics* (New York: The Free Press, 1975), p. 157.
3. Vincent Harding, "Out of the Cauldron of Struggle: Black Religion and the Search for a New America," *Soundings* 61 (Fall 1978): 339–340.
4. See, respectively, Jürgen Habermas, *Legitimation Crisis*, trans. T. M.

McCarthy (Boston: Beacon Press, 1975); Robert Heilbroner, *Business Civilization in Decline* (New York: W. W. Norton, 1976); Henry S. Kariel, *Beyond Liberalism* (New York: Harper and Row, 1977); Robert Nisbet, *Twilight of Authority* (New York: Oxford University Press, 1975); Michael Harrington, *The Twilight of Capitalism* (New York: Simon and Schuster, 1976).

5. Alfred North Whitehead, *Religion in the Making* (New York: Meridian Books, 1960), p. 86.

6. Jacques Maritain, *Integral Humanism,* trans. Joseph W. Evans (Notre Dame, Ind.: University of Notre Dame Press, 1973).

7. Eduard Heimann, *Reason and Faith in Modern Society: Liberalism, Marxism and Democracy* (Middletown, Conn.: Wesleyan University Press, 1961).

8. Philip Hefner, "The Foundations of Belonging in a Christian Worldview," in *Belonging and Alienation,* ed. P. Hefner and W. W. Schroeder (Chicago: Center for the Scientific Study of Religion, 1976), pp. 167–168.

9. Whitehead, *Religion in the Making,* p. 86.

10. Bernard Eugene Meland, *Faith and Culture* (New York: Oxford University Press, 1953), pp. 111–112.

11. John Dewey, *The Public and Its Problems* (Chicago: Swallow Press, 1954, originally published in 1927), see chapter 4.

12. Ibid., p. 126.

13. Ibid., p. 134.

14. Hannah Arendt, *Between Past and Future* (New York: Penguin Books, 1978, originally published in 1954).

15. Robert J. Pranger, *The Eclipse of Citizenship* (New York: Holt, Rinehart, and Winston, 1968).

16. Richard Sennett, *The Fall of Public Man* (New York: Alfred A. Knopf, 1977).

17. Thomas Luckmann, *The Invisible Religion* (New York: Macmillan Company, 1967).

18. Johann Metz, *Theology of the Word,* trans. William Glen-Doepel (New York: Seabury Press, 1969).

19. David Easton, *The Political System* (New York: Alfred A. Knopf, 1953).

20. Thomas Spragens, *The Politics of Motion: The World of Thomas Hobbes* (Lexington, Ky.: University Press of Kentucky, 1973).

21. Unger, *Knowledge and Politics,* p. 63.

22. Frank M. Coleman, *Hobbes and America* (Toronto: University of Toronto Press, 1977), p. 74.

23. C. B. Macpherson, *The Political Theory of Possessive Individualism* (London: Oxford University Press, 1962).

24. Coleman, *Hobbes and America,* p. 58.

25. Thomas Hobbes, *Leviathan* I.xiii.

26. William Ernest Hocking, *The Coming World Civilization* (New York: Harper and Brothers, 1956), p. 30.

27. John MacMurray, *Persons in Relation* (London: Faber and Faber, 1961), p. 17.

28. Bernard Eugene Meland, *The Realities of Faith* (New York: Oxford University Press, 1962), p. 201.

29. MacMurray, *Persons in Relation*, p. 163.

30. Easton, *The Political System*, p. 148.

31. Harold Lasswell, *Politics: Who Gets What, Where, How* (Cleveland and New York: The World Publishing Company, 1936, 1958).

32. Kariel, *Beyond Liberalism*, p. 5.

33. Ibid., p. 21.

34. Coleman, *Hobbes and America*, p. 99.

35. Ibid., pp. 12–23.

36. A. D. Lindsay, *The Modern Democratic State* (London: Oxford University Press, 1943), p. 249. See also Heimann, *Reason and Faith in Modern Society*, pp. 224–236.

37. Sebastian de Grazia, *Errors of Psychotherapy* (Garden City, N.Y.: Doubleday & Co., 1952), p. 218.

38. Sebastian de Grazia, *The Political Community* (Chicago: The University of Chicago Press, 1948).

39. Hefner, "Foundations of Belonging," p. 162.

40. John Smith, *Experience and God* (New York: Oxford University Press, 1968).

41. Arendt, *Between Past and Future*, pp. 168, 170.

42. E. P. Thompson, "Notes on Exterminism: The Last Stage of Civilization," *New Left Review* 121 (May-June 1980): 3–31.

43. John Cobb, *Is It Too Late? A Theology of Ecology* (Beverly Hills, Calif.: Bruce, 1972).

44. See Vincent Harding, *There is a River: The Black Struggle for Freedom in America* (New York: Harcourt Brace Jovanovich, 1981) and Letty Russell, *Human Liberation in a Feminist Perspective* (Philadelphia: Westminster Press, 1974).

45. Michael Harrington, *Decade of Decision: The Crisis of the American System* (New York: Simon and Schuster, 1980), pp. 319–320.

46. George Armstrong Kelly, "Mediation versus Compromise in Hegel," in *Compromise in Ethics, Law, and Politics*, ed. Roland Pennock and John W. Chapman (New York: New York University Press, 1979), pp. 89–92.

47. Theodore M. Benditt, "Compromising Interests and Principles," in Pennock and Chapman's *Compromise*, pp. 26–37.

48. Quoted in ibid., p. 28.

49. Martin P. Golding, "The Nature of Compromise: A Preliminary Inquiry," in Pennock and Chapman's *Compromise*, p. 15.

50. See John Rawls, *A Theory of Justice* (Cambridge, Mass.: Harvard University Press, 1971) and David A. J. Richards, *The Moral Criticism of Law* (Belmont, Calif.: Dickenson Publishing Company, 1977).

51. Jacques Maritain, *Man and the State* (Chicago: University of Chicago Press, 1951).

52. Jürgen Moltmann, *The Crucified God*, trans. R. A. Wilson and John Bowden (New York: Harper & Row, 1974).

53. See below, chapter 5.

54. See Douglas Sturm, "Constitutionalism: A Critical Appreciation and an Extension of the Political Theory of C. H. McIlwain," *Minnesota Law Review* 54 (December 1969): 215–244. See also below, chapter 6.

55. Carl J. Friedrich, *Transcendent Justice: The Religious Dimension of Constitutionalism* (Durham, N.C.: Duke University Press, 1964).

56. Brian Barry, *Political Argument* (New York: Humanities Press, 1965).

57. Robert Bellah, "Commentary and Proposed Agenda: The Normative Framework for Pluralism in America," *Soundings* 61 (Fall 1978): 367.

58. Whitehead, *Religion in the Making*, p. 58. See also Douglas Sturm, "Prolegomenon to the Reconstruction of the Public Interest," *American Society of Christian Ethics Selected Papers*, ed. F. Sherman (Chicago: ASCE/Scholars Press, 1975).

59. Aldo Leopold, *A Sand County Almanac* (New York: Oxford University Press, 1949), p. 214.

60. Scott Buchanan, "Natural Law and Teleology," in *Natural Law and Modern Society* (Cleveland and New York: The World Publishing Company, 1963), p. 150.

61. Whitehead, *Religion in the Making*, pp. 58–59.

62. Albert Somit and Joseph Tanenhaus, *The Development of American Political Science: From Burgess to Behavioralism* (Boston: Allyn and Bacon, 1967).

63. See Unger, *Knowledge and Politics*, pp. 46–49.

64. Heinz Eulau, *The Behavioral Persuasion in Politics* (New York: Random House, 1963), pp. 9–10. See also Douglas Sturm, "Politics and Divinity: Three Approaches in American Political Science," *Thought* 56 (December 1977): 333–365.

65. Alfred North Whitehead, *Science and the Modern World* (New York: Macmillan Company, 1939), pp. 72, 75, 85.

66. Ibid., p. 251.

67. Bernard Eugene Meland, *Higher Education and the Human Spirit* (Chicago: University of Chicago Press, 1953), p. 24.

68. Jürgen Habermas, *Knowledge and Human Interests*, trans. J. J. Shapiro (Boston: Beacon Press, 1971).

69. See Fred R. Dallmayr, *Beyond Dogma and Despair: Toward a Critical Phenomenology of Politics* (Notre Dame, Ind.: University of Notre Dame Press, 1981).

70. MacMurray, *Persons in Relation*, p. 185. See also David Tracy, *The Analogical Imagination* (New York: Crossroads, 1981), p. 343.

71. George Cabot Lodge, *The New American Ideology* (New York: Alfred A. Knopf, 1976), p. 226.

72. Ibid., p. 329.

2. Process Thought and Political Theory: A Communitarian Perspective

1. Alfred North Whitehead, *Adventures of Ideas* (New York: The Free Press, 1967), p. 4.

2. Alfred North Whitehead, *Science and the Modern World*, p. 80. See also *Knowledge and Politics*, p. 30.

3. Whitehead, *Science and the Modern World*, p. 25.

4. Ibid., p. 80.

5. Ibid., pp. 72, 75, 85.

6. Ibid., p. 14.

7. Ibid., pp. 133, 251.

8. Floyd W. Matson, *The Broken Image: Man, Science and Society* (Garden City, N.Y.: Doubleday and Company, Anchor Books, 1966).

9. For a more complete account of these schools of political science, see Douglas Sturm, "Politics and Divinity: Three Approaches in American Political Science."

10. Two summaries of political behavioralism are the following: (1) Heinz Eulau, *The Behavioral Persuasion in Politics* and (2) David Easton, "Introduction: The Current Meaning of 'Behavioralism' in Political Science," in *The Limits of Behavioralism in Political Science*, ed. James C. Charlesworth (Philadelphia: American Academy of Political Science, 1962).

11. Thomas A. Spragens, Jr., *The Dilemma of Contemporary Political Theory: Toward a Post-behavioral Science of Politics* (New York: Dunellen, 1973), pp. 73–74.

12. Two summaries of political traditionalism are the following: (1) Eric Voegelin, *The New Science of Politics* (Chicago: University of Chicago Press, 1952) and (2) Leo Strauss, *What Is Political Philosophy?* (Westport, Conn.: Greenwood Press, 1973).

13. Spragens, *Dilemma of Contemporary Political Theory*, p. 146.

14. Dorothy Emmet, *Whitehead's Philosophy of Organism* (New York: St. Martin's Press, 1966), p. 77.

15. Richard J. Bernstein, *The Restructuring of Social and Political Theory* (New York: Harcourt, Brace, Jovanovich, 1976).

16. Henry S. Kariel, *Saving Appearances: The Reestablishment of Political Science* (Belmont, Calif.: Duxbury Press, 1976).

17. Strauss, *What is Political Philosophy?* p. 40.

18. See Thomas A. Spragens, Jr., *The Politics of Motion: The World of Thomas Hobbes*.

19. Thomas Hobbes, *Leviathan* III.xlvi.

20. Ibid., "The Introduction."

21. For a compact summary of this controversy, see Spragens, *Politics of Motion*, chapter 1.

22. Hobbes, *Leviathan* I.xi.

23. See Frank Coleman, *Hobbes and America: Exploring the Constitutional Foundations.*

24. Alfred North Whitehead, *Symbolism: Its Meaning and Effect* (New York: Capricorn Books, 1959), p. 68.

25. Ibid, 88. The centrality of the symbolic factor in the dialectic between self and society lends credence to the effort to associate process philosophy with communications theory in political thought. See Emmet, *Whitehead's Philosophy of Organism*, p. xxvi, footnote 2; Robert W. Hoffert, "A Political Vision for the Organic Model," Process Studies 5 (Fall 1975): 175–186; Douglas Sturm, "Rule of Law and Politics in a Revolutionary Age," *Law and Philosophy: Readings in Legal Philosophy*, ed. Edward Allen Kent (New York: Appleton-Century-Crofts, 1970), pp. 371–387. In the almost poetic phrasing of Karl W. Deutsch, the concern at the heart of the communications model of politics is "to preserve for any finite mind or group some open pathway to the infinite, that is, to preserve for it the possibility of communication with a potentially inexhaustible environment and a potentially infinite future" (*The Nerves of Government: Models of Political Communication and Control* [New York: The Free Press, 1966], p. xiv). Such a vision calls to mind Henri Bergson's concept of an open society in *The Two Sources of Morality and Religion* (Garden City, N. Y.: Doubleday and Co., Anchor Books, 1954).

26. Note Philip Green's assertion that "In the end, a political science which does not know who the victims are is no political science at all" in *Power and Community: Dissenting Essays in Political Science*, ed. Philip Green and Stanford Levinson (New York: Pantheon Books, 1970). See below, chapter 3.

27. Whitehead, *Adventures of Ideas*, p. 10.

28. Ibid., p. 34.

29. Ibid., pp. 62–63.

30. Morton A. Kaplan, *Alienation and Identification* (New York: The Free Press, 1976), p. 115.

31. This is the striking thesis of a study by Bertell Ollman, *Alienation: Marx's Conception of Man in Capitalist Society* (Cambridge: Cambridge University Press, 1976). See also Carol Gould, *Marx's Social Ontology* (Cambridge, Mass.: MIT Press, 1978), who, while critical of Ollman's rendition of the principle of internal relations, agrees that it is essential to Marx's concept of alienation. For a contrasting interpretation, see John Torrance, *Estrangement, Alienation, and Exploitation* (New York: Columbia University Press, 1977). Torrance insists that Marx clearly distinguishes between estrangement (*Entfremdung*) and alienation (*Entausserung*). The antitheses of the two terms are, respectively, solidarity and appropriation.

32. Alfred North Whitehead, *Process and Reality: An Essay in Cosmology*, corrected edition (New York: The Free Press, 1978), pp. 226–227.

33. Whitehead, *Symbolism*, pp. 7–8.

34. Whitehead, *Process and Reality*, p. 168.

35. John T. Noonan, Jr., *Persons and Masks of the Law: Cardozo, Holmes, Jefferson, and Wythe as Makers of the Masks* (New York: Farrar, Straus and Giroux, 1976).

36. Martin Buber, *Good and Evil* (New York: Charles Scribner's Sons, 1953), pp. 7–14.

37. Don Browning, "Psychological and Ontological Perspectives on Faith and Reason," *Process Philosophy and Christian Thought*, ed. Delwin Brown, Ralph E. James, Jr., and Gene Reeves (Indianapolis: Bobbs-Merrill Co., 1971), pp. 128–142.

38. Walter Lippmann, *Public Opinion* (New York: Macmillan, 1961), Part III.

39. Albert Camus, *The Rebel: An Essay on Man in Revolt*, trans. Anthony Bowen (New York: Vantage Books, 1962).

40. Jürgen Habermas, "On Systematically Distorted Communication," *Inquiry* 13 (1970): 205–218.

41. Bertell Ollman, *Alienation*, pp. 133–134. See also P. M. John, *Marx on Alienation: Elements of a Critique of Capitalism and Communism* (Columbia, Mo.: South Asia Books, 1976), pp. 177–180.

42. See Fritz Pappenheim, *The Alienation of Modern Man: An Interpretation Based on Marx and Tönnies* (New York: Monthly Review Press, Modern Reader Paperbacks, 1968), pp. 84ff.

43. Kaplan, *Alienation and Identification*, Part II.

44. See the parallels and problems discussed in Howard L. Parsons, "History as Viewed by Marx and Whitehead," *The Christian Scholar* 50 (1967): 273–289; George V. Pixley, "Justice and Class Struggle: A Challenge for Process Philosophy," *Process Studies* 4, no. 3 (Fall 1974): 159–175; Clark M. Williamson, "Whitehead as Counter-Revolutionary? Toward Christian-Marxist Dialogue," *Process Studies* 4, no. 3 (Fall 1974): 176–186.

45. On the relation between the philosophy of internal relations and the principle of the dialectic in Marx, see Bertell Ollman, *Alienation*, chapters 3, 5, and 6. To deal with the assertion in the text, one should distinguish various types of dialectic as does Richard McKeon in the second section of his "Dialectic and Political Thought and Action," *Ethics* 65, no. 1 (October 1954): 1–33. McKeon isolates three types of dialectic: a dialectic of rationality, a dialectic of materiality, and a dialectic of experience. Similarly, Gregory Vlastos, in a paper originally published in 1937, distinguishes (1) homogeneous dialectical idealism (Hegel), (2) homogenous dialectical materialism (Marx), and (3) heterogeneous dialectic (Whitehead). The paper, "Organic Categories in Whitehead," is republished in *Alfred North Whitehead: Essays in His Philosophy*, ed. George Kline (Englewood Cliffs, N.J.: Prentice-Hall, 1963), pp. 158–167. Some more current interpretations of the thought of Karl Marx would raise serious question about Vlastos' classification and might provide a basis for effecting the comparison of Marx and Whitehead suggested in the text. See, for instance, Raymond Williams, *Marxism and Literature* (Oxford: Oxford University Press, 1977) especially Parts One and Two. In any case, both White-

head's doctrine of internal relations and the Marxian principle of dialectic provide a means of understanding forms of life as containing, albeit uneasily and in tension, their own contradictions. That is one basis of the dynamics of ethical criticism and historical transformation.

46. See Bertell Ollman's description of evidences of alienated relations in contemporary capitalist society (*Alienation*, pp. 250–252) and David L. Hall's interpretation of "the cultural problem" (*The Civilization of Experience: A Whiteheadian Theory of Culture* [New York: Fordham University Press, 1973], pp. 167–181).

47. Whitehead, *Adventures of Ideas*, pp. 251, 293.

48. Hoffert, "A Political Vision for the Organic Model."

49. Michael Weinstein, *Philosophy, Theory, and Method in Contemporary Political Thought* (Glenville, Ill.: Scott, Foresman and Company, 1971), chapter 4.

50. Hall, *Civilization of Experience*.

51. Samuel H. Beer, *The City of Reason* (Cambridge, Mass.: Harvard University Press, 1940).

52. William M. Sullivan, "Two Options in Modern Social Theory: Habermas and Whitehead," *International Philosophical Quarterly* 15, no. 1 (March 1975): 83–98. See also Sullivan's doctoral dissertation, *The Process Social Paradigm and the Problem of Social Order* (Fordham University, 1971).

53. Beer, *City of Reason*, p. 141.

54. Ibid., p. 191.

55. Ibid., p. 201.

56. Ibid., p. 212.

57. Whitehead, *Adventures of Ideas*, p. 83.

58. Ibid., p. 63.

59. Whitehead, *Process and Reality*, p. 203.

60. See Whitehead, *Adventures of Ideas*, pp. 56, 69, 257. Compare Sullivan's argument in his dissertation, abstracted in *Process Studies* 2, no. 1 (Spring 1972): 88–89.

61. Whitehead, *Adventures of Ideas*, pp. 66–67.

62. Whitehead, *Process and Reality*, pp. 222, 255.

63. Ibid, pp. 222–223.

64. On this issue, see Howard Press, "Whitehead's Ethic of Feeling," *Ethics* 81, no. 3 (February 1971): 161–168, and the critique of Press by J. B. Spencer in *Process Studies* 1, no. 3 (Fall 1973): 244–245. Spencer's side of the argument seems supported by Whitehead's statement that by peace he is "not referring to political relations" but to "a quality of mind steady in its reliance that fine action is treasured in the nature of things." But Press might invoke this affirmation: "The essence of Peace is that the individual whose strength of experience is founded upon this ultimate intuition, thereby is extending the influence of the source of all order" (*Adventures of Ideas*, pp. 274, 292).

65. Whitehead, *Adventures of Ideas*, p. 292.

66. Ibid., p. 293.

67. On communitarianism, see George C. Lodge, *The New American Ideology*, pp. 162–197 and Roberto Mangabeira Unger, *Knowledge and Politics*, pp. 263–295.

68. Whitehead, *Adventures of Ideas*, p. 295.

3. IDENTIFYING PROBLEMS OF PUBLIC ORDER: A RELATIONAL APPROACH

1. John E. Smith, *Experience and God*, p. 172.

2. Thomas A. Spragens, Jr., *Understanding Political Theory* (New York: St. Martin's Press, 1976), p. 20.

3. J. W. Gough, *John Locke's Political Philosophy*, 2nd ed. (Oxford: Clarendon Press, 1973).

4. C. B. Macpherson, *The Political Theory of Possessive Individualism: Hobbes to Locke* (London: Oxford University Press, 1964).

5. John Dunn, *The Political Thought of John Locke: An Historical Account of the Argument of the 'Two Treatises of Government'* (Cambridge: Cambridge University Press, 1969).

6. John Locke, *Two Treatises of Government*, ed. Peter Laslett (Cambridge: Cambridge University Press, 1964) II.ii.4 (p. 287).

7. Ibid., II.ii.6 (p. 289).

8. Ibid., II.ii.8 (p. 290).

9. Ibid., II.v.27 (pp. 305–306).

10. Ibid., II.ix.123 (p. 368).

11. Quoted in John Kleinig, "Human rights, legal rights and social change," *Human Rights*, ed. Eugene Kamenka and Alice Erh-Soon Tay (New York: St. Martin's Press, 1978), p. 40, footnote 12.

12. *Bentham's Political Thought*, ed. Bhikhu Parekh (London: Croom Helm, 1973), p. 269.

13. Quoted in Ross Harrison, *Bentham* (London: Routledge & Kegan Paul, 1983), p. 79.

14. Jeremy Bentham, *An Introduction to the Principles of Morals and Legislation* (New York: Hafner Publishing Co., 1948), pp. 2–3.

15. Ibid., p. 3.

16. Lee Cameron McDonald, *Western Political Theory: From Its Origins to the Present* (New York: Harcourt, Brace & World, 1968), p. 467.

17. I have been unable to locate the exact context of this quip. *An Introduction to the Principles of Morals and Legislation*, chapter 9, is sometimes cited for it, but the statement does not in fact appear in that location in the editions I have examined.

18. John Stuart Mill, *Utilitarianism*, ed. George Sher (Indianapolis: Hackett Publishing Company, 1979), p. 10.

19. The debate over where exactly Bentham stood on this issue and

whether there was a change in his views over the course of years may be seen in the following sources: David Lyons, *In the Interest of the Governed: A Study in Bentham's Philosophy of Utility and Law* (Oxford: Clarendon Press, 1973); James Steintrager, *Bentham* (Ithaca, N.Y.: Cornell University Press, 1977), chapter 3, "Polity and Economy"; and Ross Harrison, *Bentham*, chapter 5, "The Duty and Interest Junction Principle."

    20. Kariel, *Beyond Liberalism*, pp. 5–6.

    21. Unger, *Knowledge and Politics*, p. 196.

    22. See ibid., p. 227.

    23. Locke, *Two Treatises of Government*, II.v.27 (p. 306).

    24. William T. Blackstone, "Ethics and Ecology," *Philosophy and Environmental Crisis*, ed. William T. Blackstone, (Athens, Ga.: University of Georgia Press, 1974), pp. 30–36.

    25. Bentham, *Principles of Morals*, pp. 310–311.

    26. Peter Singer, *Practical Ethics* (Cambridge: Cambridge University Press, 1979), especially chapters 3 and 5.

    27. See "Section Two: Rights, Duties, and the Environment," *Environmental Ethics*, ed. K. S. Shrader-Frechetter (Pacific Grove, Calif.: The Boxwood Press, 1981) and Christopher D. Stone, *Should Trees Have Standing? Toward Legal Rights for Natural Objects* (Los Altos, Calif.: William Kaufmann, Inc., 1974).

    28. Frederick Elder, quoted in Cobb, *Is It Too Late?* pp. 83–84.

    29. Dean E. Mann, "Introduction," *Environmental Policy Formation: The Impact of Values, Ideology, and Standards*, ed. Dean E. Mann (Lexington, Mass.: Lexington Books, D. C. Heath and Company, 1981), pp. 15–17.

    30. Tom Regan, "Introduction," *Earthbound: New Introductory Essays in Environmental Ethics*, ed. Tom Regan (Philadelphia: Temple University Press, 1984) pp. 34–35.

    31. Leopold, *A Sand County Almanac*, p. viii.

    32. Ibid., p. 216.

    33. Ibid., p. 203.

    34. Ibid., p. 204.

    35. Ibid., pp. 224–225. See also John B. Cobb, Jr., *Is It Too Late?* pp. 55–56.

    36. William Pollard, "The Uniqueness of the Earth," *Earth Might Be Fair: Reflections on Ethics, Religion, and Ecology*, ed. Ian G. Barbour (Englewood Cliffs, N.J.: Prentice-Hall, Inc., 1972), pp. 96–97.

    37. Susan Moller Okin, *Women in Western Political Thought* (Princeton: Princeton University Press, 1979), p. 200.

    38. Locke, *Two Treatises of Government*, II.vi.52 (p. 321).

    39. Ibid., II.vii.82 (p. 339).

    40. *A Wollstonecraft Anthology*, ed. Janet M. Todd (Bloomington, Ind.: Indiana University Press, 1977), "Part II: Works of Controversy."

    41. "Declaration of Sentiments and Resolutions, Senaca Falls," *Feminism: The Essential Historical Writings*, ed. Miriam Schneir (New York: Random House, 1972), pp. 76–82.

42. Okin, *Women in Western Political Thought*, p. 200.

43. John Stuart Mill, "The Subjection of Woman," *Essays on Sex Equality: John Stuart Mill & Harriet Taylor Mill*, ed. Alice S. Rossi (Chicago: The University of Chicago Press, 1970), p. 125.

44. Ibid., pp. 148, 150.

45. Carol C. Gould, "The Woman Question: Philosophy of Liberation and the Liberation of Philosophy," *Women and Philosophy: Toward a Theory of Liberation*, ed. Carol C. Gould and Marx W. Wartofsky (New York: G. P. Putnam's Sons, Capricorn Books, 1976), pp. 5–44.

46. Valerie C. Saiving, "Androgynous Life: A Feminist Appropriation of Process Thought," *Feminism and Process Thought*, ed. Sheila Greeve Davaney (New York: The Edwin Mellen Press, 1981), p. 18.

47. See John B. Cobb, Jr., "Feminism and Process Thought: A Two-Way Relationship," in Davaney's *Feminism and Process Thought*, pp. 32–61.

48. Saiving, "Androgynous Life," p. 17.

49. Ibid., p. 26.

50. Unger, *Knowledge and Politics*, p. 222 (italics added).

51. Barry Bluestone and Bennett Harrison, *The Deindustrialization of America: Plant Closings, Community Abandonment, and the Dismantling of Basic Industry* (New York: Basic Books, Inc., 1982), p. 6.

52. Quoted in Staughton Lynd, *The Fight Against Shutdowns: Youngstown's Steel Mill Closings* (San Pedro, Calif.: Singlejack Books, 1982), pp. 164–165.

53. Ibid., p. 166.

54. Ibid., p. 176.

55. See Maurice Cranston, *What Are Human Rights?* (London: The Bodley Head, 1973). Cranston reports, but is extremely critical of, this shift. In appendices, Cranston includes the Universal Declaration of Human Rights proposed by the United Nations and, as well, the two covenants resulting from the Declaration: (1) International Covenant on Economic, Social and Cultural Rights and (2) International Covenant on Civil and Political Rights.

56. Martin Carnoy, Derek Shearer, and Russell Rumberger, *A New Social Contract: The Economy and Government After Reagan* (New York: Harper & Row, 1983), pp. 230–231.

57. Lester C. Thurow, *The Zero-Sum Society: Distribution and the Possibilities for Economic Change* (New York: Basic Books, Inc., 1980), pp. 80–81.

58. Ibid., p. 204.

59. Peter F. Koslowski, "The Ethics of Capitalism," *Philosophical and Economic Foundations of Capitalism*, ed. Svetozar Pejovich (Lexington, Mass.: Lexington Books, D. C. Heath and Company, 1983), pp. 33–64.

60. Joseph A. Schumpeter, *Capitalism, Socialism, and Democracy* (New York: Harper & Brothers, 1942), p. 63.

61. Bluestone and Harrison, *Deindustrialization of America*, p. 63.

62. Marie Jahoda, *Employment and unemployment: A social-psychological analysis* (Cambridge: Cambridge University Press, 1982). See also Terry F.

Buss and F. Stevens Redburn with Joseph Waldron, *Mass Unemployment: Plant Closings and Community Mental Health* (Beverly Hills, Calif.: Sage Publications, 1983).

63. Bluestone and Harrison, *Deindustrialization of America*, p. 79.

4. On Meanings of Public Good

1. Glenn Tinder, *The Crisis of Political Imagination* (New York: Charles Scribner's Sons, 1964), p. 241.

2. Several typologies differentiating meanings of public interest have been constructed over the past two decades. The typologies vary in part because of the data taken into account, in part because of the methods employed, and in part because of the theoretical or practical purposes governing the constructions. To explore these differences might be illuminating, but must be left to some other occasion. See Frank J. Sorauf, "The Public Interest Reconsidered," *Journal of Politics* 19, no. 3 (November 1957): 616–639; Wayne A. R. Leys and Charner Marquis Perry, *Philosophy and the Public Interest* (Chicago: Committee to Advance Original Work in Philosophy, 1959); Glendon Schubert, *The Public Interest: A Critique of the Theory of a Political Concept* (Glencoe, Ill.: Free Press, 1960); Gerhart Niemeyer, "Public Interest and Private Utility," *The Public Interest*, ed. C. J. Friedrich (New York: Basic Books, 1970); Sturm, "Prolegomenon to the Reconstruction of the Public Interest"; Clarke E. Cochrane, "Political Science and 'The Public Interest,'" *Journal of Politics* 36, no. 2 (May 1974): 327–355.

3. Arthur L. Kalleberg and Larry Preston, "Normative Political Analysis and the Problem of Justification: The Cognitive Status of Basic Political Norms," *Journal of Politics* 37, no. 3 (August 1975): 650–684; see esp. p. 652.

4. Arthur Bentley, *The Process of Government* (Bloomington, Ind.: Principia Press, 1949), p. 222.

5. See David B. Truman, *The Governmental Process* (New York: Alfred A. Knopf, 1951), p. 50.

6. See the arguments in Sorauf, "The Conceptual Muddle," in Friedrich's *The Public Interest*; Sorauf, "The Public Interest Reconsidered"; Schubert, The Public Interest; and Schubert, "Is There a Public Interest Theory?" in Friedrich's *The Public Interest*. In his book-length study, Schubert is driven to conclude "political scientists might better spend their time nurturing concepts that offer greater promise of becoming useful tools in the scientific study of political responsibility" (p. 224).

7. Barry, *Political Argument*, esp. chaps. 11–15.

8. Richard E. Flathman, *The Public Interest: An Essay Concerning the Normative Discourse of Politics* (New York: John Wiley & Sons, 1966), esp. summary passages on pp. 66 ff. and 82 ff.

9. Virginia Held, *The Public Interest and Individual Interests* (New York: Basic Books, 1970), esp. chap. 6.

10. Brian Barry's analysis of aggregative want-regarding principles is much more complex and detailed than this paragraph indicates. He distinguishes, for example, uses of the terms "public interest," "public good," "general welfare," and "public conscience." He sorts out negative from positive applications of these terms in political association. He illustrates instances in which judgments employing these terms result in conflicting policies. And he explores the difficult question of how to ensure that the force of government will be used on behalf of public interest. But the paragraph in the text presents enough of the substance of Barry's analysis to demonstrate the importance and the status of the principle in his interpretation of political argument.

11. Dewey, *The Public and Its Problems*, chap. 1.

12. In William J. Meyer's recent restatement of Dewey's position, "The public good can be said to be the best regulation and control of the indirect consequences of social transactions as determined by the public through the satisfactoriness of actions it takes in pursuit of authoritative agreements about its goals" (*Public Good and Political Authority: A Pragmatic Proposal* [Port Washington, N.Y.: Kennikat Press, 1975], p. 133).

13. Dewey, *The Public and Its Problems*, chap. 4.

14. See Leo Strauss, *What Is Political Philosophy?*, esp. chap. 1; and Eric Voegelin, *The New Science of Politics*.

15. Edward Shils, *Center and Periphery: Essays in Macrosociology* (Chicago: University of Chicago Press, 1975), pp. 3–16.

16. Julius Cohen has argued that the term "public interest" is used in American law in a dual sense: "First, in a logical sense—i.e., to explicate the *meaning* of the established basic values of the community. Thus, it would be in the public interest to pursue a certain goal because it would be consistent with the *meaning* of a basic community value. Second, it is used in an instrumental sense—i.e., that a policy would be in the public interest if its consequences would implement one or more of the established basic values of the community" ("A Lawman's View of the Public Interest," in Friedrich's *The Public Interest*, p. 156).

17. See Jacques Maritain, *The Person and the Common Good*, trans. John J. Fitzgerald (Notre Dame, Ind.: University of Notre Dame Press, 1966); and Yves Simon, *The Tradition of Natural Law* (New York: Fordham University Press, 1965).

18. Dante Germino, *Beyond Ideology: The Revival of Political Theory* (1967; reprint, Chicago: University of Chicago Press, 1977), p. 6.

19. In one essay, William Ernest Hocking distinguishes between a "widened empiricism," which he also calls a "broadened or heightened empiricism," and an "empiricism of the immediate" ("Marcel and the Ground Issues of Metaphysics," *Philosophy and Phenomenological Research* 15 [June 1954]: 429–441, 446–447). In another study, he distinguishes between a "scholastic empiricism" and a "working empiricism" (*Experiment in Education: What We Can Learn from Teaching Germany* [Chicago: Henry Regnery, 1954], pp.

242–244). See also Floyd W. Matson, *The Broken Image: Man*, Science and Society.

20. Meland, *Faith and Culture*, pp. 98 ff.

21. Ibid., pp. 111–112.

22. Ibid., p. 91.

23. For a recent expression of classical conservatism, see Bertrand de Jouvenal, *Sovereignty: Inquiry into the Public Good* (Chicago: University of Chicago Press, 1957), esp. chap. 7.

24. Meland, *The Realities of Faith*, p. 208.

25. Meland, *Faith and Culture*, p. 206.

26. See John B. Cobb, Jr., *God and the World* (Philadelphia: Westminster Press, 1969), esp. chap. 2.

27. The term "open society" has been used in at least three appreciably different senses—a more organic, processual sense (Henri Bergson); a more individualistic, institutional sense (Karl Popper); and a more transcendental, levels-of-being sense (Eric Voegelin). See Dante Germino, "Preliminary Reflections on the Open Society," in *The Open Society in Theory and Practice*, ed. Dante Germino and Klaus von Beyme (The Hague: Martinus Nijhoff, 1974), pp. 1–25. The sense intended in this text is closer to Bergson than to Popper or Voegelin. The influence of Henry Nelson Wieman's concept of "creative intercommunication" must also be acknowledged; see *Man's Ultimate Commitment*.

28. *Laws* 1.7.23.

29. 94 U.S. 113 (1877).

30. 94 U.S. 113, 126.

31. 291 U.S. 502 (1934).

32. 290 U.S. 398 (1934).

33. 290 U.S. 398, 435–436.

34. 310 U.S. 586 (1940).

35. 310 U.S. 586, 596.

36. 310 U.S. 586, 600.

37. 319 U.S. 624, 642 (1943).

38. 326 U.S. 501 (1946).

39. 323 U.S. 192 (1944).

5. On Meanings of Justice

1. Ernst Troeltsch, *The Social Teaching of the Christian Churches*, trans. Olive Wyon (London: George Allen & Unwin, Ltd., 1931, originally published 1912), p. 1010.

2. Simone Weil, *Oppression and Liberty*, trans. Arthur Wills and John Petrie (Amherst, Mass.: University of Massachusetts Press, 1973), p. 146.

3. Ibid., p. 103.

4. José Miranda, *Marx and the Bible*, trans. John Eagleson (Maryknoll, N.Y.: Orbis Books, 1974), pp. 78–106.

5. Dante Germino, "The Revival of Political Theory," *Ideology, Politics and Political Theory*, ed. Richard Cox (Belmont, Calif.: Wadsworth Publishing Co., 1969), p. 97.

6. Rawls, *A Theory of Justice*, p. 3.

7. Edmond Cahn, *The Sense of Injustice* (Bloomington, Ind.: Indiana University Press, 1964).

8. Dorothy Emmet, *The Moral Prism* (New York: St. Martin's Press, 1979), p. 1.

9. Luke 4:18.

10. Wieslaw Lang, "Marxism, Liberalism, and Justice," *Justice*, ed. Eugene Kamenka and Alice Erh-Soon Tay (New York: St. Martin's Press, 1980), pp. 123ff.

11. Weil, *Oppression and Liberty*, p. 83.

12. Richard Flathman, *The Practice of Rights* (Cambridge: Cambridge University Press, 1976), p. 171.

13. William Ernest Hocking, *The Lasting Elements of Individualism* (New Haven, Conn.: Yale University Press, 1937), p. 23.

14. L. T. Hobhouse, *Liberalism* (New York: Henry Holt and Company, 1911), p. 19.

15. Hocking, *Lasting Elements of Individualism*, p. 136.

16. Robert Nozick, *Anarchy, State, and Utopia* (New York: Basic Books, 1974), p. 160.

17. Galatians 3:38.

18. Sanford A. Lakoff, "Christianity and Equality," *Equality*, ed. J. Roland Pennock and John W. Chapman (New York: Atherton Press, 1967), p. 117. See also Sanford A. Lakoff, *Equality in Political Philosophy* (Cambridge, Mass.: Harvard University Press, 1964) and Stephen Charles Mott, "Egalitarian Aspects of the Biblical Theory of Justice," *The ASCE Selected Papers*, ed. Max Stackhouse (1978), pp. 8–26.

19. Troeltsch, *Social Teaching of the Christian Churches*, pp. 77–78.

20. Ferenc Feher and Agnes Heller, "Forms of Equality," in Kamenka and Tay's *Justice*, p. 151.

21. Ibid., p. 152.

22. Brian Barry, "Justice as Reciprocity," in Kamenka and Tay's *Justice*, pp. 75–76.

23. Ibid.

24. Julius Stone, "Justice Not Equality," in Kamenka and Tay's *Justice*, p. 112. For a refined statement of this theme, see Michael Walzer, *Spheres of Justice* (New York: Basic Books, 1983).

25. A. M. Honoré, "Social Justice," *Essays in Legal Philosophy*, ed. Robert S. Summers (Berkeley and Los Angeles: University of California Press, 1976), pp. 62–63, 91 (italics removed).

26. Lang, "Marxism, Liberalism, and Justice," p. 148.

27. 1 Corinthians 12:12, 27.

28. Bertell Ollman, *Alienation: Marx's Conception of Man in Capitalist Society*, pp. 133–134.

29. Gould, *Marx's Social Ontology*, p. 153.

30. In his article on "The Quest for Distributive Justice and the Liberal Outlook," *Liberalism and the Modern Polity*, ed. Michael J. Gargas McGrath, (New York and Basel: Marcel Dekker, 1978), Mulford Q. Sibley formulates the principle of justice that should guide those whose political aim is a "communist society":

> Every human being, simply because he is a human being and regardless of his native capacity or culture, has a right equal to that of all other human beings to receive those goods and services needed to sustain his life, to enable him to use his talents for the community, and to permit the fulfillment of his own unique nature so long as that fulfillment does not involve harm to the community. Inseparably connected with this right is a corresponding duty—that he serve the community in ways most suitable to his talents and to the full extent of his ability. (p. 166)

The goal, he writes, "is a society in which each contributes according to his or her individually evaluated ability and receives in accordance with individually defined but ethically defensible needs" (p. 166). This principle of justice is distinguished from justice as equality by conjoining both right and duty relative to the formation and maintenance of a social order constructed on the "premise of fraternity."

31. Gould, *Marx's Social Ontology*, pp. 173, 171, 175, 177.

32. Robert O. Johann, "Rationality, Justice and Dominant Ends," *The Value of Justice*, ed. Charles A. Kelbley (New York: Fordham University Press, 1979), pp. 20–21.

33. Ibid.

34. See Jürgen Habermas, "On Systematically Distorted Communication," and "Towards a Theory of Communicative Competence," *Inquiry* 13 (Winter 1970): 360–375.

35. Unger, *Knowledge and Politics*, pp. 284–295.

36. Romans 12:2.

37. For Leo Strauss, see his *Natural Right and History* (Chicago: The University of Chicago Press, 1953) and *What is Political Philosophy?* For Eric Voegelin, see his *The New Science of Politics* and *Science, Politics and Gnosticism* (Chicago: Henry Regnery Co., 1968). Voegelin's orientation is succinctly stated in this passage from his *Science, Politics, and Gnosticism*, p. 18:

> The decisive event in the establishment of *politike episteme* was the specifically philosophical realization that the levels of being discernible within the world are surmounted by a transcendent source of being and its order. And this insight was itself rooted in the real movements of human spiritual soul toward divine being experienced as transcendent. In the experiences of love for the world-transcendent origin of being, in

philia toward the *sophon* (the wise), in *eros* toward the *agathon* (the good) and the *kalon* (the beautiful), man became philosopher. From these experiences arose the image of the order of being. At the opening of the soul . . . the order of being becomes visible even to its ground and origin in the beyond, in the Platonic *epekeina*, in which the world participates as it suffers and achieves its opening. Only when the order of being as a whole, unto its origin in transcendent being, comes into view, can the analysis be undertaken with any hope of success; for only then can current opinions about right order be examined as to their agreement with the order of being.

38. Strauss, *What is Political Philosophy?* p. 10.
39. Ibid., p. 34.
40. Ibid., pp. 80–81.
41. Strauss, *Natural Right*, p. 147.
42. Strauss, *What is Political Philosophy?* p. 11.
43. Strauss, *Natural Right*, p. 151.
44. Strauss and Voegelin cast the principle of justice as wisdom in the framework of classical metaphysics with its hierarchical and static doctrine of the structure of being. In the thought of Alfred North Whitehead, there is an alternative rendering of the principle in the framework of a metaphysics of process. See, for instance, Whitehead's "concept of an Adventure in the Universe as One," in his *Adventures of Ideas*, p. 295. Without Adventure, civilization languishes and dies; with Adventure, civilization is provoked into new possibilities and finds, at the same time, a sense of fulfillment and ultimate Peace. While there is no explicit doctrine of justice in Whitehead's writings, Lois Livezey has constructed the outlines of such a doctrine in her unpublished doctoral dissertation on *Whitehead's Conception of the Public World* (University of Chicago, 1983) as well as in an unpublished paper, "Rights, Goods, and Virtues: Toward An Interpretation of Justice in Process Thought" (1986).
45. Paul Tillich, *The Socialist Decision*, trans. Franklin Sherman (New York: Harper and Row, 1977), p. 2.
46. Weil, *Oppression and Liberty*, p. 103.

6. Corporations, Constitutions, Covenants: The Problem of Legitimacy

1. See the Appendix at the end of the chapter for a summary table of the characteristics of these three forms of human relation.
2. Dow Votaw, *Modern Corporations* (Englewood Cliffs, N.J.: Prentice Hall, 1965), p. 1.
3. William T. Gossett, *Corporate Citizenship* (Lexington, Va.: Washington and Lee University, 1957), p. 180.

4. Ibid., p. 157. See also the closing paragraphs of Adolf A. Berle and Gardiner C. Means, *The Modern Corporation and Private Property*, rev. ed. (New York: Harcourt, Brace, and World, 1968), p. 313.

5. Votow, *Modern Corporations*, pp. 25–26.

6. 4 Wheat. 518, 636. See also Lord Coke's definition of a corporation aggregate in the 1613 case of Sutton's Hospital. 10 Coke's Rep. 1, 32.

7. John Kenneth Galbraith, *The New Industrial State* (Boston: Houghton Mifflin Co., 1971), chapters 15 and 7. The trend toward amalgamation and merger was predicted by Marx and Engels, who anticipated monopolization within particular industries. While sheer monopolization has been, by and large, prevented, the trend has been toward the formation of "concentrates" (Berle) and "oligopolies" (Galbraith).

8. Peter F. Drucker, *The Concept of the Corporation* (New York: New American Library, 1964), p. 48.

9. Douglas MacGregor, *The Human Side of Enterprise* (Englewood Cliffs, N.J.: Prentice Hall, 1960), p. 60. Italics added.

10. William H. Whyte, Jr. *The Organization Man* (Garden City, N.Y.: Doubleday Anchor Books, 1956).

11. W. Lloyd Warner, *The Corporation in the Emergent American Society* (New York: Harper and Row, 1962), p. 48.

12. Neil H. Jacoby, "The Multinational Corporation," *The Center Magazine* 3, no. 3 (May 1970): 54.

13. The articles were collectively published in Richard Austin Smith, *Corporations in Crisis* (Garden City, N.Y.: Doubleday and Co., 1963).

14. Edward S. Mason, "Introduction," *The Corporation in Modern Society*, ed. Edward Mason (New York: Atheneum, 1969), p. 1.

15. Amitai Etzioni, "The Search for Political Meaning," *The Center Magazine* 5, no. 2 (March-April 1972): 2, 3.

16. Seymour Martin Lipset, *Political Man* (London: Mercury Books, 1967), p. 77. For an extended consideration of the nature of legitimacy in political theory, see Carl J. Friedrich, *Man and His Government* (New York: McGraw Hill, 1967), chapter 13, especially pp. 232–246.

17. James Willard Hurst, *The Legitimacy of the Business Corporation in the Law of the United States 1780–1970* (Charlottesville, Va.: University of Virginia Press, 1970), p. 58.

18. Ibid., p. 70.

19. Charles Howard McIlwain, *Constitutionalism: Ancient and Modern*, rev. ed. (Ithaca, N.Y.: Cornell University, 1947), p. 21. See also Douglas Sturm, "Constitutionalism: A Critical Appreciation and An Extension of the Political Theory of C. H. McIlwain," *Minnesota Law Review* 54, no. 2 (December 1969): 215–244.

20. Francis D. Wormuth, *The Origins of Modern Constitutionalism* (New York: Harper and Bros., 1949), p. 9.

21. See Alan Gewirth's discussion of three meanings of consent—occur-

rence, dispositional, and opportunity—and his argument that the western liberal democratic tradition most intelligibly means by "consent" the provision of institutional means for citizen participation and dissent within the political process. "Political Justice," *Social Justice*, ed. Richard B. Brandt (Englewood Cliffs, N.J.: Prentice Hall, A Spectrum Book, 1962), pp. 119–169, especially 128–141.

22. See Francis Wormuth, *Origins of Modern Constitutionalism*, chapter 16.

23. Adolf A. Berle, Jr., *The Twentieth Century Revolution* (New York: Harcourt and Brace, 1959), p. 188.

24. See John Courtney Murray, "Natural Law and the Public Consensus," *Natural Law and Modern Society* (Cleveland and New York: World Publishing Company, 1963), and Wieman, *Man's Ultimate Commitment*, chapter 10 "Industry Under Commitment."

25. See Milton Friedman, *Capitalism and Freedom* (Chicago: University of Chicago Press, 1962) and Eugene V. Rostow, "To Whom and For What Ends is Corporate Management Responsible?" in Edward Mason's *The Corporation in Modern Society*.

26. John Kenneth Galbraith, *American Capitalism* (Boston: Houghton Mifflin, 1956).

27. Abram Chayes, "The Modern Corporation and the Rule of Law," in Edward Mason's *The Corporation in Modern Society*, p. 41.

28. Ibid., p. 43. See also Kingman Brewster, "The Corporation and Economic Federalism," in Edward Mason's *The Corporation in Modern Society*.

29. Robert A. Dahl, *After the Revolution? Authority in a Good Society* (New Haven and London: Yale University Press, 1970), pp. 115–140. The use of Yugoslavia for illustrative purposes should make clear that there is nothing inherently incompatible between the socialization of industry and constitutionalism, Friedrich Hayek's arguments to the contrary notwithstanding. Dahl has expanded his position on this issue in his recent book, *A Preface to Economic Democracy* (Berkeley, Calif.: University of California Press, 1985). Other current books arguing for economic democracy include: David W. Ewing, *Freedom Inside the Organization* (New York: E. P. Dutton, 1977), Martin Carnoy and Derek Shearer, *Economic Democracy* (Armonk, N.Y.: E. P. Sharpe, 1980), and Carnoy, Shearer, and Rumberger, A New Social Contract.

30. Henry Nelson Wieman, *The Directive in History* (Boston: Beacon Press, 1949), p. 35.

31. Ibid., p. 52.

32. Walther Eichrodt, in his *Theology of the Old Testament*, vol. 1, trans. J. A. Baker (Philadelphia: Westminster Press, 1962), argues that the Sinaitic covenant is the central motif for understanding the entire history of Israel. This view has been subjected to heavy criticism subsequently. See, e.g., Ronald Clements, *Abraham and David: Genesis XV and Its Meaning for Israelite Tradition* (Naperville, Ill.: Alec R. Allenson, Inc., 1967) especially chapter 7 "The Covenant Tradition in Israel," and Dennis J. McCarthy, S.J., *Old Testa-*

ment Covenant: A Survey of Current Opinion (Richmond, Va.: John Knox Press, 1972). I am indebted to Professor Phyllis Trible of Union Theological Seminary for assistance on this point and in connection with other aspects of this portion of the study.

33. Gerhard Von Rad, *Old Testament Theology*, vol. l, trans. D. M. G. Staller (New York: Harper Bros., 1962), p. 129.

34. George Mendenhall, "Covenant," *Interpreter's Dictionary of the Bible*, vol. 1 (New York: Abingdon Press, 1962), p. 714. The remainder of this paragraph assumes Mendenhall's thesis about the possible origin and structure of covenants. Mendenhall's thesis has not been without its critics, however. See McCarthy, *Old Testament Covenant* and, in addition, his *Treaty and Covenant: A Study in Form in the Ancient Oriental Documents and in the Old Testament* (Rome: Pontifical Biblical Institute, 1963).

35. Eichrodt, *Theology of the Old Testament*, pp. 37–38.

36. Ibid., pp. 74–75.

37. See George Mendenhall as quoted in Delbert R. Hillers, *Covenant: The History of a Biblical Idea* (Baltimore: Johns Hopkins Press, 1969), p. 88.

38. Eichrodt, *Theology of the Old Testament*, p. 76.

39. Johannes Pedersen, *Israel: Its Life and Culture* I-II, trans. Mrs. Aslauf Moller (London: Geoffrey Cumberlege, Oxford University, 1926), p. 271.

40. Ibid., p. 276.

41. Ibid., p. 308. For another rendering of the meaning of the term *"shalom"* in Hebrew scriptures, see John I. Durham, "Shalom and the Presence of God," *Proclamation and Presence: Old Testament Essays in Honor of Gwynne Henton Davies*, ed. John I. Durham and J. R. Porter (Richmond, Va.: John Knox Press, 1970). Durham's basic contention is that *shalom* is the gift of God and is received only in God's presence. *Shalom* signifies the fulfillment, the completion, the perfection of humankind.

42. Von Rad, *Old Testament Theology*, p. 371. See also Eichrodt, *Theology of the Old Testament*, p. 240.

43. Pederson, *Israel: Its Life and Culture*, p. 342.

44. Ibid., p. 345.

45. Eichrodt, *Theology of the Old Testament*, p. 232.

46. Von Rad, *Old Testament Theology*, p. 37. Italics added. In this connection it would be instructive to examine Harry Orlinsky's article on "Nationalism, Universalism and Internationalism in Ancient Israel," *Translating and Understanding the Old Testament: Essays in Honor of Herbert Gordon May* (Nashville and New York: Abingdon Press, 1970). In passages where others have argued that there is an internationalist strain in Israel, Orlinsky finds instead either a form of nationalism or some conjunction of nationalism and universalism in which Israel as the people of God occupy a special role.

47. Friedrich, *Transcendent Justice*.

7. Corporate Culture and the Common Good

1. Voegelin, *New Science of Politics*, p. 27.

2. Berle, *Twentieth Century Capitalist Revolution*, p. 114.

3. Votaw, *Modern Corporations*, p. 2.

4. Sandra Salmans, "New Vogue: Company Culture," *New York Times*, January 7, 1983, p. D 1.

5. Terrence Deal and Allan Kennedy, *Corporate Culture: The Rites and Rituals of Corporate Life* (Reading, Mass.: Addison-Wesley, 1982), p. 19.

6. James O'Toole, *Making America Work: Productivity and Responsibility* (New York: Continuum, 1981), see chapter 1, "The Wealth of the Nation."

7. Meland, *Fallible Forms and Symbols*, p. xiii.

8. O'Toole, *Making America Work*, p. 184.

9. Clifford Geertz, *The Interpretation of Cultures* (New York: Basic Books, 1973), p. 5.

10. Ibid., p. 24.

11. Anthony Giddens, *New Rules of Sociological Method: A Positive Critique of Interpretive Sociologies* (New York: Basic Books, 1976), p. 53. See also Anthony Giddens, *Central Problems in Social Theory: Action, Structure and Contradiction in Social Analysis* (Berkeley, Calif.: University of California Press, 1979).

12. Marvin Harris, *Cultural Materialism: The Struggle for a Science of Culture* (New York: Vintage Books, Random House, 1979), p. 59.

13. Giddens, *New Rules*, pp. 103–113, 157, 161.

14. Whitehead, *Adventures of Ideas*, p. 6.

15. Thomas Donaldson, *Corporation and Morality* (Englewood Cliffs, N.J.: Prentice-Hall, 1982), pp. 109–112.

16. Yet see William P. Sexton, "The Human Ecology of Modern Corporations," *The Judeo-Christian Vision and the Modern Corporation*, ed. Oliver Williams and John Houck (Notre Dame, Ind.: University of Notre Dame Press, 1982), pp. 55–72.

17. Deal and Kennedy, *Corporate Culture*, pp. 107–127.

18. O'Toole, *Making America Work*, p. 158.

19. Bebe Moore Campbell, "Black Executives and Corporate Stress," *The New York Times Magazine*, December 12, 1982, p. 39.

20. Ibid., p. 100.

21. Catherine B. Cleary, "Women in the Corporation: A Case Study About Justice," in Williams and Houck's *The Judeo-Christian Vision and the Modern Corporation*, p. 299.

22. Rosabeth Moss Kanter, *Men and Women of the Corporation* (New York: Basic Books, 1977).

23. O'Toole, *Making America Work*, p. 124.

24. Robert L. Heilbroner, *The Limits of American Capitalism* (New York: Harper & Row, Torchbooks, 1967).

25. Phillip I. Blumberg, *The Megacorporation in American Society: The Scope of Corporate Power* (Englewood Cliffs, N.J.: Prentice-Hall, 1957).

26. Richard Eells, quoted *The Corporation Take-Over*, ed. Andrew Hacker (Garden City, N.Y.: Doubleday & Co., Anchor Books: 1965), p. 105.

27. "Corporate Culture: The Hard-to-Change Values That Spell Success or Failure," *Business Week*, October 27, 1980, p. 148.

28. Gould, *Marx's Social Ontology*, p. 43.

29. Galbraith, *New Industrial State*.

30. Arthur Selwyn Miller, "Toward the 'Techno-Corporate State?'—An Essay in American Constitutionalism," *Villanova Law Review* 14, no.1 (Fall 1968): 1–73.

31. Lodge, *New American Ideology*.

32. John Braithwaite, "The Limits of Economism in Controlling Harmful Corporate Conduct," *Law and Society Review* 16, no. 3, (1981–1982): 481–504.

33. Arthur Selwyn Miller, *The Supreme Court and American Capitalism* (New York: The Free Press, 1968).

34. Lodge, *New American Ideology*.

35. Richard J. Barnet and Ronald E. Muller, *Global Reach: The Power of Multinational Corporations* (New York: Simon and Schuster, 1974).

36. John P. Davis, *Corporations* (New York: Capricorn Books, 1961), vol. 2, p. 254.

37. Votaw, *Modern Corporations*, p. 25.

38. Heilbroner, *Business Civilization in Decline*, p. 9.

39. Robert L. Heilbroner, "Foreword: The Long-Run Challenge to a Business Civilization," *Corporate Social Policy: Selections from Business and Society Review*, ed. Robert L. Heilbroner and Paul London (Reading, Mass.: Addison- Wesley, 1975), p. ix.

40. Barnet and Muller, *Global Reach*, pp. 386–387.

41. Meland, *Fallible Forms*, p. 105

8. A New Social Covenant: From Democratic Capitalism to Social Democracy

1. Whitehead, *Adventures in Ideas*, p. 12.

2. Schumpeter, *Capitalism, Socialism, and Democracy*, p. 82.

3. Meland, *Faith and Culture*, p. 124.

4. Augustine *City of God* (trans. Marcus Dods) 14.1

5. Franklin I. Gamwell, "Freedom and the Economic Order: A Foreword to Religious Evaluation," *Christianity and Capitalism*, ed. Bruce Grelle and David A. Kreuger (Chicago: Center for the Scientific Study of Religion, 1986), p. 51.

6. Murray N. Rothbard, *Individualism and the Philosophy of the Social Sciences* (San Francisco: Cato Institute, 1979), p. 15.

7. Giddens, *Central Problems in Social Theory*, pp. 49–96.

8. Meland, *Faith and Culture*, pp. 111–112.

9. Philip Hefner, "Foundations of Belonging in a Christian Worldview," p. 162.

10. Michael J. Sandel, *Liberalism and the Limits of Justice* (Cambridge: Cambridge University Press, 1982), p. 179.

11. Rawls, *Theory of Justice*, p. 3.

12. Alasdair MacIntyre, *After Virtue* (Notre Dame, Ind.: University of Notre Dame Press, 1981), pp. 175–189.

13. Unger, *Knowledge and Politics*, pp. 191–235.

14. Maritain, *Person and the Common Good*, pp. 40–41 (italics in the original).

15. Ibid., p. 45. See also Jacques Maritain, *Man and the State*, pp. 188–216.

16. Friedrich A. Hayek, *The Mirage of Social Justice* (Chicago: University of Chicago Press, 1976), p. 111.

17. Hobhouse, *Liberalism*, p. 115.

18. Joyce Appleby, *Capitalism and A New Social Vision* (New York: New York University Press, 1984).

19. Louis Hartz, *The Liberal Tradition in America* (New York: Harcourt, Brace and World, 1955).

20. Michael Novak, *The Spirit of Democratic Capitalism* (New York: Simon and Schuster, 1982).

21. Robert Benne, *The Ethic of Democratic Capitalism* (Philadelphia: The Fortress Press, 1981).

22. Ludwig von Mises, *Epistemological Problems of Economics* (Princeton: Van Nostrand Press, 1960).

23. Immanuel Wallerstein, *The Modern World System*, 2 vols. (New York: Academic Press, 1974, 1980). See also his *Historical Capitalism* (London: Verso, 1983).

24. Adam Smith, *The Wealth of Nations* (New York: The Modern Library, 1937).

25. Hayek, *Mirage of Social Justice*, p. 115.

26. Ibid., p. 110.

27. Bruno Hildebrand, *Die Nationaloekonomie der Gegenwart und Zukunft* (Frankfort, 1848).

28. George F. Will, *Statecraft as Soulcraft* (New York: Simon and Schuster, 1983).

29. See Daniel Bell, *The Cultural Contradictions of Capitalism* (New York: Basic Books, 1976).

30. See Bertell Ollman, *Alienation: Marx's Conception of Man*.

31. Wallerstein, *Historical Capitalism*, pp. 13–43.

32. See Oskar Lange, "On the Economic Theory of Socialism," in *On the Economic Theory of Socialism*, ed. Benjamin Lippincott (Minneapolis, Minn.: University of Minneapolis Press, 1938).

33. Karl Marx and Friedrich Engels, *The Communist Manifesto*, in *Property*, ed. C. B. Macpherson (Toronto: University of Toronto Press, 1978).

34. See A. D. Lindsay, *Modern Democratic State*, pp. 117–121.

35. Schumpeter, *Capitalism, Socialism, and Democracy*, pp. 269–284.

36. Dahl, *Preface to Democratic Theory*.

37. Lindsay, *Modern Democratic State*, p. 116.

38. See Alan Gewirth, "Political Justice," pp. 119–169.

39. Eduard Heimann, *Reason and Faith in Modern Society* (Middletown, Conn.: Wesleyan University Press, 1961), p. 283.

40. Lindsay, *Modern Democratic State*, p. 245.

41. Dewey, *The Public and Its Problems*, pp. 143, 147.

42. Joshua Cohen and Joel Rogers, *On Democracy* (New York: Penguin Books, 1983), pp. 50–51.

43. Carole Pateman, *Participation and Democratic Theory* (Cambridge: Cambridge University Press, 1970), p. 38.

44. MacMurray, *Persons in Relation*, pp. 118–119.

45. Wallerstein, *Historical Capitalism*, chapter 2.

46. See, e.g., Heilbroner, *Business Civilization in Decline*; Unger, *Knowledge and Politics*; Habermas, *Legitimation Crisis*; Bell, *Cultural Contradictions of Capitalism*.

47. Appleby, *Capitalism and A New Social Vision*.

48. Smith, *Wealth of Nations*.

49. Gibson Winter, *Being Free* (New York: MacMillan, 1970).

50. See Paul Tillich, *Socialist Decision*, Part I.

51. See Hildebrand, *Die Nationaloekonomie*.

52. Robert Johann, *The Pragmatic Meaning of God* (Milwaukee: Marquette University Press, 1966), p. 46.

53. See Jürgen Moltmann, *The Church in the Power of the Spirit*, trans. Margaret Kohl (New York: Harper and Row, 1977), pp. 114–121, 314–317.

54. Gustavo Gutierrez, *A Theology of Liberation*, trans. Sister Caridad Inda and John Eagleson (Maryknoll: Orbis Books, 1973).

55. See Pateman, *Participation and Democratic Theory*; Bell, *Cultural Contradictions of Capitalism*; Unger, *Knowledge and Politics*; Alec Nove, *The Economics of Feasible Socialism* (London: George Allen and Unwin, 1983); Harrington, *Decade of Decision*; Martin Carnoy and Derek Shearer, *Economic Democracy* (Armonk, N.Y.: M. E. Sharpe, 1980); and Dahl, *Preface to Economic Democracy*.

56. Meland, *Fallible Forms*, pp. 97–98.

57. Johann, *Pragmatic Meaning of God*, pp. 49–66; Charles Hartshorne, *Reality as a Social Process* (Glencoe, Ill.: The Free Press, 1953), pp. 29–43.

9. American Legal Realism and the Covenantal Tradition

1. Cited in James Luther Adams, "God and Economics," in *Belief and Ethics*, ed. W. Widick Schroeder and Gibson Winter (Chicago: Center for the Scientific Study of Religion, 1978), p. 89.

2. George Christie, *Jurisprudence* (St. Paul, Minn.: West Publishing Co., 1973), p. 644.

3. Harry Jones, "Legal Realism and Natural Law," in *The Nature of Law*, ed. M. P. Golding (New York: Random House, 1966), p. 262.

4. Karl Llewellyn, *Jurisprudence* (Chicago: University of Chicago Press, 1962), pp. 68–69.

5. H. L. A. Hart, *The Concept of Law* (Oxford: Clarendon Press, 1961), pp. 121–132.

6. See Lois Forer, *The Death of the Law* (New York: McKay, 1975).

7. Llewellyn, *Jurisprudence*, p. 16.

8. Karl Llewellyn, *Bramble Bush* (New York: Oceana Publications, 1960), pp. 12–13.

9. Ibid.

10. Ibid., pp. 75–76.

11. Llewellyn, *Jurisprudence*, p. 67. See also his *Bramble Bush*, p. 39.

12. Llewellyn, *Jurisprudence*, pp. 31–32.

13. 347 U.S. 483 (1954) (initial decision); 349 U.S. 294 (1954) (implementing order).

14. 370 U.S. 421 (1962).

15. Lon Fuller, *Anatomy of the Law* (New York: F. A. Praeger, 1968), p. 66.

16. William Douglas, "Stare Decisis," *Essays on Jurisprudence from the Columbia Law Review* (New York and London: Columbia University Press, 1963), pp. 18–41.

17. 217 N.Y. 382; 111 N.E. 1050 (1916). See Edward Levi, *An Introduction to Legal Reasoning* (Chicago: University of Chicago Press, 1948), pp. 14–18.

18. Llewellyn, *Bramble Bush*, p. 68.

19. Ibid., pp. 157–160.

20. Llewellyn, *Jurisprudence*, p. 111.

21. Ibid., p. 115.

22. Llewellyn, *Bramble Bush*, p. 13.

23. Oliver Wendell Holmes, "The Path of the Law," *An Introduction to Law* (Cambridge: Harvard Law School Association, 1962), pp. 39–60.

24. Llewellyn, *Jurisprudence*, p. 36.

25. Ibid., p. 37.

26. Llewellyn, *Bramble Bush*, p. 9. See also pp. 107–118, 153–154. Compare *Jurisprudence*, pp. 37, 111, 115.

27. Jones, "Legal Realism and Natural Law," p. 269.

28. Llewellyn, *Jurisprudence*, p. 86.

29. Ibid., pp. 199–201.

30. Llewellyn, *Bramble Bush*, p. 118; see also *Jurisprudence*, pp. 37, 205, 212.

31. Llewellyn, *Jurisprudence*, pp. 202, 204, 212.

32. Meland, *Fallible Forms*, p. 3.

33. Jeremiah 7:4–8.

34. Meland, *Fallible Forms*, p. 123.

35. Ibid., p. 122.

36. See Gustavo Gutierrez, *A Theology of Liberation* and José Miguez Bonino, *Doing Theology in a Revolutionary Situation* (Philadelphia: Fortress Press, 1975).

37. Meland, *Realities of Faith*, p. 91.

38. Ibid., pp. 192–193.

39. Unger, *Knowledge and Politics*. For an earlier expression of this alternative, see Roscoe Pound, "The New Feudal System," *Kentucky Law Journal* 19 (1930): 1.

40. Ibid., p. 196.

41. Noonan, *Persons and Masks of the Law*, p. 17.

42. Ibid., p. 19.

43. Forer, *Death of the Law*, p. xi.

44. Ibid., p. 196.

10. Context and Covenant: Social Theory and Theology in Bioethics

1. Alfred North Whitehead, *The Function of Reason* (Boston: Beacon Press, 1958), pp. 65–66.

2. Daniel Callahan, "Bioethics as a Discipline," *Hastings Center Report* 1 (1973): 68.

3. Robert M. Veatch, *A Theory of Medical Ethics* (New York: Basic Books, 1981), p. 3.

4. K. Danner Clouser, "Bioethics," *Encyclopedia of Bioethics*, vol. 1, 115–127.

5. Edmund D. Pellegrino and David C. Thomasma, *A Philosophical Basis of Medical Practice* (New York: Oxford University Press, 1981).

6. Van Rensselaer Potter, *Bioethics: Bridge to the Future* (Englewood Cliffs, N.J.: Prentice-Hall, 1971).

7. Gordon D. Kaufman, *An Essay in Theological Method* (Missoula, Mont.: Scholars Press, 1975), p. ix.

8. Max Horkheimer, *Die Sehnsucht nach dem ganz Anderen* (Hamburg: Furche-Verlag, 1979), p. 60.

9. Paul U. Unschuld, "Medical Ethics, History of: South and East Asia: General Historical Survey," *Encyclopedia of Bioethics*, vol. 3, 901. Italics added.

10. Callahan, "Bioethics as a Discipline," p. 68.

11. Ibid., p. 72.

12. Daniel Callahan, "Shattuck Lecture—Contemporary Biomedical Ethics," *The New England Journal of Medicine* 302 (1980): 1228–1233. In recent personal correspondence (1986), Callahan reports that his work has moved more completely in the direction of a contextual form of bioethics.

13. Van Rensselaer Potter, "Bioethics for Whom?" *The Social Responsibility of Scientists: Annals of the New York Academy of Sciences* 196 (1972): 201.

14. Potter, *Bioethics*, p. 2.

15. See Potter's "Bioethical Creed for Individuals," in his *Bioethics*, p. 196, and in his "Bioethics for Whom?" p. 204.

16. See Potter's proposal for a "Council on the Future" as a fourth branch of government in his *Bioethics*, pp. 75–82.

17. Paul Ramsey, *The Patient as Person* (New Haven and London: Yale University Press, 1970), p. xii.

18. Ibid., p. xiii.

19. Ivan Illich, *Medical Nemesis* (New York: Pantheon Books, 1976), pp. 270–271. Italics added.

20. David F. Horrobin, *Medical Hubris* (Montreal and Lancaster: Eden Press, 1977), pp. 1, 115.

21. Richard Zaner, "Embodiment," *Encyclopedia of Bioethics*, vol. 1, 361–366 and *The Context of Self* (Athens, Ohio: Ohio University Press, 1981).

22. David Schench, Glenn Graber, and Charles Reynolds, "Encyclopedia of Bioethics," *Religious Studies Forum* 7, no. 1 (1981): 6.

23. Michael Gordy, "Sociality," *Encyclopedia of Bioethics*, vol. 4, 1605.

24. René Dubos, *Man, Medicine, and Environment* (New York: Frederick A. Praeger, 1968), p. 91.

25. Roy Branson, "Bioethics as Individual *and* Social: The Scope of a Consulting Profession *and* Academic Discipline," *The Journal of Religious Ethics* 3 (1975): pp. 111–139.

26. Renée Fox, *Essays in Medical Sociology: Journeys into the Field* (New York: John Wiley and Sons, 1979), p. 525.

27. Branson, "Bioethics as Individual *and* Social."

28. See Clouser, "Bioethics," pp. 121–123.

29. Giddens, *New Rules for Sociological Method*, p. 22.

30. Giddens, *Central Problems in Social Theory*.

31. Flathman, *The Practice of Rights*, pp. 11–15.

32. Talcott Parsons, "Definitions of Health and Illness in the Light of American Values and Social Structure," in *Concepts of Health and Disease*, ed. Arthur L. Caplan, H. Tristram Engelhardt, Jr., and James J. McCartney (Reading, Mass.: Addison and Wesley Publishing Company, 1981), p. 69.

33. Talcott Parsons, *The Social System* (Glencoe, Ill.: The Free Press, 1951), pp. 436–437. See also Parsons, "Definitions of Health," p. 70.

34. Henry E. Sigerist, *Civilization and Disease* (Chicago: University of Chicago Press, 1962), p. 236.

35. Eliot Freidson, *Profession of Medicine: A Study of the Sociology of Applied Knowledge* (New York: Dodd, Mead, and Co., 1979), Part II.

36. Ibid., p. 249.

37. Ibid., p. 331. See also Part IV.

38. Barbara Ehrenreich and John Ehrenreich, "Medicine and Social Control," in *The Cultural Crisis of Modern Medicine*, ed. John Ehrenreich (New York: Monthly Review Press, 1978), p. 73.

39. David Mechanic, *Politics, Medicine, and Social Sciences* (New York: John Wiley and Sons, 1974), p. 116; see also pp. 59–67.

40. David Mechanic, "Medicine, Sociology of," *Encyclopedia of Bioethics*, vol. 3, 1056.

41. Ibid., p. 1057.

42. Ibid. See also Eliott Krause, *Power and Illness: The Political Sociology of Health and Medical Care* (New York: Elsevier, 1977), pp. 33–67.

43. See, e.g., *Poverty and Health*, ed. John Kosa, Aaron Antonovsky, and Irving Kenneth Zola (Cambridge, Mass.: Harvard University Press, 1969); Carter L. Marshall and Carol Paul Marshall, "Poverty and Health in the United States," *Encyclopedia of Bioethics*, vol. 3, 1316–1321; John H. Bryant, "Poverty and Health in International Perspective," *Encyclopedia of Bioethics*, vol. 3, 1321–1327; Harold S. Luft, *Poverty and Health* (Cambridge: Balinger Publishing Co., 1978).

44. Mechanic, *Politics, Medicine, and Social Sciences*, pp. 55–56 and "Medicine, Sociology of," p. 1056.

45. James H. Jones, "Racism and Medicine," *Encyclopedia of Bioethics*, vol. 4, 1405–1410.

46. John Ehrenreich, *Cultural Crisis of Modern Medicine*, Part 2.

47. Ibid.

48. Krause, *Power and Illness*, p. 1.

49. Ibid., p. 296.

50. Ibid., p. 319.

51. Barbara Ehrenreich and John Ehrenreich, *The American Health Empire* (New York: Random House, 1970), pp. 4–17.

52. Tom Levin, *American Health: Professional Privilege vs. Public Need* (New York: Praeger Publishers, 1974), pp. 11–12.

53. Ibid., pp. 13–14.

54. Ibid., pp. 28–31.

55. Fox, *Essays in Medical Sociology*, pp. 499–529.

56. *Henry E. Sigerist on the History of Medicine*, ed. Felix Marti-Ibanex (New York: MD Publications, 1960), p. 26; Henry E. Sigerist, *Civilization and Disease* (Chicago: University of Chicago Press, 1962), pp. 66, 241.

57. Sigerist, *Civilization and Disease*, p. 7.

58. Ibid., p. 55.

59. Ibid., p. 40.

60. Ibid., p. 59.

61. Dubos, *Man, Medicine, and Environment*, pp. 65–66.

62. Ibid., pp. 52–53.

63. Ibid., p. 72.

64. René Dubos and Jean-Paul Escande, *Quest: Reflections on Medicine, Science and Humanity*, trans. Patricia Ranum (New York: Harcourt Brace Jovanovich, 1980), pp. 10–11.

65. Giddens, *Central Problems in Social Theory*, p. 5.

66. William A. Glaser, "Medical Care: Social Aspects," *International Encyclopedia of the Social Sciences*, vol. 10, 95.

67. Mechanic, *Politics, Medicine, and Social Sciences*, pp. 1–2.

68. Ibid. See also Parsons, "Definitions of Health," pp. 79–81, and Krause, *Power and Illness*, pp. 123–155.

69. Kaufman, *Essay in Theological Method*, p. 30.

70. Schubert Ogden, *The Reality of God and Other Essays* (New York: Harper and Row, 1966), p. 57.

71. Whitehead, *Process and Reality*, p. 166.

72. Ibid., p. 190.

73. Meland, *Realities of Faith*, p. 206.

74. Whitehead, *Religion in the Making*, p. 59.

75. Meland, *Realities of Faith*, p. 207.

76. Meland, *Faith and Culture*, pp. 111–112.

77. See Bernard Eugene Meland, *Fallible Forms*, pp. 96–101.

78. H. Tristram Engelhardt, "The Concepts of Health and Disease," in Caplan, Engelhardt, and McCartney, *Concepts of Health and Disease*, p. 42.

79. Ibid., p. 43.

80. Warren Reich, "Toward a Theory of Autonomy and Informed Consent," *Annual of the Society of Christian Ethics*, ed. Larry L. Rasmussen (1982): 191–215.

81. Leon Kass, "Regarding the End of Medicine and the Pursuit of Health," *Public Interest* 40 (1975): 29.

82. Sigerist, *Civilization and Disease*, p. 66.

83. Ibid., p. 242. Italics added.

84. Parsons, "Definitions of Health," p. 69. Italics removed.

85. Potter, *Bioethics*, p. viii.

86. Albert R. Jonsen and Andre E. Hellegers, "Conceptual Foundations for an Ethics of Medical Care," in *Ethics in Medicine*, ed. Stanley Joel Reiser, Arthur J. Dyck, and William J. Curran (Cambridge, Mass.: MIT Press, 1977), p. 133.

87. Ramsey, *Patient as Person*, p. xiii.

88. Veatch, *Theory of Medical Ethics*, pp. 110–126. See also L. W. Sumner, "Does Medical Ethics Have Its Own Theory?" *The Hastings Center Report* 12 (1982): 38–39.

89. William F. May, "Code and Covenant or Philanthropy and Contract," in Reiser, Dyck, and Curran, *Ethics in Medicine*, pp. 65–76.

INDEX

adventure, 51, 99, 255n44
affirmative action, 149
alienation, 5, 21–24, 29–30, 32, 42–46,
    51, 62, 66, 73–74, 92, 95, 97,
    103–104, 108–111, 185, 244n31
analytic principle, 27–28, 76–78, 83, 111,
    211
Appleby, J., 173
appreciative consciousness, 4, 29, 165
Arendt, H., 14, 21
aristocratic conservatism, 96–97,
    108–109, 111
Aristotle, 3, 16, 32, 36–37, 40–41, 167,
    235
Augustine, 166, 199
autonomy, principle of, 164, 233, 235

Bacon, F., 141
Barnet, R., 161–162
Barry, B., 78, 101, 111, 251
Beer, S., 47–50
behavioralism, 27–28, 35–37, 76–77,
    79–80, 243n10
Bell, D., 185
Bellah, R., 26
Benne, R., 173
Bentham, J., 54, 57–59, 64, 74, 174, 184
Berdyaev, N., 85, 99
Berkeley, Bishop, 33
Berle, A. A., 125, 140
Bernstein, R., 36
bioethics, 210–237
    contextual, 210, 212–219, 222–237
    diachronic dimensions, 221–222,
        226–229
    personalist, 212–219
    synchronic dimensions, 221–226, 229
Black, Justice, 91
Blackstone, W. T., 64

Bluestone, B., 70, 73
Branson, R., 219–220
bread, problem of, 85
Browning, D., 45
Buber, M., 45
Buchanan, S., 27
bureaucracy, 145, 152
Burke, E., 41, 49, 67

Callahan, Daniel, 212, 215
Camus, A., 45, 97
capitalism, 45–46, 71, 94, 103, 140, 160,
    164–166, 172–176, 178, 180–184.
    See also democratic capitalism
    heterodox interpretation, 166,
        173–176
    orthodox interpretation, 166, 173–176
Cardozo, Justice, 194
Carnoy, M., 71, 185–186
Chayes, A., 126–127
Chesterton, G. K., 187
Christie, G., 189, 208
Cicero, 75, 85
civil liberties, 76, 85–87, 90–92, 181
civility, 15, 109–110
civilization, 42–43, 46, 49–51, 89, 99,
    109–110, 160, 198
Cobb, J., 23
Cohen, Joshua, 179
Cohen, Julius, 251n16
Cole, G. D. H., 179–180, 185
Coleman, F. M., 16, 17, 20
common good, 26–27, 50–51, 73–74, 81,
    102, 162, 165–167, 170–172, 180,
    182, 184–186, 196, 211, 233–237
    typologies of public interest, 250n2
communication, 29, 91, 104–105, 163,
    244n25